DESIRING THAI MEN

DESIRING THAI MEN

Asian Gay Media and
Transforming Masculinities

**Narupon Duangwises
and Peter A. Jackson**

SOUTHEAST ASIA PROGRAM PUBLICATIONS

an imprint of

CORNELL UNIVERSITY PRESS

Ithaca and London

First published 2025 by Cornell University Press

Library of Congress Cataloging-in-Publication Data

Names: Naruphon Duangwises, author. | Jackson, Peter A., author.
Title: Desiring Thai men : Asian gay media and transforming masculinities /
    Narupon Duangwises and Peter A. Jackson.
Description: Ithaca : Cornell University Press, 2025. | Includes
    bibliographical references and index.
Identifiers: LCCN 2025004856 (print) | LCCN 2025004857 (ebook) | ISBN
    9781501783623 (hardcover) | ISBN 9781501783630 (paperback) | ISBN
    9781501783654 (epub) | ISBN 9781501783647 (pdf)
Subjects: LCSH: Gay culture—Thailand—History—20th century. | Gay
    culture—Thailand—History—21st century. | Gay men—Thailand—Social
    life and customs—20th century. | Gay men—Thailand—Social life and
    customs—21st century. | Male homosexuality—Thailand—History—20th
    century. | Male homosexuality—Thailand—History—21st century. | Gay
    men—Thailand—Identity. | Masculinity—Thailand—History—20th century. |
    Masculinity—Thailand—History—21st century.
Classification: LCC HQ76.2.T5 N37 2025 (print) | LCC HQ76.2.T5 (ebook) |
    DDC 306.76/6209593—dc23/eng/20250221
LC record available at https://lccn.loc.gov/2025004856
LC ebook record available at https://lccn.loc.gov/2025004857

Contents

Figures and Tables

Figures

Tables

Acknowledgments

I began collecting information for this book as an insider familiar with the gay community in Bangkok. My gay friends at Thammasat University and the members of the gay networks I know in Bangkok's bars, pubs, karaoke venues, and saunas as well as on the internet and social media have all been exceptionally generous in relating their life stories and experiences to help us appreciate the rapidly changing patterns of Thailand's diverse gay worlds. I especially wish to thank the members of the gay fitness group for their reflections on the construction of masculinity and the coyote boy performers at pubs in Bangkok's Lam Salee area for their insights on working-class gay masculinity. Participating in live streaming events on the Camfrog online chat platform provided unparalleled insights into young men's desires for masculinity and the importance of sexual contact with other men.

Peter Jackson and I have worked together closely throughout this project, exchanging ideas, theories, and analyses in comparing the wealth of information we gathered on the similarities and differences across the social hierarchies that structure the divides within Thai gay cultures. We have made extensive use of the digital data in the Thai Rainbow Archive, which we collaborated in developing with support from the British Library and the Australian National University. The extensive records of Thailand's gay print media in this database have helped us trace the changes in Thai gay masculinities over the past four decades. This book has only been made possible by the analysis of historical data and fieldwork studies of the actual practices of gay men in public spaces. We would also like to thank the many Thai gay academic friends who provided useful advice and comments in writing this book.

Narupon Duangwises
Bangkok

I have often felt an uncanny parallel between my academic career and the modern history of gay Bangkok. Thailand's first commercially successful gay magazine, *Mithuna Junior*, was published in 1983 during my first extended stay in the country to conduct fieldwork research for my PhD. While at that time I was in Bangkok to study Thai Buddhism, I saw how important the publication of *Mithuna Junior* was for my Thai gay friends. The excitement and pride that the appearance of this magazine generated among Thai gay men in the early 1980s made it clear to me that this was a watershed event for the country's gay community and deserved wider recognition and focused academic study. It is a rare gift to be present at the beginning of a transformative cultural phenomenon and to be able to follow its development over the decades, and I have long felt a deep sense of responsibility to bring awareness of the historical importance of Thai gay print media to the international academy and to LGBTQI+ communities more broadly. I have also been deeply honored by the goodwill and collegial spirit of collaboration that Thai gay academic and community friends have shown in bringing this long-term study to fruition. I have learned so much from Narupon Duangwises and it is such a pleasure to help bring some of his pivotal contributions to Thai queer studies to an international readership. Special thanks to Nikorn Chimkhong and Vitaya Saeng-aroon of the Bangkok Rainbow Organization and Parathakorn Nimsang for their dedication in helping make the digital archive of Thai gay magazines in the Thai Rainbow Archive a reality. Carolyn Brewer at the Australian National University and the digital archive staff at the National Library of Australia also provided invaluable training and support in the technologies and techniques of transferring print media into online formats. Many thanks also to our research and project sponsors. The research for this book and for the Thai Rainbow Archives Project were made possible with a grant from the Australian Research Council Discovery Program and with funding from the British Library's Endangered Archives Programme.

Peter A. Jackson
Sydney and Bangkok

Note on Transcription, Referencing, and Currency

Transcribing Thai

There is no generally agreed-upon system of representing Thai in roman script, and all systems have some limitations because the twenty-six letters of the roman alphabet are not sufficient to represent all the consonants, vowels, diphthongs, and tones of Thai. In this book we adopt a modified version of the Thai Royal Institute system of romanizing Thai. This system makes no distinction between long and short vowel forms, and tones are not represented. We differ from the Royal Institute system in using "*j*" for the Thai "*jor jan*," not "*ch*," except in accepted spellings of royal titles and personal names. Hyphens are used to separate units of compound expressions that are translated as a single term in English, such as *khwam-pen-chai*, "masculinity."

Some exceptions to the transcription system are made for words where there might be some confusion. For example, we use *mee* not *mi*, for a Thai gay "bear," *ee* not *i* to represent the colloquial feminine title used before names, and *hee* not *hi* for the crude term "cunt." Other exceptions to the transcription system are that terms borrowed from English are written as in English even if they are pronounced differently in Thai. This makes it easier to highlight the impact of English on much contemporary Thai gay usage. These borrowed English terms are italicized, although "gay" has such widespread usage in Thailand and internationally that we do not italicize it here. Some of the most common Thai terms in this book that follow English spelling rather than the transcription system used elsewhere are *bi* (from bisexual), *both*, *king*, *man*, and *queen*.

Referencing of Thai Names

We follow the Thai academic norm of referring to Thai authors by given names, not surnames, and all citations by Thai authors are alphabetized in the references and elsewhere by given names. We follow authors' preferred spellings of their names in English when this is known rather than following the transliteration system used elsewhere in this book.

Thai Currency Exchange Rate

The Thai currency is the baht. For most of the period covered in this study the exchange rate for the baht hovered around thirty baht to one US dollar. However, during the Asian economic crisis from mid-1997 to 1999, the baht lost almost 50 percent of its value and for a couple of years the exchange rate fell to fifty baht to one US dollar.

DESIRING THAI MEN

ACTING THE MAN IN GAY THAILAND

This book describes the multiple, evolving masculinities of men who have sex with men in Thailand that emerged between the 1980s and 2010s from the intersecting influences of commercial gay media and gay venues of bars, pubs, and saunas. Our book details the history of class-based, contextualized, and flexible masculinities that evolved among Thai men who desire and seek out sex with other men in a capitalist setting of print and online media and expanding consumerist lifestyles. Our analyses reveal the transformative influences that nationally distributed Thai-language gay magazines had on Thailand's gay cultures, lifestyles, and gendered identities across the four-decade period beginning in the early 1980s. The forms of desire represented in Thai gay print media form an important archive for the study of same-sex histories and the formation of contemporary masculine identities in this Southeast Asian society. Studying the shifting forms of masculine presentation among Thai men who desire other men also provides a foundation for rethinking issues in comparative transnational queer studies, such as the importance of class in the formation of modern gay masculinities and the relevance of notions of hegemonic masculinity (Connell 1995, 2002) outside of the West.

The period from the 1980s to the 2010s contrasts with earlier eras in Thailand, when there were no local media produced by or for Thai gay men, as well as the period since the later 2010s, when digital technologies of the internet and smartphones have seen the relocation of gay communications to online platforms. While the national press had often featured gay and transgender (*kathoey*) stories from the 1960s (see Jackson 2009), these reports were almost always framed in terms of demeaning stereotypes that sensationalized, lampooned, and lambasted homosexual and trans people. Commercial Thai-language gay magazines published from the early 1980s were the first venues in the country that disseminated positive images and discourses of homosexual identity at the national level and found ready markets among large numbers of gay men in the country's rapidly expanding urban middle classes. Our research complements the work of authors who have analyzed the important place of gay print media in the development of other modern Asian same-sex cultures. Tom Boellstorff (2005; 2007, 35–40) has considered gay "zines," small-print-run magazines, in Indonesia in the 1980s and 1990s and Mark McLelland (2000, 2005) has detailed the history of both print and early online gay media in Japan since World War II.

The Transformative Influence of Thai Gay Print Media

The case studies in the following chapters trace the dramatic transformations that gay print media brought about in Thai gay men's understandings of their gendered identity, with older feminine models of the male homosexual being replaced with increasingly masculine, and indeed hypermasculine, images of the middle-class gay man. The major shifts in the gendering of male same-sex relations in Thailand began with a progressive differentiation of masculine-identified homosexual men, who appropriated the identity label "gay," from feminine-identified trans women or *kathoey*. In earlier decades of the twentieth century, all homosexual men and trans women had been conflated under the Thai category of *kathoey*, which was formerly an all-encompassing term that included all forms of nonnormative gender and sexual difference (see Jackson 2016). However, from the 1970s, masculine- and feminine-identified males were progressively differentiated with distinct masculine and feminine identities respectively forming around the terms "gay" and *kathoey*.

A second major gender shift subsequently took place within communities of masculine-identified gay men in the 1990s and early 2000s, with receptive anal sex being reconfigured in masculine rather feminine terms and male-male sex being reimagined as a pairing of two masculine partners rather than of a feminine receptive and masculine insertive partner. These intersecting gender transformations—involving differentiation of distinct masculine homosexual and feminine trans identities followed by a masculinization of male same-sex relations—were reflected in discursive shifts that were popularized and consolidated in same-sex and trans cultures across the country through commercial print and online media.

Gay print media in the form of commercial Thai-language gay magazines were also central to the development of the gay scene of bars, pubs, discos, and saunas in Bangkok and other major cities and the associated evolution of distinctive class-based forms of middle-class and working-class masculinity among Thai gay men. There is no single dominant model of masculinity within Thailand's gay cultures. Rather, diverse class-based gay masculinities have come into being within local structures of socioeconomic disparity and hierarchical status differentiation. Our research highlights both the multiplicity and contextuality of the diverse forms of gendering among Thai gay men and reveals how men from different classes and in different contextual settings incorporate both masculine and feminine forms of gendered embodiment and self-representation into their individual presentation and social relations.

The different contextual forms of gendered practice in Thailand's gay communities are often most prominently manifested and expressed in discourse and for this reason analyses of speech acts in Thai are central to our accounts of gendering within Thai gay cultures. The large number of Thai-language gay magazines published from the early 1980s to the later 2010s provide a comprehensive corpus and an extensive historical record of the modern transformations of the country's gay cultures and communities and are a key source for our research. The gay magazines considered here have largely been sourced from the Thai Rainbow Archives Project, which we initiated. It was generously funded by the British Library's Endangered Archives Programme to digitize over one thousand individual publications. Some more sexually explicit Thai gay magazines were not digitized for the Thai Rainbow Archives Project because their images were deemed inappropriate for the British Library's open-source archive. Those magazines have been accessed from private collections.

The era of gay print media is now over in Thailand. The last commercial Thai gay magazine, the Thai-language edition of the English gay magazine *Attitude*, ceased publication in April 2018. Free advertorial magazines distributed from commercial gay venues continued to be published for another couple of years, until the lockdowns and border closures instituted to control the spread of the COVID-19 virus decimated Thailand's commercial gay scene in early 2020. No Thai gay print magazine survived the COVID-19 pandemic. Like so much of social life during the pandemic, Thai gay communication and expression moved online, where it has continued to blossom in diverse and expanding dimensions. The COVID-19 pandemic further accelerated the shift from print to online media that had already been gaining pace from the early 2000s.

The final chapter of this book details further transformations of Thai gay cultures that took place with the arrival of the first online digital platforms. In the 2000s and early 2010s, the emerging virtual spaces of online gay chat rooms initially existed in parallel with print media. However, by the mid-2010s, Thai gay print media found it increasingly difficult to compete with the interactive immediacy and multidimensional scope of digital media. The historical narratives of the evolution of Thai gay masculine gendering outlined in this book end in the early 2010s, just before the arrival of smartphone technologies and dating applications once again transformed patterns of communication and sexual networking. While the opening chapters of this book trace the transformations wrought by Thailand's commercial gay print media, the closing chapter points to the ongoing changes brought about by the digital technologies that have superseded gay print magazines.

Contemporary media studies often focus on novel technologies and applications. Indeed, the internet, smartphones, digital transmission, and streaming continue to revolutionize communications and all domains of gay social life. However, the forms of digital media have built on the not-so-distant era of print-based media, which for the first time provided a basis for the development of an "imagined" national community of Thai gay men beyond the local social networks that could be sustained by direct human contact (see Anderson 1983; Jackson 2009, 2011b). It was Thailand's commercial gay print media that gave birth to and nurtured the development of gay identity as an imagined possibility for homosexual men across the country. While often regarded as a symbol of a now past era, it was the medium of gay print magazines that first opened the door to the prospect of exploring expanding dimensions of queer being. It was through print magazines that the generation of gay men who now lead many of Thailand's most important queer community organizations—such as Bangkok Rainbow, MPlus, and The Rainbow Sky Association of Thailand—came to understand their sexual identities and arrive at social and political consciousness of LGBTQI+ rights. While the era of Thailand's gay print media may have passed, its influences continue to resonate through today's community organizations and digital technologies, whose forms have built on the pioneering efforts of the editors and publishers of the country's gay magazines. Our historical research on gay print media thus provides crucial insights into the origins of contemporary patterns of Thai gay community organization and communication in the era of online digital media.

Capitalism and Media in the Rise of Gay Thailand

Technologies of mass mediatization, and the capitalist market that enabled them to reach national and indeed international readerships and audiences, are central to the analyses in all the chapters in this book. Capitalism and media are at the core of the emergence of modern gay Thailand. While simplistic accounts of glo-balization often mistook the market and new media as forces for cultural homog-enization, our research highlights the distinctiveness of the Thai gay cultures that have been brought into being by local forms of capitalism and indigenous Thai-language media. The case studies in this book describe the Thai gay worlds that evolved in interaction with international Western and Asian gay discourses and imagery, often existing in parallel with expatriate and tourist gay spaces and venues in Bangkok and other major Thai urban centers.

Nevertheless, the print and online media and commercial gay venues con-sidered here were almost exclusively domestic cultural and sexual domains for relations and interactions among Thai men. Despite a clear awareness of Western and other gay worlds, there is a marked absence of Western gay men in the print magazines, online domains, and gay venues detailed in the following chapters. Indeed, a stand-out feature of the more than three decades of Thai gay magazines that we study is a general lack of images of Caucasian men. While Western gay cultures and political activism are widely reported and English gay terms and expressions are well-known, the men represented as sexually attractive models of modern Thai manhood are overwhelmingly Thai and East Asian. Thailand has been at the center of globally dominant Western influences since the period of Anglo-French high imperialism in the nineteenth century and the post–World War II and Cold War eras of American dominance. However, the Caucasian men who were the agents of the increasingly dominant imperialist and neo-imperialist geopolitical and cultural influences in Thailand did not become models of sexual desirability. This is no doubt related to the fact that Thailand was the only South-east Asian country that was never colonized by a Western power. Known as Siam until 1939, Thailand is the only society in the region that remained independent throughout the colonial era and charted its own course of modernization. In this historical setting, indigenous Thai-language gay media and local gay entrepre-neurs responding to the domestic market within Thailand have been the most important factors in the emergence of the country's modern gay cultures (see Jackson 2009). The combination of local discursive, media, and economic forces has determined the localization of modern gay cultures in Thailand's major cit-ies. Our analyses of the domestic processes within Thailand that enabled and fostered the growth of internally diverse and socioeconomically stratified gay communities provide perspectives that contrast with accounts that focus on the transnational dimensions of the development and growth of modern queer Thailand. This book reveals that the emergence of a thriving Thai-language gay press in the early 1980s, which responded to demand from a domestic national gay market, was *the* crucial factor that enabled the rapid expansion of Bangkok's commercial gay scene of bars, discos, and saunas in the later 1980s and 1990s.

Our research also indicates that distinct middle-class and working-class styles of gay masculinity emerged within a sexual culture based on commercial sexual relations. Commercial sex, in which middle-class Thai men have bought the sexual services of working-class men, lies at the center of the modern history of gay Thailand. English-language accounts of sex work in Thailand have often focused on the foreign clients of Thai sex workers, both women and men (see, for example, Bishop and Robinson 1998). Such studies create a mistaken impression that the Thai sex industry is predominantly foreign-oriented although, in fact, the foreign sector is built on a substantial local industry.

Thailand's gay middle class formed amid multiple influences mediated by both commercial gay venues and print media. These venues and media created homosexual spaces for the Thai gay middle class in two important ways. First, gay bars and other venues served as sites of consumption where the male body was transformed into a sexual commodity. In these places, middle-class gay identity was performed through paying a fee for the sexual services of working-class male sex workers. Second, the print media provided educated gay men with ideas by which to imagine fashioning a gay lifestyle amid the rapidly expanding consumer culture of urban life. In the early 1980s, the urban lifestyle of Bangkok's gay middle class was built around the consumption of sexual commodities such as sex workers, gay pornographic videos, and photos of nude male models. These two spaces—gay bars and the virtual field of gay magazines—were both constituted as domains for the marketing of sexual commodities for middle-class gay men.

Gay Thailand in International Perspective

Thailand has an important place in the comparative transnational study of queer histories and cultures. Since the 1990s, research on the country's same-sex and trans communities and cultures has expanded rapidly both internationally and in Thailand.[1] Historically, gender and sexual minorities in Thailand were tolerated but nonetheless suffered widespread discrimination and lacked legally recognized rights. The dominant religion of Theravada Buddhism did not condemn homosexuality or transgenderism as sins but rather saw them as unfortunate conditions that, according to the law of karma, resulted from immoral deeds such as adultery committed in a previous life (Jackson 1995, 1998). Compared to the intense forms of religiously sanctioned and legally enforced homophobia experienced in many Western and other societies, premodern Thailand had a comparatively open culture that can be characterized as somewhat tolerant but not genuinely accepting of sexual and gender minorities (Jackson 1999).

In the second half of the twentieth century, Thailand became home for large, vibrant communities of gay men, lesbians, and trans women, and, since the early 2000s, trans men. Since the 1970s, Thailand's extensive commercial gay and trans scenes, together with the country's significant tourism infrastructure, have seen the country become a magnet, first for Western gay tourists and, since the 1990s, for gay tourists from across Southeast and East Asia. The economic development of the Asian region has seen the rise of gay middle classes in an increasing number of countries, and many of these men have been keen to travel and experience gay life in other countries. Thailand has come to play an important role as a queer-friendly location of intraregional gay tourism within Asia.

Thailand's more open society has proved important in the broader development of LGBTQI+ communities and activism across the region. Gay men from more repressive Southeast Asian societies have often been able to socialize more easily in the gay scenes in Bangkok and other Thai cities than in their home country. Alex Au (2011) argues that in the 1990s socializing among Singaporean gay tourists in the more open environment of Bangkok's gay venues enabled networks to be established that were crucial to the development of gay community activism in the city-state. Until that time, Singapore's more repressive legal and cultural environment had restricted the development of homosexual community organizations and identity politics.

Bangkok has also been chosen as the site for several regional queer organizations, such as APCOM, the Asia Pacific Coalition on Male Sexual Health. The United Nations' first independent expert on protection against violence and discrimination based on sexual orientation and gender identity (often shortened to the UN independent expert on sexual orientation and gender identity [UN IE SOGI]) was internationally recognized Thai human rights lawyer Vitit Muntarbhorn, who held the position from 2016 to 2017.

In many Western countries homosexual rights movements emerged in parallel with commercial gay scenes. However, while Thailand had a queer-tolerant (but not queer-accepting) culture that nurtured flourishing commercial gay and trans scenes, the country had only a limited movement for LGBTQI+ political and human rights until the 2000s. In the 1980s and 1990s, Thai gay media, commercial venues, and male erotica proliferated largely in the absence of a political movement calling for gay visibility based on "coming out," such as marked gay scenes and the politics of gay liberation in some other parts of the world from the late 1960s and early 1970s (see, for example, Altman 1993 [1971]). Ironically, the lack of a political movement to advance the legal rights of queer people resulted from the country's comparatively tolerant sexual and gender culture and the fact that same-sex behavior was not criminalized. Not having been colonized, European anti-sodomy laws were not implemented in Thailand. In the West, homosexual rights movements often began as forms of activism to overturn anti-sodomy laws that had been used to prosecute and often imprison homosexual men. In the absence of such oppressive laws, Thai homosexual men had no need to organize to change their legal status. Instead, the forms of discrimination they suffered emerged from antipathetic cultural attitudes that were diffuse and more difficult to confront or challenge by the forms of political activism that character-ized homosexual rights movements in the West.

In Thailand, sexual and gender minorities first became the focus of public attention and state policies in the 1960s and 1970s, when newly introduced anti-prostitution laws led to trans women sex workers being arrested and sent to men's prisons (Jackson 2009). In the 1960s, high profile crimes, including the murders of some prominent homosexual men, also led the country's sensationalist press to highlight the emergence of communities of men in Bangkok who identified with the new label of "gay" (Jackson 1999). At this time, the antigay views of state actors and the sensationalist mainstream media did not incite any gay organized political movement, although a small number of individual gay men did publicly challenge the negative stereotypes of homosexuality and transgenderism.

As was the case in several other Southeast Asian countries, the first time that sexual minorities in Thailand became the concerted focus of public policies was in the 1980s, when HIV was spreading among gay men and public health mea-sures were introduced. It was in response to state interventions in gay men's and trans women's lives in the 1980s and 1990s that gay and trans activists working on HIV issues formed the first LGBTQI+ organizations. In addition to engaging in education to promote safe sexual practices among the homosexual men and trans women who were threatened by the HIV virus, these organizations also took on community development roles with the aims of engendering a sense of pride in gay and trans identity and promoting acceptance of gender and sexual differ-ence in the mass media and among government agencies and the wider public. The 1990s also saw the emergence of the first lesbian community organization, which in the early 2000s often joined with gay and trans women organizations in public education activities and calls to end discrimination in media reporting, work, education, access to health care, and other fields. Thai LGBTQI+ activism has accelerated considerably since the 2010s, with concerted lobbying leading to the passing of a marriage equality bill in 2024. Another issue at the forefront of community activism is the legal recognition of the gender status of trans women and trans men. In the early twenty-first century, exchanges between and within Asian societies have become increasingly important influences in the develop-ment of LGBTQ+ activism and queer cultural change across the region. Thomas Baudinette (2024) provides a salient example of this in his study of how the boom in Boys Love or BL media across East and Southeast Asia since the mid-2010s reflects the growth in queer cultural exchanges between Thailand, Japan, China, the Philippines, and other regional societies. While the BL genre of manga and young adult novels of romance between young men began in Japan, the significant development of this genre in Thailand has had major impacts internationally, including in Japan.

Thailand's Semicolonial Queer Modernity

Historically, Thailand has been a site of multiple complex cultural intersections from China, India, the Middle East, and the West (see Harrison and Jackson 2010). The case studies detailed here reflect the diversity of gay Thailand at a historical moment of transnational queer transition when twentieth-century influences from Western gay cultures and communities blended with the impact of twenty-first-century trends from emerging East Asian gay communities. While multiple influences of the gay West and gay East Asia are apparent in this book's chapters, our analyses focus on the ways that Thai gay men communicated with and related to other Thai gay men. This book thus considers the commodified and mediatized circuits of male same-sex desire and gay sexual interaction that circulated within Thailand during the era of print media dominance. And as in Thailand, capitalism and new media have been central to the emergence of modern gay cultures in other Southeast Asian societies such as the Philippines (see Garcia 2009) and Singapore (see Yue and Zubillaga-Pow 2012).

However, the religio-cultural traditions and distinctive histories of colonialism under various European and American sex-political regimes have led to much disparity across the region. Indeed, Southeast Asia is one of the world's most diverse regions. Historically, its civilizations emerged across archipelagos of thousands of islands and within mainland river valleys separated by major mountain chains. Its societies formed from diverse religious and cultural traditions: Islam in Malaysia and Indonesia; Buddhism in Thailand, Myanmar, Laos, and Cambodia; Confucianism in Vietnam; and Christianity in the Philippines. Furthermore, neighboring societies experienced markedly different colonial regimes: Hispano-American Philippines; Dutch Indonesia; Portuguese Timor; British Burma, Malaya, and Singapore; French Vietnam, Cambodia, and Laos; and noncolonized Siam.

While Siam/Thailand remained independent through the colonial era, critical historiography nonetheless contends that the country was subject to a range of influences from politically and economically more powerful Western countries that rendered the society subordinate to the West in many dimensions. The colony-like status of independent Siam/Thailand in the global order has been variously described as semicolonialism (Jackson 2010a, 2010b) or crypto-colonialism (Herzfeld 2010). This semicolonial or crypto-colonial position of Thailand in relation to modern forms of power—neither fully independent of hegemonic Western influences nor completely colonized—places Thai queer studies outside of some dominant theoretical narratives. This means that some elements of queer theory need to be rethought in analyzing the country's queer history and cultures.

The Primacy of Gender: Heteronormativity and Thai Nationalism

One consequence of Siam/Thailand's semicolonial relation to Western imperial power is that modern forms of biopower have had as much, if not more, influence over the expression of masculine and feminine gendering as the formation of heteronormative constraints on sexuality (see Jackson 2003). In formerly colonized Southeast Asian societies such as Singapore and Malaysia, the imposition of British anti-sodomy laws and their continued implementation even after independence has had lasting negative impacts on these countries' queer communities (see Yue and Zubillaga-Pow 2012). In contrast, Thai governments had little concern with homosexuality. Rather, in the middle decades of the twentieth century, the militarist ideology of the modernizing Thai state emphasized normative masculine and feminine gender roles and governments sought to legislate modern forms of masculine and feminine fashion and presentation. A feature of modern Thai gender and sexual cultures that distinguishes them from Western and neighboring Southeast Asian societies is that gender expression has been more stringently policed by the state than sexuality. Dominant forms of heteronormativity in Thailand emerged from a nationalist project that required men and women to respectively embody what the mid-twentieth-century state viewed as civilized forms of masculinity and femininity, and Thai gay masculinities have evolved from and in relation to these statist gender dictates. Nattapol Wisuttipat argues that in Thailand sexual orientation, whether homosexual or heterosexual, is not the center of attention in Thai forms of cultural surveillance. Rather, for gay men, "it is gender performance [as masculine] that induces the pressure to conform and assimilate" (2022, 238n5). This emphasis on masculine gender performance as the defining core of modern Thai gay identities is a central theme that we return to throughout this book.

As revealed in our research, a lasting impact of this distinctive form of modern biopower is that, for many Thai men, a masculine gender identity may be more important than sexual identity. The fact that the performance of gender identities has been subject to intense social scrutiny and surveillance in modern Thai history while sexuality per se has rarely been regulated has produced a gender-sex regime in which there may be more anxiety surrounding gender performance than the sex or gender of one's sexual partner. Indeed, the continuing impact of semicolonial biopower over Thai gender is manifested among the men in our study for whom the eroticization of masculinity is of more concern than notions of homosexual or heterosexual identity.

Queer Thailand as Method in International Queer Studies

Thailand's semicolonial position in globally dominant forms of Western political and economic power and discursive authority requires us to take a critical stance regarding scholarship on male sexualities in order to accurately represent the distinctiveness of the modern histories of gender and sexuality in this predominantly Buddhist Southeast Asian society. By foregrounding discourses and images that circulate among Thai men who desire and seek out other men we contribute to efforts to decolonize Western sexology and queer studies (see, for example, Luther et al. 2024). Our analyses highlight the importance for international queer studies of taking case studies from the "Global South" as constituting bases of theorical construction, and our approach develops Kuan-Hsing Chen's (2010) call for taking "Asia as method" to the fields of comparative transnational gender and sexual history.[2] We aim to move beyond Euro-American perspectives by locating Thai discourses as the starting point of analysis and not merely as forms of local data to be fed into Western theories. Our work also responds to Dipesh Chakrabarty's (2000) call to "provincialize Europe" in studies of Asian histories, cultures, and societies. That is, we regard Europe and North America as other provinces of knowledge alongside Asia, which we place on an epistemological and theoretical status on par with the West.

While distinctive, we do not suggest that Thai sexual and gender cultures possess any essential uniqueness. We place the transnational, globalizing influences of capitalism and print and online media at the heart of the analyses in all the chapters. However, we do point to the unevenness of the sway of the market and the influence of media that emerge from the compound influences of Thailand's semicolonial position in the imperial world order, the dominance of Theravada Buddhist views on sex and gender, and the dramatic class disparities that continue to structure Thai gay society. This understanding is informed by the literature on multiple modernities (see Eisenstadt 2000), which reveals the ways that global processes produce different outcomes as they cross cultural, linguistic, and national borders.

Our comparative focus is primarily on studies of gender and sexuality in the West and East Asia. This is because, since the nineteenth century, Thai gender and sexual cultures, both queer and heteronormative, have had the strongest interactions with and been most influenced by Europe, the United States, China, Japan, and Korea. While neighboring countries in Southeast Asia are geographically closer, they have had comparatively little impact on Thai same-sex cultures. Indeed, this is a broader pattern and is not only characteristic of gender and sexual cultures. The diverse histories of British, French, Dutch, Spanish, and American colonialism in Southeast Asia, and the lack of direct colonization in the case of Thailand, mean that neighboring countries in the region have often had stronger relations with their respective former colonial powers than with their immediate neighbors (see Harrison and Jackson 2010).

"Gay" in Thailand: Between Desire for Masculinity and Sexual Identity

While we emphasize how Thai masculinities, homosexual practices, and gendered identities have developed in ways that differ from Western gender and sexual regimes, and we consider Thai discourses and practices nonreductively through a local lens, our accounts nonetheless do draw on the term "gay." This is because we base our studies on analyzing discourses within communities of Thai men who identify with the borrowed term "gay" and the print media publications produced by and marketed to these men. We use "gay" throughout this book because even men who do not claim a gay identity participate in spaces that are labeled as "gay" in local discourses, such as the "gay" chat rooms in the Camfrog online platform analyzed in the last chapter.[3]

The critical insights of Western queer theory have been adapted by scholars of gender and sexual diversity (see, for example, Narupon and Jackson 2021a, 2021b, 2023). However, the term "queer" itself has only limited resonance in Thai and is not widely used beyond academic circles. Instead, since the early 2000s, a newly coined local expression for "gender/sex diversity," *khwam-lak-lai-thang-phet*, has been used by Thai LGBTQI+ groups and by queer-friendly media, academics, and bureaucrats as an accepted expression to refer collectively to all forms of same-sex, transgender, and transsexual identity. In many ways this neologism is now used in Thailand in ways that parallel the uses of "queer" in English, with related expressions such as *khon thi mi khwam-lak-lai-thang-phet* being used to describe "gender and sexually diverse people."

Analytical Focus on Gay Masculinities and Acting the (Gay) Man

In both the West and in many Asian societies there is a widespread fascination with Thailand's highly visible cultures of trans women, who are often called "ladyboys" in sensationalizing accounts (see, for example, Totman 2003; Aldous and Pornchai 2008). However, this focus on trans women and queer femininities can render the country's cisgendered gay men invisible and no previous study of queer Thailand has taken the diversity of gay masculinities as its primary focus. The significant size of the Thai gay print media industry across the four decades of our study indicates the existence of a substantial local market for male-male erotica (see the appendix). The fact that this large archive of sources on modern Thai gay history was published in Thai, and was often of an ephemeral nature, has also led to it largely evading the gaze of Western observers. Our book is then a corrective to the omission of gay masculinities from accounts of Thailand's modern homosexual communities and histories.

An important result of the focus on the gay masculinities that emerged within circuits of local media and domestic capitalism is the revelation of the internal diversity of gay Thailand, which is structured by significant class-based differences between working-class and middle-class gay men. These class-based differences in the forms of gay masculinity underlie the commercially mediated relations between working-class men as sex-service providers and middle-class gay men as consumers of sexual services. Studies that focus on the transnational dimensions of gay Thailand by considering the roles of foreign Western and Asian gay tourists risk obscuring the local patterns of socioeconomic differentiation from which Thailand's commercial gay scenes have emerged and that have determined Thai gay men's different modes of masculine expression.

Discourses of *Kek Man* and *Ab Man* Straight Acting and the Fetishization of Straight Men

While the social lives of large numbers of gay-identified Thai men may be characterized by feminine discourses and practices, their sexual lives are strongly marked by an at times affected, even exaggerated, masculinity. This affectation of masculinity to appear sexually attractive is called *kek man* or *ab man*, "to act the man." Texts and images in gay print magazines, and, since the early 2000s, in online media, have been fundamental to changes in the enactment of eroticized forms of *kek man* and *ab man* masculinity. This includes both gay-identified men and males who do not claim or acknowledge a gay identity but interact with other men in spaces and venues labeled as "gay."

Women are largely absent from the Thai gay media that we study, although trans women are represented. Thai gay men may act and speak in feminine ways when socializing with other gay men, but representations of femininity in Thai gay media are usually limited to featuring trans women, especially cabaret performers. This is not unique to Thai gay media but is equally true of gay publications and media internationally in both the West and Asian societies such as Japan. The absence of females in Thai gay media reflects the fact that the primary roles of these publications and online spaces has been to represent and respond to male same-sex desire that is refracted through the lens of notions of masculinity.

The class-based differences within Bangkok's gay communities are much more than patterns of socioeconomic relations; they extend to markedly different cultures of masculinity. In contrast to the Western notion of "hegemonic masculinity" (Connell 1995, 2002), which tends to assume that a singular model of normative masculinity is dominant within any given society, our research indicates that there is no single hegemonic model of masculinity within Thailand's class-stratified gay cultures. Rather, there are distinctive class-based norms of Thai gay masculinity, with each class grouping of men having its own forms and images of sexually attractive manhood. Our chapters on middle-class gay gym culture and working-class coyote boy dance performers respectively reflect the development of these class-based forms of gay masculine gendering. The muscular bodies of gay men called *kam pu*, "crab claws," men with large biceps developed through intensive gym work and food supplements, and the slim, lithe look of coyote boy dancers both emerged out of the complex gender cultures that were nurtured by the first generation of print media gay magazines in the 1980s. The final chapter on gay chat rooms captures the early impact of the internet on the masculine gender culture of gay Thailand that had emerged in the late twentieth century.

A significant dimension of the masculine sexual culture of Thai gay men has been the role of heterosexual men as male sex workers and as the cover and centerfold models of gay magazines. It was mostly straight working-class men whose bodies were commodified both in commercial sex work and on the pages of gay magazines. Throughout most of the period when print magazines were the dominant form of Thai gay media, heterosexually identified men, called *phu-chai* in Thai, were the prime objects of the gay male gaze. *Phu-chai* literally means "a man." However, since the emergence of gay-identified men, it has taken on the specific sense of "a heterosexual man" and in common usage is contrasted with "gay," which has the sense of "a gay man."

In further contrast to the notion of hegemonic masculinity, our studies reveal that even within class-based social groupings, individual gay men move between different contextual forms of masculine and feminine presentation. Not only does each social class have a distinctive ideal of Thai gay masculinity; individual gay men within each class also daily enact a diverse repertoire of genderings. This repertoire is reflected not only in embodied self-presentation but just as importantly in language use. Thai gay men mark their movement through, and their temporary positionings within, differently gendered habitus by distinctive forms of language use, including masculine and feminine pronouns, sentence particles, and other terms. The gender-specific discourses of middle-class and working-class gay men are central to our analyses because labile forms of self-referencing are some of the most notable features of Thai gay cultures.

In terms of theories of queer identity, gender, and sexual practices our study highlights the importance of dismantling the binary thinking of a polarized gender divide between masculinity and femininity that dominated Western culture during the colonial and early neocolonial eras. In modern Thai gay cultures, men with same-sex attraction express behaviors, language, and emotions that are both feminine and masculine, depending on the dynamic social context. For Thai gay men, the alternation between masculine and feminine speech and presentation is not only about identity. Just as crucially, this alternation is about skillfully moving between "masculine" contexts of building sexual relationships and constructing an acceptable public image, on the one hand, and "feminine" settings of forming gay social networks, on the other.

The Archive of Thailand's Gay Magazines

This book is the outcome of a collaborative project that has had a long gestation period. Our research began over a decade ago as part of a project funded by the Australian Research Council, and we initially envisioned our book as a contemporary account of Thai gay publications and gay gender culture in the early 2000s. However, rapid changes in the Thai print media industry brought on by the internet and new digital technologies, as well as the failure of Thai libraries and archives to collect gay publications, meant that our collaboration soon morphed into a historical project of salvaging and preserving the endangered archive of gay magazines. Our collaboration has not only involved analyzing gay print media; it has also required us to spend considerable time and energy accumulating and preserving the gay publications considered here. We did not have access to an existing archive of Thai gay magazines. No public library or research archive in Thailand or any other country held copies of the several thousand magazine issues published over the past few decades.

From the 1980s to the 2010s, Thailand had one of the world's largest gay print industries. We have found 163 separate magazine titles totaling over 3,250 issues that were published from 1983 to 2018. We are not aware of any other

Asian country in which so many gay magazines were published across these decades. The large volume of vernacular Thai gay materials documents the modern history of a major non-Western sexual and gender culture and is an academic research trove, with Thailand's gay magazines constituting a resource of genuine international importance. However, like the communities they have emerged from and represent, Thai gay magazines are socially marginalized and culturally stigmatized. Because of cultural sensitivities and anti-homosexual bias, neither the National Library of Thailand nor any university or institutional archive collected these materials, with most established institutions considering gay publications unworthy of preservation. Thai academic libraries have also declined to accept donated copies of these magazines offered freely by Thai gay community organizations. Many Thai gay publications were also ephemeral and of an underground nature known only to the members of these marginalized communities. Thai gay magazines existed in a gray borderland between legitimate publications and under-the-counter erotica and pornography and as such were often at risk of being shut down by the Thai police, who enforce the country's anti-pornography laws.

While only produced since the 1980s, these materials were in danger of disappearing completely, with the only remaining copies being in the hands of private collectors. In this setting, we established the Thai Queer Resources Centre (TQRC) in Bangkok in collaboration with the Bangkok Rainbow Organization, a Thai gay community organization, to draw on their membership networks to access private collectors and undertake a recovery mission to save Thailand's rapidly disappearing gay publications. The objective of the TQRC was to obtain copies of endangered gay magazines from private collectors so they could be digitized. With funding from the British Library's Endangered Archives Programme and in collaboration with the Bangkok Rainbow Organization we were subsequently able to collect and digitize just over one thousand magazines, which are now an open-access online resource available for download from the British Library's (n.d.) website. The only substantial publicly available collection of Thai gay magazines is now held offshore in the UK in digital format.

The large number of titles and issues of Thai gay magazines provides an important indication of the actual size and significance of the country's gay communities over the past several decades and reflects the existence of an extensive local market for Thai-language gay publications since the early 1980s. In the appendix, we list the title, decade of publication, and number of issues of each of the magazines that we discovered during our research. In summary, in the 1980s, 9 separate commercial magazines were published while in the golden age of Thai gay print media, in the 1990s, 61 separate titles of commercial gay magazines appeared on Thai newsstands together with 3 free community magazines. In the first decade of the 2000s, 46 titles of commercial gay magazines were published, 7 different free bar magazines were distributed from gay venues, and 2 free community magazines also appeared. In the final decade of Thai gay print in the 2010s, 27 commercial gay magazine titles were published as well as 8 free bar magazines distributed from gay venues. Despite this large number of titles and issues, gay publishing in Thailand was never an easy undertaking. Some titles were published for only a handful of issues before shutting down. Nevertheless, many magazines were commercially successful for several years and had print runs of over a hundred issues across their lifetime.

Erotica, Pornography, and Gay Identity

While the first generation of gay magazines in the 1980s were broadly oriented lifestyle publications, from the 1990s Thai gay print and online media became increasingly oriented toward sex. We draw on these periodicals and online chat rooms because these media have been key influences in the transformations of Thai gay masculinities and notions of gay identity. Visual imagery, let alone homoerotic or pornographic visual imagery, is rarely given a place in Thai or Southeast Asian area studies or even in Asian gender studies. This is the case even though visual imagery through print, film, and other media has been central to the modern histories of masculine and feminine gender transformations globally. More particularly, Thai gay media have not served merely as forms of sexual entertainment but rather have stimulated imaginings and fantasies of ways of living and being outside of heterosexual social norms. Gay media created spaces for experiences that transgress established social rules and provided foundations for the emergence of new forms of sexual and gender subjectivity.

While Thai gay magazines were often considered obscene (*lamok*) by the Thai authorities, many homosexual men nonetheless came to understand their same-sex desires as being central to their identity by consuming eroticized images of the male body in these sources. In Thailand the history of homoerotic publications has been pivotal to the emergence of modern gay identity as a sense of selfhood founded on awareness of same-sex attraction. For Thai gay men, print and online media representations of sexually desirable masculinity have functioned as social tools that reinforce understandings of same-sex identity and selfhood by mobilizing sexual fantasies that center on the male body.

The narratives and images of sex in gay magazines and chat rooms formed social spaces in which previously isolated Thai homosexual men came to understand their shared interest in other men, and these mediatized spaces of male eroticism in turn provided a foundation for the emergence of forms of gay sociality and community. Communities could only emerge as dimensions of gay cultural life once gay identity itself came into being. And a gay sexual identity could only emerge from a conscious awareness of same-sex interest, which was often forged through the consumption of erotic images. In summary, national forms of gay sociality and gay community in Thailand emerged from a foundation of the national distribution of gay erotica.

Approaches

We have adopted a multidisciplinary approach in this book, drawing on a range of research methods including text analysis, online ethnography, and face-to-face interviews and focus group discussions. The methods used in researching the different case studies are described in detail in the relevant chapters. Our interpretations of Thai sources draw on extensive fieldwork that we have each undertaken among LGBTQI+ communities in Thailand over several decades. Our method draws on critical discourse analysis that pays close attention to changes in both the languaging and the visual representation of masculine desire and identity among Thai men over the decades from the 1980s to the 2010s. The forms of discourse that we consider include narratives, interviews, and other texts published in gay magazines and internet posts as well as online chat in digital platforms and early social media.

Narupon adds that the information and analyses in this book also draw on his own experiences. Narupon grew up in Ayutthaya in central Thailand and moved to Bangkok to study at the university. He has had many gay and *kathoey* friends and colleagues from elementary school to university as well as after graduating and starting work in government organizations. Living and working with gay and bisexual friends has helped frame his understanding of the language and practices of trans and homosexual people. Narupon has also gathered information from visits to gay spaces and venues such as bars, restaurants, pubs, and saunas as well as parks, swimming pools, sports fields, and barracks. He has also interacted with gay informants online.

Structure of the Sections and Chapters

Our book is divided into three parts. In chapters 1 to 3 we study the transformative influence of Thai gay magazines from their inception in the early 1980s to their diversification in the 1990s and early 2000s. Chapters 4 and 5 present ethnographic studies of the class-based forms of gay masculinity that emerged in the early 2000s from the images and discourses that had circulated in gay magazines in the preceding two decades. In chapter 6 we describe the further transformation of Thai gay masculinities that was brought about by digital media in the early 2000s.

In chapter 1 we analyze discourses from a range of Thai gay magazines and online sources to detail how Thai gay men are especially flexible in their gender performances of both effeminacy and masculinity in daily life as well as in romantic relationships and sexual encounters. In addition to gendered forms of comportment and behavior, we consider Thai gay men's multiple performances of gender expressed through masculine and feminine forms of language. While Thai gay social lives are often characterized by camp expressions and effeminacy, Thai gay sex lives are strongly marked by the embodiment and discourses of masculinity. We detail how the language of gay effeminacy is found in the context of in-group social interactions, while the language of gay masculinity predominates in the field of sexual culture and ideals of sexually attractive male bodies. Thai gay identity, then, is based on a contextualization of effeminate sociality and masculine sexuality. The discourses of gay gendering detailed in this chapter provide a basis for the analyses of the practices and embodiment of gay masculinities in the following chapters.

In chapter 2 we use Thailand's first commercially successful gay magazines as sources to understand the emergence of social and business connections between gay bars and middle-class gay men in Bangkok during the 1980s. Drawing on Thailand's first successful gay magazine, *Mithuna Junior*, and other early gay publications such as *Neon, Morakot*, and *Midway*, which emerged as competitor gay magazines in the mid-1980s, we describe the development of gay bars and spaces in Bangkok as well as Thailand's stratified class-based gay sexual cultures. The editors and publishers of *Mithuna Junior* collaborated with gay bars to produce new forms of homoerotic consumption and socialization in which patron-client relationships based on class stratification between working-class male sex workers and middle-class gay clients developed as a dominant pattern. We also show how in the early 1980s gay identity came to be increasingly differentiated from the trans *kathoey*, although many gay men still sought out straight men as sexual partners and were typically positioned as feminine in straight-gay sexual relations.

Chapter 3 considers the masculine imaging of the male models who posed nude for the homoerotic photos published in Thai gay magazines from the 1980s to the 2010s, analyzing how these images reflected patterns of male homosexual desire. We consider how Thai gay men perceived these masculine images and how the representation of male nudity responded to and sustained Thai gay men's sexual imaginations. It is not only the textual forms of discourse in Thai gay magazines that inform us about the transformations of gay masculinity. The images of the men photographed in these magazines also tell us much about Thai cultures of masculinity. Drawing on visual sources, we investigate the relationships between images of the male nude and gay men in the consumer culture that formed the matrix within which Thai gay identity evolved over the late twentieth and early twenty-first centuries. The full-color male centerfolds that were a mainstay of Thai gay magazines from their inception in the early 1980s reveal ideals of masculinity, underlining the fact that there are multiple paragons of gay masculinity in Thailand related to class and ethnicity.

Several body types are identified in the imaging of men in Thai gay magazines: the natural body; the muscular body; the metrosexual body; and the male body decorated with tattoos and earrings. Notable changes in the styles of masculinity imaged in Thai gay magazines are transitions from the style of Thai boxers and sportsmen to the metrosexual man and, since the later 1990s, the bodybuilder. We explore the cultural and social contexts behind these changing representations of the masculinity of the Thai male body, the Thai gay desire for masculine sexual partners, and the types of masculinity that Thai gay men have regarded as sexually desirable. As masculine ideals evolved across the decades, older images of the sexually attractive male body were not superseded but rather remained as alternatives in an increasingly complex gender culture of multiple masculinities that now exist as options and matters of taste and personal preference for different gay men. Thai gay men now negotiate and create their body images from a range of patterns, with several ideals of male sexual attractiveness now coexisting in urban gay gender cultures in the country.

Chapters 4 and 5 present case studies of the distinctive middle-class and working-class masculinities that respectively came to characterize Thailand's diverse gay cultures in the 1990s and early 2000s. Thailand's gay magazines both reflected and supported the development of these class-based forms of gay masculinity. In the early 2000s, fitness centers emerged as gay spaces where middle-class men came to find friends and sexual partners in Bangkok's cosmopolitan consumer culture. The mainstream perception of fitness centers in Thailand today is that they are gay spaces where homosexual men exercise to build up their muscle mass in order to enhance their masculine profile and become more sexually attractive. Although urban Thai gay men have shared some characteristics with gay men in other parts of the world, they experience the spaces of fitness centers in terms of their own distinctive experiences and meanings. In contrast to the situation in some Western countries, gay physical exercise in Thailand has not developed in the context of a gay rights movement but rather for the sole purpose of becoming sexually attractive to other gay men.

Chapter 5 then details the alternative masculinity of working-class coyote boy dancers who performed in gay bars and pubs in Bangkok in the early 2010s. Coyote boy troupes were composed of working-class men of diverse sexualities—heterosexual, bisexual, and homosexual—and their erotic dancing for gay audiences reflected the way these men negotiated their masculine gender roles and sexual desires in different situations. The coyote boy dance phenomenon was primarily a feature of Bangkok gay venues that catered to a local market of younger Thai gay men rather than the bars and pubs whose main clienteles were international gay tourists. We explore the bodily practices by which coyote boy dancers performed their erotic shows and the forms of gendering they embodied in their stage personas as well as their offstage lives.

The slim physiques of coyote boy performers contrasted with the muscularity of middle-class gay men who worked out in gyms and took muscle-developing supplements. Coyote boys represented a distinctive working-class masculinity that was regarded as an ideal of male sexual attractiveness among working-class and lower-middle-class gay men in the early 2010s. Coyote boy performances also reflected a stylization of working-class understandings of what it meant to act like a man—*kek man* or *ab man* in Thai gay parlance—creating performances that eroticized the masculine image in stylized forms of expression.

In chapter 6 we analyze the impact of digital media on the culture of Thai gay masculinity. Commercial digital media have not merely represented images and discourses of Thai gay masculinity. In the years immediately before smartphone technologies became widely available in Thailand and gay dating apps like Grindr, Hornet, and Blued became influential platforms for gay hookups in the country, Camfrog was the most important platform for online sexual encounters for both homosexual and heterosexual men and women. In the early 2010s, Thailand ranked third in the world for use of Camfrog, following the United States and China. The immediacy afforded by online interactive platforms such as Camfrog created virtual cybersex domains that accentuated the performance of masculinity in Thai gay sexual culture. The internet contributed to a more intense masculine gendering of same-sex relations, such that even heterosexual men could participate in gay chat rooms, not necessarily to find a male sexual partner but rather to affirm their own masculinity. In marked contrast to earlier eras when male same-sex relations were seen as feminizing, in the early twenty-first century participating in a gay chat room functioned to demonstrate the masculinity of the users in these virtual domains.

While the men who met and engaged in virtual sexual interactions on Camfrog largely remained silent on the question of their identity as "gay," male same-sex practices were nonetheless framed as strong confirmations of masculine gender identity. As an online video platform devoted almost wholly to sexual interaction, relations on Camfrog took place within intensified patterns of the *ab man* or straight-acting style of gay masculinity. The medium of web-based video brought into even sharper relief the patterns of eroticized masculine performance that had been nurtured by gay print magazines in earlier decades. The sexual activities of the male users of Camfrog did not constitute forms of sexual identity but rather were expressions and confirmations of masculine gender identity. The extent to which same-sex erotic practices enacted by male Camfrog users took place in a highly masculine expressive and discursive setting was underscored by the common idiom among users: "Men who have sex with men are real men" (*chai dai chai kheu yort chai*).

Part I
DISCOURSES AND IMAGES IN THAI GAY MAGAZINES

THAI GAY LANGUAGE OF MASCULINITY AND EFFEMINACY

In this chapter we detail how Thai gay men are especially flexible in their gender performances of both effeminacy and masculinity in the various social situations in their daily lives as well as in their romantic relationships and sexual encounters. In addition to gendered forms of comportment and behavior, Thai gay men's multiple performances of gender are expressed using both masculine and feminine forms of language. Gendered language forms are respectively used to communicate and express both effeminacy and masculinity within circles of gay friends and with sexual partners. Thai gay social lives are often characterized by camp expressions and effeminacy. However, Thai gay sex lives are strongly marked by the embodiment and discourses of masculinity. Thai gay male identity is based on a contextualization of femininity and masculinity, and the alternation between masculine and feminine forms of behavior and language use in different contexts permits gay men to adapt their public social and private sexual relations according to the interactions in the different domains of their lives. The Thai gay discourses of gender detailed in this chapter provide a basis for the analyses of the practices and embodiment of gay masculinities in the chapters that follow.

We use a multidisciplinary research method in this chapter. Our sources include texts from Thai gay magazines from the 1980s, 1990s, and early 2000s that include information on community building, sexual identity, social relationships, and sexual experiences. Beginning in 2012, we also undertook searches of Thai gay internet sites and social media. From Thai gay websites, chat rooms, discussion boards, and mobile phone applications we analyzed messages and reports of experiences that gay men shared in describing their sexual activities, gender identity, and perceptions of masculinity and femininity both in themselves and their sexual and romantic partners. We have also drawn on participant observation from our experiences as scholars who have participated in networks of gay friends and attended gay social events in Bangkok from the 1980s to the early 2020s. We have made use of our experiences and understanding as insider researchers in interpreting Thai gay discourses and behavior in interviews and group discussions. To ensure informant confidentiality assumed names are used throughout the book.

Contextuality and the Enactment of Gender Plurality

Our research confirms Penny Van Esterik's (2000) account of the importance of contextual sensitivity in the realization of multiple patterns of gendering in Thai gay men's lives. Van Esterik observes that "Thais socialize themselves, their children and their visitors to develop contextual sensitivity" (2000, 39), with the term *kala-thesa*, literally "time and place," denoting the ability to move with ease between contexts structured by different normative expectations. In this culture of multiple time and place contexts, Van Esterik argues that Thai gender is "a context-sensitive process. . . . It is Thai sensitivity to context—expressed as *kala-thesa*, knowing how time, space, and relationships between people intersect to create appropriate contexts—that allows for a flow of multiple gender identities. Identities slip easily over each other like tectonic plates, alternately revealing and concealing what lies beneath. . . . Surfaces are transformable, temporary, and aesthetically pleasing, while the self remains hidden and ultimately unknowable, an argument compatible with the Buddhist concepts of 'non-self' (Pali: *anatta*) and 'impermanence' (Pali: *anicca*)" (Van Esterik 1999, 278).[1] Nattapol Wisuttipat argues that because of their movement between forms of masculine and feminine gendering, and in particular the need to conform to dominant norms of masculine presentation, Thai gay men "acquire heightened sensitivity towards time-place appropriateness of *kala-thesa*" (Nattapol 2022, 249).

Feminine *Sao Taek* and Masculine *Ab Man* in Thai Gay Gendering

Thai gay men's alternation between effeminacy in gay social interaction and masculinity in sexual encounters is encapsulated in the key in-group terms *sao taek* and *ab man*. The paired colloquial expressions *sao taek* and *ab man* respectively denote feminine and masculine actions and speech by gay men and can be used either to describe gay in-group camaraderie in friendly banter or as derogatively bitchy put-downs. *Sao taek* refers to camp feminine behaviors and conversational styles during socializing among gay friends in private gay spaces, while *ab man* is the situational masculinity performed in public heteronormative settings within the family, at work, and in everyday life in society as well as when seeking a sexual partner.

A widespread belief in Thai gay culture is that every gay man has a feminine part.[2] The enactment of gay effeminacy is variously referred to as *khwam-pen-ying* ("being lady-like"), *khwam-sao* ("girliness"), *taek sao* ("to break out one's [inner] girl"), or more commonly *sao taek* ("for one's [inner] girl to break out"). It is a form of in-group social play that works as a tool in making and maintaining relationships among gay friends. *Khwam-pen-ying* is a more formal and technical term while *khwam-sao* is informal with a more intimate "cute" (*na-rak*) and "sweet" (*wan*) sense. In expressions of male femininity and effeminacy, the term *ying*, which refers to a mature woman of marriageable age, conveys somewhat formal yet nonetheless polite nuances, while *sao*, which denotes a young woman, has a nice, sweet sense. The most common expressions for gay femininity are formed with *taek*, "to break" or "to break out," and suggest that a gay man either intentionally expresses his inner femininity, *taek sao*, or his femininity breaks out, *sao taek*, perhaps unintentionally or despite attempts to be masculine or straight acting.

While gay effeminacy is expressed in private social spaces, in contrast Thai gay masculinity, *khwam-pen-chai* or "being manly," is enacted in sexual and romantic situations. Gay men also act like a man in family and public settings within heterosexual institutions. In the early twenty-first century, *ab man* is the most common Thai gay idiom for masculine straight acting and can have either a playful teasing sense or a derogatory connotation of putting on airs and pretending to be butch while in fact having an inner "girl" (*sao*). *Man* is borrowed from the English "man" and has been used since at least the 1970s to signify a masculine identity or presentation. Nattapol (2022, 228) describes *man* in Thai as meaning "heterosexual-presenting."

Ab man is derived from a slang expression, *ab bao*, which first came into use in the early 2000s.[3] *Ab bao* is a mildly derogatory idiom that describes a young woman who affectedly feigns innocence to appear attractive and cute while in fact being worldly and sexually experienced. *Bao* is a slang term that describes childlikeness or childishness. There are two schools of thought on the origin of the term *ab*. Some Thai linguists suggest that *ab* is derived from the term *aep*, which means to be furtive or sneaky and to do something covertly or by stealth. *Aep* entered Thai gay slang in the 1980s as part of the expression *aep jit*, literally "a sneaky mind/persona," coined by the American-educated former academic and gay media personality Seri Wongmontha to translate "to be closeted" into Thai. However, other scholars suggest that *ab* is an abbreviation for the English term "abnormal." Whatever its origin, *ab* spread into wider usage to mean to pretend or feign, so in Thai gay speak *ab man* means to pretend to be masculine while in fact being gay or effeminate.

An earlier Thai gay expression for "straight acting," *kek man*, was used in the 1980s and 1990s but is now less common. *Kek* is a loanword from the Southern Chinese Teochew (Thai: Tae Jiw) language that means to put on airs or act affectedly and *kek man* means to pretend to be masculine or act in an exaggerated and affectedly masculine way.[4] The straight-acting tactics of passing—that is, not expressing feminine characteristics so as not to be identified as gay in public—are also called *mai sadaeng ork*, which means "not to show or demonstrate" femininity or effeminacy. *Mai sadaeng ork* is the negative form of *sadaeng ork*, which means to express or show femininity or effeminacy and hence be publicly identifiable as gay. Gay men who conform to heteronormative patterns of masculinity can also be described by the idiom *du mai ork*, "I can't tell [that he's gay]." Nattapol reports that, among gay musicians in genres of Thai classical music, the expressions *kep akan*, "to keep [a masculine] position," and *khip luk*, from the English "keep [a masculine] look," describe "withholding any bodily gestures that reveal their gender nonconformity and thus lead to homosexual suspicion" (2022, 29). He describes Thai gay men's public performances of *kep akan* or *khip luk* masculinity as "curated gender" and "curated bodily practices" (29).

Gay men stand at the intersection of Thailand's multiple cultures of masculinity and femininity, variously enacting distinctive forms of both genders depending on the context and setting. In Thai gay communities developing skill in these different contextualized performances of masculinity and effeminacy is important for successful socializing and in establishing sexual and romantic relationships. The nuanced and often complex expression of both masculinity and femininity denoted in Thai gay language use detailed below reflects gay men's ability to adapt to the contextual demands imposed on them by the dominant heteronormative gender/sex regime. Thai gay discourses also reveal an indigenous view of nonessential gender, of feminine and masculine genders as enacted, with the feminine expression *sao taek* and the masculine *ab man* both emphasizing notions of gender affectation or pretense. And within Thai gay communities there are also distinctive class-based forms of gendering. As discussed in subsequent chapters, forms of masculine and feminine gendering differ significantly between socioeconomically stratified classes of gay men.[5]

The Changing Gendering of Thai Gay Men's Sex

Straight-acting *ab man* masculinity has become increasingly central in Thai gay cultures since the 1970s, when a series of major transformations began to take place in Thai gay cultures. Since the middle decades of the twentieth century, Thai homosexual men have increasingly sought to distinguish themselves from trans women *kathoey* (Jackson and Sullivan 1999). The 1970s was the decade when a modern gay culture first emerged widely in Thai society and was a transitional period during which Thai homosexual men began to become more confident in identifying as gay. The 1970s saw the beginnings of the transformative influence of print media, when many Thai homosexual men learned about modern gay life and identity from the lonely-hearts column "The Sad Life of Gays" (*chiwit sao chao gay*) written by an agony uncle who used the pen name Uncle Go Pak-nam in the nationally distributed sensationalist fortnightly magazines *Plaek* ("Strange") and *Mahatsajan* ("Miraculous") (see Jackson 2016). The following decade of the 1980s saw Thailand's first commercially successful gay magazines, *Mithuna Junior* and *Neon*, which we analyze in chapter 2. These publications introduced increasing numbers of middle-class homosexual men to the expanding commercial scene of gay bars, pubs, and massage parlors in Bangkok and Chiang Mai as well as the tourist cities of Pattaya and Phuket.

The decades of the 1970s and 1980s also saw changing attitudes about being gay and the performance of manhood. In this period, it was still the case that most Thai homosexual men felt that they could only identify as gay in private, while they should act like a man, *kek man* or *ab man*, in public places. The first experiences of gay life for many middle-class Thai homosexual men were in visiting gay venues, especially gay bars, where they met straight young men who worked as male sex workers. Rather than seeking out other gay men, large numbers of middle-class homosexual men in these decades had sex with male sex workers. At this time, homosexual men who identified as gay usually took a sexually receptive position, called *gay queen* in the Thai gayspeak of the period. Gay-identified men were usually expected to take the receptive role in anal intercourse with a male sex worker, who was expected to play the active role, which was labeled as *king* or *gay king*. The *gay queen* identity and personality of this period was widely taken as signifying an effeminate person who expressed his sexual desire through engaging in receptive anal intercourse with a more masculine, and ostensibly heterosexual, male sex worker.

Peter Jackson and Gerard Sullivan (1999) have observed that the paired opposite sexual roles of *gay queen* and *gay king* reflected understandings of *phet*, the indigenous Thai discourse of gender and sexuality, which in gay cultures of the period were realized through different degrees of masculine and feminine expression and under which ascribed gender was central to regulating and clas-sifying sexual status.[6] The paired 1970s terms *gay king* and *gay queen* reflected how normative masculine and feminine gender roles were interpreted and evalu-ated within homosexual practices. At this time, many homosexual men perceived their sexual identity in terms of the binary model of masculine insertive and feminine receptive sexual relations, with the two sexual roles of masculine *gay king* top and feminine *gay queen* bottom exemplifying the normative male and female gendering of gay relationships and identities.

However, major changes took place in Thai gay sexual culture in the 1990s, when gay men increasingly turned to other gay men as their preferred sexual partners rather than heterosexual male sex workers. The terms *gay king* and *gay queen* are now outdated among younger generations of gay men, who regard these expressions as reflecting the way that gay identity was restricted by het-eronormative gender roles in earlier decades. The terms *king* and *queen* have become old-fashioned because they denoted a masculine/feminine binary in gay sexual relations. Since the 1990s, sexual roles have become increasingly delinked from gendered expression, with gay men who are the receptive partners seeking to express masculinity in equal degree to those who take the insertive role. Thai gay men have come to see themselves as masculine whatever their sexual role. The gendered associations of the sexually receptive *gay queen* as feminine and the sexually insertive *gay king* as masculine are now avoided by the use of a newer set of terminologies that describe sexual roles without implying any sense of gen-dering. As detailed further in the following chapter, the terms *ruk*, "to advance, invade," and *rap*, "to receive," are now respectively preferred instead of *king* and *queen*. The terms *ruk* and *rap* have been borrowed from the masculine sport of Muay Thai, Thai boxing, in which offensive punches are called *tha ruk*, "an attacking stance," and defensive positions are called *tha rap*, "a receptive stance" (Kukdej 2010). While now superseding the terms *king* and *queen*, *ruk* and *rap* nonetheless perpetuate a cultural classification of sexual knowledge that sepa-rates different roles in sexual practices and reflects the idea that people are identi-fied by their preferred sexual conduct.

The opening of a large number of gay saunas in Bangkok in the 1990s pro-vided increasing numbers of gay men in the capital with expanded opportu-nities for sexual experimentation with multiple partners who were other gay men, not male sex workers.[7] Saunas were especially important sexual spaces for urban gay men in learning how to transcend stereotypes of gay effeminacy and behave in masculine ways in romantic and sexual relationships with other men. It was in the context of a shift of the center of gay sexual and social life from bars to saunas that *ab man* performances of eroticized masculinity became increasingly important. In the 1990s, it was more common for gay men to say that *gay queens* could change and play an insertive role, *fai ruk*, in anal sexual intercourse, just as a *gay king* could be the receptive partner, *fai rap*. Sometimes, both *queens* and *kings* could be both receptive and insertive, now known in Thai as either "can do everything" (*dai mot*) or by the borrowed English term *both*, that is, "*both* top (*ruk*) and bottom (*rap*)." By the late 1990s and early 2000s, as the binary masculine-feminine gendering of gay men's sexual roles declined, the terms *king* and *queen* were replaced by *ruk* "insertive," *rap* "receptive," and *both* "versatile," which referred to male-male sexual activity without ascribing either a masculine or feminine gendering to sexual positions. Nevertheless, it is still the case that in Thai gay culture the insertive partner or *fai ruk* may also playfully be called a "husband" (*phua*) while the receptive partner or *fai rap* can be called a "wife" (*mia*).

One of the most notable transformations that took place in Thai gay culture in the 1990s was an increasingly widespread acknowledgment that even effeminate gay men may take any role in bed and that being either top or bottom in sexual relations may be unrelated to either masculine or feminine presentation or behavior. Thai gay and *kathoey* communities now use the playful expression *sao siap*, "a penetrating girl," to refer to effeminate gay men who can play the insertive *ruk* role. *Sao siap* was first used in *kathoey* communities to denote preoperative trans women who play the insertive role in anal sex with male partners and subsequently spread to be used among gay men.

As Thailand's commercial gay scene of bars, pubs, discotheques, and saunas expanded in the later decades of the twentieth century, increasing numbers of homosexual men were able to meet others in safe, private spaces that provided them with opportunities to learn how to identify as gay and to differentiate themselves from traditional images of the gender-crossing *kathoey*. They were also able to express sexual desires and engage in forms of sociality with gay friends by adopting and negotiating characteristics of both masculinity and femininity. Contextualized *kala-thesa* "time and place" social and cultural spaces are important for Thai homosexual men to learn about the different situations in which masculinity and femininity may respectively be expressed. Among Thai gay men, femininity and effeminacy are not the sole foundations of gendered identity, as is the case among trans women *kathoey*. For Thai gay men, effeminacy and femininity are more matters of play than of gendered identity. Thai gay men alternate between *sao taek* feminine and *ab man* masculine performances depending on the *kala-thesa* social context, often expressing feminine and effeminate characteristics in paradoxical relationship with masculine forms of expression. The following chapters present case studies of how Thai gay men of different classes have negotiated the alternation between feminine *sao taek* sociality and masculine *ab man* sexuality in different decades over the past half century. We show how the transformations in Thai gay sexual culture across this period, which saw progressively greater emphasis on the performance of masculinity, was nurtured by commercial print and online media.

In the remainder of this chapter, we describe the nuanced discourses of femininity and masculinity in Thai gay communities as language use is central to gendered being and presentation in Thailand. We first summarize the general features of gendered discourse in Thai and language use in trans women *kathoey* communities as Thai gayspeak draws heavily from their vocabularies and discursive forms.

The Thai Language and Gendered Discourse

In the modern national language of Thailand, based on the dialect of the country's central region surrounding Bangkok, pronouns, particles, and other parts of speech are highly diversified in terms of expressing different nuances of masculine and feminine gender. Men and women have distinctive ways of speaking that both demonstrate and specify their respective sexual and gender identities. This gendering of the language has come to reflect the modern official forms of sexuality and the gender ideals promoted by the Thai state since the time of Prime Minister Field Marshal Plaek Phibunsongkhram during World War II. Since then, the Thai nation-state has sought to socialize and regulate its citizens under a patriarchal heteronormative ideology as part of a nationalist paradigm for engendering forms of sexual civilization that, it was believed, would enable Thailand to compete against Western colonial powers (Reynolds 1999; Kongsakon 2002; Jackson 2003). This social control of the binary gendering of men and women has now permeated every dimension of Thai social life, with state gender controls being found in family law, dress, body language, and forms of intimacy as well as in the spoken and written languages.

Thailand's national language is structured primarily in terms of heterosexual norms. The "good Thai citizen" (*phonlameuang di*) should both speak and act properly according to state regulations. Men and woman have their own gendered vocabularies and associated forms of bodily comportment that are linked with speech norms. These forms of speech are important reflections of masculine and feminine characteristics and modern Thai culture is highly sensitive to discursive references to gender, for both the speaker and interlocutors. Gendered pronouns, sentence particles, and titles have become so central to the norms of proper spoken Thai that it is all but impossible to avoid gendered references in most everyday situations. Thai requires the speaker to specify their gender identity as either masculine or feminine as well as the assumed or presumed gender identity of persons spoken to and spoken about.

Thai first-person pronouns—that is, terms translated by the gender-neutral English pronoun "I"—are almost all gendered. There are multiple Thai first-person pronouns, whose use is not determined by grammatical rules but rather by social conventions to reflect degrees of politeness and intimacy as well as the masculine or feminine gender identity of the speaker. Thai also has politeness particles that are used at the end of sentences. These gendered particles are also used to express agreement—that is, to say "yes." In polite speech, men use the sentence particle *khrap* while women use *kha* at the end of sentences to express courtesy as well as to agree with another speaker. These two particles respectively mark the masculine or feminine identity of the speaker. *Khrap* is also used by trans men and masculine-identified lesbians or *tom*, while *kha* is used by feminine-identified trans women *kathoey*. Among masculine-identified Thai men, regardless of their sexuality as either straight or gay, gendered pronouns and sentence particles are formalized expressions of masculine identity and behavior. Masculine-identified Thai men do not use speech forms that are employed by women.

Kathoey and the Language of Gender Transition and Transformation

While Thai gay and trans women *kathoey* identities and communities are increasingly differentiated, they nonetheless continue to overlap and intersect in many ways and Thai gay men often playfully borrow and adapt the language of *kathoey*. Thai has rich vocabularies of *kathoey* transgendering in multiple registers that include Buddhist religious terminologies, technical biomedical and legal terms as well as both derogatory and appreciative terms that are used in the general community. Many usages within *kathoey* communities have also become known widely in Thai society and have been incorporated into mainstream colloquial and slang discourse. Thai gay men draw on all these diverse terms and language levels in context-specific and often playful ways.

The ancient North Indian language Pali, the classical language of the Theravada Buddhist scriptures, has contributed the terms *napungsaka*, "hermaphrodite," and *bandor* as technical expressions to describe both cross-gender behavior and intersex people. While the Central Thai term *kathoey* is now dominant across the country—a result of nation-building policies in the twentieth century that promoted Central Thai as the national language of administration, education, and media—regional varieties of Thai formerly had their own distinctive dialectical terminologies. In northern Thailand an effeminate man was previously called *pu-mia*, "male-wife/female," while in northeastern Thailand effeminate men were called *phu-mae*, "male-mother/female." In these varieties of Thai, the terms for "wife" (*mia*) and "mother" (*mae*) were commonly used as general terms to refer to sexually mature women, who in Central Thai are termed *phu-ying*.

Under the modernizing regime of the fascist-inspired Prime Minister Phibunsongkhram from the late 1930s to the late 1950s, Thai society was subjected to an intense regularization of the heteronormative system in which the sex/gender binary that separated the culture of men and masculinity from women and femininity was promoted as an instrument of state cultural policy. Under this system, femininity among men was increasingly problematized (Kongsakon 2002). It was in the aftermath of this state-ordered system that the first program of academic research into what was then described as the "social problem" of the *kathoey* was begun in the 1960s (see Jackson 1997b). Nattapol describes how government officers in Thailand are still expected to embody the official gender norms that were introduced in the mid-twentieth century. "The employees who are government officials . . . face the necessity to abide by the binarized gender ideals not only because they are regarded as exemplifying those with civil manners, but also because they are viewed as the preservers of the national culture . . . and as cultural exemplars (teachers). . . . Government institutions are places that straighten any display of queerness" (Nattapol 2022, 243).

Men who do not conform to the state-imposed gender binary and act in an effeminate manner face social sanctions and discrimination, experience less social respect, and are often treated as sexual objects by heterosexual men (Jackson 1995). They are viewed as "artificial women" (*phu-ying thiam*) and popular discourses and media representations often portray them as being ill-fated in love, finding it difficult to establish a lasting romantic relationship with men. Nevertheless, in many rural areas of Thailand *kathoey* beauty contests are often popular events at festivals such as temple fairs held to raise funds for Buddhist monasteries. In these public beauty contests, *kathoey* have a chance to demonstrate their feminine beauty through female fashion and makeup. And in this specific context they can achieve respect and may receive respectful titles such as *nang-fa jamlaeng*, "an angel transformed [into a human being]" or "an angel in human form" if they are judged as succeeding in embodying normative ideals of feminine beauty. Formerly, local *kathoey* beauty contests had evolved to a high level and achieved acceptance as nationally televised tourist attractions in events such as the annual Miss Tiffany's Universe beauty contest for trans women *kathoey* in the coastal resort city of Pattaya. It has become increasingly common to find *kathoey* who live as women working in female professions such as dancers, makeup artists, hairdressers, and fashion designers. The relationship between *kathoey* identity and feminine beauty has achieved general recognition in Thailand's mass media, and many trans women *kathoey* are now appreciated for their embodiment of modern ideals of femininity.

A wide range of terms continue to be used to refer to *kathoey* and, depending on the context, may variously reflect attitudes of either disparagement or admiration. One strongly disparaging term is *tut*. When used by heterosexual speakers, this term is strongly homophobic and transphobic. *Tut* is also used by gay men in anger with other gay men or *kathoey* as a form of verbal abuse. Another common term widely used in gay circles is *taeo*, which is like "queen" in English gayspeak expressions such as drag queen, drama queen, or to act queeny. *Taeo* is a softer, less confrontational term than *tut*. *Taeo taek*, formed on the model of the idiom *sao taek* noted earlier, means to act queeny. *Sao praphet sorng*, "a second type of girl," and *phu-ying praphet sorng*, "a second type of woman," are more formal expressions that were popularized by trans-identified people in the 1980s and 1990s as more acceptable, polite expressions. *Phu-ying thiam*, "an artificial woman," while less common nowadays, was used in the later decades of the twentieth century to refer to both preoperative and postoperative trans women. The Thai man's name *Pratheuang* became another term for *kathoey* in popular discourse in the 1990s after a pop song with this title was released. The song described a man who meets an old school buddy named *Pratheuang*, who has since undergone gender reassignment surgery. Since the early 2000s, *phu-ying kham-phet* has become increasingly widely used as a polite formal expression for trans women and *trans*—abbreviated from *trans*gender and *trans*sexual—has also been borrowed and used as a self-identifying label by some trans women.

There are many diverse identities in the broader cultures and communities of *kathoey*, several of which do not conform to dominant norms of heterosexual feminine beauty. While some *kathoey* undergo medical procedures of full gender reassignment and are called *kathoey plaeng phet*, "changed-sex *kathoey*" or "transsexual *kathoey*," others do not have surgery but rather feminize their bodies by taking female hormones such as estrogen. In more formal settings this latter group is often described as *kathoey mai plaeng phet*, "nontranssexual *kathoey*." In colloquial settings preoperative trans women are called *kathoey mi ngu*, a "*kathoey* with a snake"—that is, a *kathoey* with a penis—an expression that was first used within *kathoey* circles but is now widely known among the public. After completing sex reassignment surgery, they may describe themselves as *pha laeo*, "having been operated on," or more colloquially *chor laeo*, "having been snipped or chopped."

Some working-class *kathoey* on low incomes may not have enough money to pay for either cosmetic surgery or female hormones, and while cross-dressing and wearing makeup retain a more visible male physiology. These working-class *kathoey* may be disparagingly called "water-buffalo *kathoey*," *kathoey khwai*, because of their dark skin and masculine musculature. Economic status is a prerequisite for undergoing the medically assisted transformation that enables a female-identifying *kathoey* to successfully embody feminine beauty and achieve respect as "an angel in human form" rather than being disparaged as having a buffalo-like body.

In a study of *kathoey* performers in Pattaya cabaret shows Prempreeda Pramoj na Ayutthaya (2003) has outlined the differently nuanced ways by which *kathoey* identify themselves in terms of the extent to which they embody both the performance of femininity and have undergone medically assisted transformation into femaleness. In Thailand's modern communities of trans women, the feminization of the body through surgical removal of the male organs and the sculpting of a female sexual physiology is the final stage of the journey of personal transformation. With the attainment of a feminized body, *kathoey* develop an enhanced sense of self-confidence. The contemporary, self-confident *kathoey* identity has been forged in a historical context of social and cultural learning that Thai trans women have undertaken as members of evolving communities aided by advances in medical technologies of gender reassignment, hormone treatment, and cosmetic surgery.

Kathoey Femininity and Gay Effeminacy

The femininity of *kathoey* is realized through modification and transformation of the male body into a desired female form. This is different from the situation for gay men, whose effeminacy is not judged by bodily transformation but rather by speech and behavior. Gay men who enact and express femininity nonetheless derive their sexual identity from sexual intimacy and romantic involvement with men. The physiology of the male body is of paramount significance for gay men, who rely on the male physique and sex organs while engaging in sexual relations with other men. In contrast to trans women *kathoey*, gay men do not desire to undergo gender reassignment surgery, as the penis is central to their identity based on same-sex desire for males who embody masculine characteristics. While the gendering and identity of the trans woman *kathoey* are based on surgical removal of the penis, or the obscuring of the penis among preoperative *kathoey mi ngu*, the gendering and identity of gay men is based on the preservation and valorization of the penis. For the trans woman *kathoey*, femininity is realized by a biomedically assisted transition from the male/masculine to the female/feminine. In contrast, for gay men, femininity and masculinity are alternate behavioral and linguistic modalities that are often expressed in playful and ironic ways in contextualized settings that are unrelated to physical embodiment.

Thai Gay Men and the Language of Effeminacy

Among Thai gay men, both masculine and feminine gendered terms are used in different situations. Thai gays select gendered words to identify both themselves and their friends, and language use is a primary field for the expression of effeminacy. *Ork sao*, abbreviated from *sadaeng ork sao*, "express or showing girliness," describes a gay man who has an effeminate demeanor in his everyday life as well as in private settings. As noted earlier, feminine mannerisms and ways of speaking used among gay friends are described as *sao taek* or, in even more informal speech, as *taeo taek*. These expressions describe situations where a gay man's inner "girl" (*sao*) or "faggot" (*taeo*) "breaks out" (*taek*) through the public performance of normative masculinity, whether intentionally or unintentionally. *Sao taek* describes a more feminine gender expression than *ork sao* and describes a context-specific social behavior in which Thai gay men act in effeminate or girly ways within their groups of friends in mostly private settings.

Ways in which a gay man may *taek sao* in private settings include the use of the polite feminine first-person pronouns *dichan* or *chan*, the female sentence particles *kha* and *ya* (the latter is used informally by Thai women), and by referring to gay friends by feminine third-person pronouns such as *lorn*, *chi* (from the English "she"), *thoe*, and *nang*, all of which denote "she/her." It is common for gay men to use terms that relate to womanlike and feminine characteristics in conversation in private settings with friends. Effeminate speech forms are not used with strangers or in public settings where a gay man wishes to present a masculine persona. For example, the informal feminine title *ee* is often used before a gay man's name, whereby a man nicknamed *Ek* may be called *Ee Ek*, "Missy Ek." This means that he is regarded as expressing feminine characteristics. Gay friends can also be referred to as *pheuan sao*, "girl friends." When surprised or excited, Thai gays may use female interjections, such as *wai!*, which is an exclamation used by women to express fright or strong displeasure. When gay men cross-dress and do drag, they may be described as "beautiful" (*suay*), "attractive" (*ngam*), or more informally as *roet*, a slang term that also means to be pretty or beautiful. If they powder their face, their friends may tease them with terms such as *deng* or *na deng*, meaning to have a powdered, whitened face.

Many Thai gays are especially adept in using feminine forms of disparagement to engage in playful banter and bitchiness. Terms of disparagement used by women usually reflect anger or disapproval, but when used by gay men among friends these same terms may not necessarily carry negative connotations. Among close friends, Thai gays often transform female terms of disparagement into amusing expressions of camaraderie and intimacy. Examples are *raet*, *ee raet*, and *dork-thorng*, all of which are bitchy, slang terms that mean "You slut!" If a gay man expresses a desire to sleep with a handsome guy, his friends might exclaim *hee khan*, "You've got an itchy cunt!"—a derogatory misogynistic expression used to describe women who are regarded as showing too much interest in sex. If it is known that a gay man has slept with many men, his friends might refer to him as *kari*, or "whore." While these are highly derogatory terms when used to refer to women and would never be used in public settings or in formal conversation, when used within circles of gay friends they are more terms of amusement that reflect friendship and engender gay in-group camaraderie. In these settings, use of these terms rarely incites an angry response. In table 1.1 we list some of the female words in different categories of parts of speech that are used by Thai gay men.

TABLE 1.1 Thai gay men's language of femininity and effeminacy

CATEGORY OF WORDS	TERMS
First-person pronouns	*Dian* (I/me—woman) (informal form of *dichan*)
	Dichan (I/me—woman)
Second-person pronoun	*Nu* ("little girl"; she/her, used of younger gay men)
Third-person pronouns (she/her)	*Chi* (from English "she"; she/her)
	Lorn (she/her)
	Nang ("miss," she/her)
	Thoe (she/her)
Feminine gender titles	*Ee* (she)—A colloquial title used before women's names and nicknames, which gay men also often use before the names and nicknames of other gay men, especially if they are effeminate or regarded as *ab man*, affecting masculinity
Feminine sentence particles	*Jao kha* (yes—very formal)
	Kha (yes—polite)
	Na ya (yes—informal)
	Phekha (yes—used by women when replying to a member of Thai royalty)
	Ya (yes—informal)
Adjectives and verbs	*Deng* (to wear face-brightening powder or makeup; literally "bouncy")
	Jik kat (to be bitchy; literally "to peck and bite")
	Ke (pretty, smart, charming, chic)
	Khan hee (to be horny; literally "My cunt is itching")
	Ngam (pretty)
	Phraeo (bright)
	Roet (perfect, gorgeous, fantastic, fabulous)
	Sao (a young woman; to be feminine acting)
	Sao taek (exposure or revelation of femininity)
	Suay (beautiful)
	Taek sao (expressing femininity)
	Taeo taek, tut taek (feminine acting)

(continued)

TABLE 1.1   (continued)

CATEGORY OF WORDS	TERMS
Interjections	*Ee!* (scream of fear)
	Taai tai! (scream of surprise)
	Ui! (scream of excitement)
	Wai! (scream of fright or shock)
Expletives and bitchy scolding	*Datjarit* (to be affected, pretentious)
	Dork-thorng (You bitch! You slut!)
	Ee dork (You bitch! You slut!)
	Ee pleuak (Damn you! Literally "You termite!")
	Ee raet (You slut!)
	Ee ran (You slut!)
	Ee sat (You cheat! Literally "You animal!")
	Hee khan (to be slutty; literally "to have an itchy cunt")
	Kadae (to show off)
	Kari (You whore!)
	Na hee (cunt face, extremely disparaging)
	Raet (to be slutty)
	Torlae (to lie, to bullshit)

The Thai Gay Language of Drag

Thai gay men also have distinctive vocabularies for drag. Humorous cross-dressing is straightforwardly called *taeng ying*, "to dress as a woman." Placing the hands on the waist and striking a pose like a female fashion model on the catwalk is called *thao eo*, "foot waist." Pointing the index finger to the front, regarded as a feminine form of body language, is called *chi niw*, "finger pointing." Pointing the foot in front of the body in a feminine way is known as *phoi thao*, an idiom that combines an abbreviation of the English word "point" and the Thai term for "foot," *thao*. This refers to imitating the pose of a female model who points a foot forward to give a better display of her dress or skirt. Putting on a longhair wig is known as *jik wig*, "to throw on a wig," while hiding any visible sign of the penis beneath the underwear is called *taep*. This latter term may be derived from either the English word "tab" or "tape" as cross-dressing drag performers often use tape to hold the penis close against the body so it is not visible when wearing tight-fitting clothes. Table 1.2 lists some common gay idioms to describe various types of feminine acting.

TABLE 1.2   Thai gay idioms for feminine body expression

BODY EXPRESSION	MEANING
Bo na; bo paeng	To brush powder on the face
Chi niw	To point the index finger
Jik wig	To put on a wig
Poi(nt) thao	To point a foot in front of the body
Taeng ying	To cross-dress as a woman
Taep	To hold the penis tightly against the body in underwear with tape
Thao eo	To place one's hands on the waist

The Language of Masculinity of Gay Men, Straight Men, and *Tom*

To accord with heterosexual gender norms, many Thai gay men seek to embody male gender roles in public settings where they use the language of masculinity. They refer to themselves as *phom*, "I/me," the same first-person pronoun used by straight men. Like straight men, in informal settings close gay friends who present a masculine persona may also refer to themselves using the pronoun *ku*, "I," while addressing the person spoken to as *meung*, "you." The pronouns *ku* and *meung* can be used by either men or women when speaking with an interlocutor of any gender. Unlike personal pronouns such as *dichan* and *phom*, which respectively indicate either a feminine or masculine gender identity, *ku* and its paired second-person pronoun *meung* do not mark the speaker as identifying with any gender. While gender neutral, *ku* can nonetheless carry the sense that the speaker views him- or herself as gender normative. For this reason it is especially widely used by men who wish to present themselves as masculine. When they are acting in a masculine way with other gay men of a similar age, they may address their interlocutors as *nai*. If the man spoken to is older, he may be called *phi*, "older brother," and if the interlocutor is younger than the speaker, he may be referred to as *norng*, "younger brother." When referring to a straight or gay male viewed in a masculine way, the third-person pronoun *khao*, "he/him," is used. The masculine title *ai* ("him") may be used before a man's name or nickname, such as a man nicknamed Daeng being referred to as *Ai* Daeng. *Ku* ("I"), *meung* ("you"), and *ai* (prenominal male title) are all impolite when used with people who are not close acquaintances but among friends they express masculine camaraderie and friendship.

Thai gay men also use the same masculine sentence particles as straight men: *khrap* in everyday situations, *khrapphom* in formal settings, and *ha* or *wa* in informal speech. Use of these sentence particles indicates both a masculine

TABLE 1.3 The language of masculinity of gay men, straight men, and *tom*

CATEGORY OF WORDS	GAY MEN	STRAIGHT MEN	TOM BOYS
Personal pronouns	*Phom* (I/me)	*Phom*	*Phom*
	Ku (I/me)	*Ku*	*Ku*
	Nai (you)	*Nai*	*Nai*
	Meung (you)	*Meung*	*Meung*
	Ai (him)	*Ai*	*Ai*
Sentence particles	*Ha*	*Ha*	*Ha*
	Khrap	*Khrap*	*Khrap*
	Khrapphom	*Khrapphom*	
Interjection	*Hoei* (Hey!)	*Hoei*	*Hoei*
Expletives	*Ai ha* (Damn you!)	*Ai ha*	*Ai ha*
	Ai hia (Damn you!)	*Ai hia*	*Ai hia*
	Ai sat (Damn!)	*Ai sat*	
	Khuay (Cock!)	*Khuay*	
	Maeng (Damn!)	*Maeng*	

identity and the performance of a masculine gender role. Masculine-identified lesbian *tom* also use the sentence particle *khrap* and the first-person pronoun *phom*. Some *tom* may also use the informal sentence particle *ha* to demonstrate their masculine gender identity. When gay men and *tom* use these words, they do not act merely as a medium of communication but rather demonstrate the masculine identity and sense of manliness of the speaker.

The interjection *Hoey* "Hey!" is used by masculine speakers and Thai also has a wide range of expletives used by men. *Ai ha*, "Damn you!" (literally, "You pestilent plague!"), *ai hia* "Damn you!" (literally, "You monitor lizard!"), and *ai sat* "Damn you!" (literally, "You animal!") are all extremely strong swear terms that are likely to elicit a strong, perhaps even violent, response from the person they are directed at. *Khuay*, a common Thai slang term for the penis or "cock," can also be used as an expletive to mean "Damn!" *Maeng* has the strong sense of "You motherfucker!" or "That motherfucker!" and is abbreviated from *yet mae meung*, "Fuck your mother!" Table 1.3 lists some of the most common masculine gender terms used by Thai gay men, straight men, and masculine-identified *tom*.

Gay men, heterosexual men, and *tom* use very similar vocabularies of masculinity. Verbal masculinity conveys strength, authority, and courage and Thai heterosexual men often speak in a curt manner to indicate that they are in control of things. *Tom* also use masculine terms to indicate that they are strong and able protect their feminine female partners, or *dee*. In the case of gay men, masculine language use symbolizes the enactment of heteronormative gendering, which, as detailed in the following chapters, is especially important in establishing sexual relationships. Thai gay men use masculine language forms for the dual purposes of social acceptance by conforming to heterosexual norms and to seek relationships with masculine gay men. Expressing masculine characteristics and using masculine terms reflect the need for social conformity by Thai gays who want to avoid discrimination and who wish to establish sexual and romantic relations with other gay men.

Thai Gay Men's Negative Attitudes Toward Public Expressions of Effeminacy

While effeminate expression is common among many groups of Thai gay men, who may be called *gay sao*, "girlie gays," some masculine gay men nonetheless hold negative attitudes toward effeminacy. These men believe that a male homosexual should act as a *man*—that is, someone who acts and talks like a *phu-chai*, "heterosexual man," in everyday life. As noted earlier, the English word "man" has been borrowed into Thai gayspeak to describe acting in a masculine way. In Thai *man* now describes a masculine presentation of either a gay-identified or heterosexual male, while *phu-chai* is used in the specific sense of denoting the masculine gender of a heterosexually identified male. English has been an important source of new terms in Thai gayspeak since "gay" was first borrowed in the 1960s. However, once borrowed into Thai, English terms often take on new meanings and distinctive resonances. Borrowed English terms are also often combined with Thai words to create new compound expressions, as in the term *kek man*, "to affect masculinity."

In table 1.4 we list some of the terms used by Thai gays to describe acting in a masculine *ab man* way.

TABLE 1.4   Idioms for masculine body expression among Thai gays

BODY EXPRESSION	MEANING
Kep meu	To keep one's hands beside the body; not being overly expressive with one's hands
Len klam	To work out; to do bodybuilding exercises
Nang khwai hang	To sit crossed-legged
Sak rangkai	To have a body tattoo
Thang kha	To spread the legs when sitting
Thort seua	To take off one's shirt
Wai nuat	To have a moustache

The terms listed in table 1.4 denote the masculine performance of *ab man*, of avoiding feminine ways of acting or embodiment. Nattapol observes that the term *samruam* is often used to refer to the type of restrained self-control, or avoidance of feminine exuberance, that is central to normative forms of masculine performance in Thailand. *Samruam* describes the ability to refrain from making immediate gestures or emotional expression in an obvious, explicit, or exaggerated manner. This includes, for example, an ability to control one's laughter, elation, anger, or even pain. *Samruam* is situational, i.e., a social etiquette that is expected in formal gatherings, as well as categorical, i.e., some groups of people are expected to be *samruam* more than others. Buddhist monks are the representative example of ones who lead a *samruam* life in its strictest sense (Nattapol 2022, 236). In the chapters that follow we trace how the cultural expression of masculinity has become increasingly central to Thai gay culture, as promoted in the imaging of the male body in successive generations of Thai gay print and online media.

THAI GAY MAGAZINES, GAY BARS, AND BAR BOYS

As Thailand's market economy grew rapidly from the 1980s, the size of the middle class and the urban area of Bangkok both expanded significantly. During this period, gay bars and commercial Thai-language gay magazines created both real and virtual social spaces for middle-class homosexual men to explore their sexual and romantic lives and to develop an enhanced sense of sexual identity based on same-sex preference. In this chapter we use the first generation of commercially successful gay magazines in Thailand, in particular *Mithuna Junior*, which was published between 1984 and 1997, as sources to analyze the development of the country's urban gay culture in the 1980s and 1990s. Drawing on *Mithuna Junior* and other early gay magazines such as *Neon*, *Morakot*, and *Midway*, which emerged as competitor gay publications from the mid-1980s, we detail the emergence of commercial gay bars and spaces in Bangkok as well as Thailand's stratified class-based gay sexual culture. The editors and publishers of *Mithuna Junior* collaborated with gay bars to produce new forms of homoerotic consumption and socialization in which gay patron-client relationships based on class stratification developed as a dominant pattern in gay Thailand.[1]

Mithuna Junior was published solely in Thai and reflected the development of the commercial gay scene for Thai gay men. Significantly, apart from reports of gay events and activism overseas, there was a notable absence in the magazine of accounts and images of Caucasian men or of men from other major contemporary Asian gay cultures such as Japan or Taiwan. The orientation of *Mithuna Junior* was overwhelmingly local, which contrasts with some stereotypes that the Thai gay scene has developed from "imported" Western gay models and in response to Western gay tourism. In comparative studies of the histories of modern gay communities in Asian metropolises such as Tokyo, Taipei, and Bangkok there has been considerable debate about whether local factors have been the driving forces in the rise of new same-sex cultures or, in contrast, Asian societies have borrowed these novel cultural forms from the West. Dennis Altman's (1996a, 1996b, 1997) accounts of the "global gay" and "global queering," which positioned Western, predominantly American, gay communities as sources of gay cultural globalization, were widely critiqued as overlooking the local origins of the often-characteristic forms of modern gay identity in many non-Western societies (see Berry 1998; Martin 1998). We argue that the distinctiveness of Thailand's class-structured gay culture reflects the fact that it has emerged from the local conditions of Thai capitalism and domestic Thai-language media.[2]

Thailand's urban gay middle class formed amid multiple social influences mediated by both commercial gay venues and print media. These locales and media contributed to the creation of homosexual spaces for the Thai gay middle class in two important ways. First, gay bars and other venues served as sites of consumption where the male body was transformed into a sexual commodity. In these places, middle-class gay identity was performed through paying a fee for the sexual services of working-class male sex workers. Second, print media such as *Mithuna Junior* provided educated gay men with ideas by which to imagine fashioning a gay lifestyle amid the rapidly expanding consumer culture of urban life. These two spaces, one real and the other virtual, were both constituted as domains for the marketing of sexual commodities for urban middle-class gay men. *Mithuna Junior* magazine was founded at the very start of the takeoff period of the Thai economy in the early 1980s, and its commercial success and that of its competitor gay magazines, as well as of the many gay venues that advertised in these publications, was based on the growing disposable incomes of the rapidly expanding Thai gay middle class.

Thai Gay Men and Class Distinctions

Thailand's gay bars and magazines emerged at a time of rapid economic growth characterized by an expansion of the middle class and increasingly urban life-styles (see Narong 1992; Chalongphob 1993; Deininger and Squire 1997; Pranee and Chalongphob 1998; Funatsu and Kagoya 2003; Siriporn 2005). The Thai middle class grew exceptionally rapidly over the decade from the mid-1980s to the mid-1990s, when the country's economy grew at rates of over 10 percent per annum. Thailand's National Statistics Office reported that in 1986 5 million people were categorized as belonging to the middle class out of a total national population of 52 million. Just a decade later in 1996, the numbers in the Thai middle class had increased to 28 million (National Statistics Office, n.d.; Narong 2005). Across the decade from 1986 to 1996, the average wage of middle-class workers increased dramatically, from 1,800 to 9,000 baht per month (Medhi 1993; Ikemoto and Uehara 2000). In this dynamic setting, middle-class Thai gay men were increasingly able to pay for the services provided in commercial venues such as bars and saunas.

Class formation and socioeconomic stratification among Thai gay men is based on occupation and educational background. Three different classes can be identified within Bangkok's gay community. The first is working- or lower-class gay men who live in poor-standard housing, have low levels of education, and earn their income from daily wage labor as construction workers, waiters, peddlers, hawkers, seasonal agricultural laborers, taxi drivers, and sex workers. The second sector is middle-class gay men who generally live in good conditions, are well-educated, and work in the business sector, education, or in government service. The gap between socioeconomic classes in Thailand is significant, and middle-class gay incomes are often several times higher than those of working-class gay men. The third group is a small but influential number of rich *hiso* (from "high society") gay men who receive significant incomes from their businesses or from inherited family estates. They typically socialize in their own private groups separate from the larger numbers of middle-class gay men who patronize gay venues and the working-class men who work in bars and pubs as waiters and sex workers.

Dredge Käng observes that *hiso* Thais are very perceptive with regard to class distinctions.

> Wealthy Thais have the elite cultural capital to differentiate international brand name products from copies, the status valences of different English accents, the relative importance of foreign cities, and other cosmopolitan references that are not readily legible to those without extensive international experience. Rich Thais typically have travelled extensively and are often educated abroad. Thus, they have extensive experiences with foreigners, most often in Western countries, and are used to the company of *farang* [Westerners]. Moreover, they are, for the most part, 'above' status concerns. Being driven by one's chauffeur to a high-end hotel restaurant in a Mercedes with a well-dressed *farang* friend or partner creates an impression that insulates one from questions about status. The same is not true for middle-class people. (Käng 2015, 111)

In a study of middle-class Thai gay men's preferences for Asian partners Käng defines middle-class status in the early 2010s as having been defined by monthly incomes that varied between 7,000 to 70,000 baht (Käng 2017, 185n6), with the low end representing the starting salaries of junior grade civil servants. However, Käng notes that income per se is not the sole determinant of perceived middle-class status in Thailand, with working in an air-conditioned environment being as important, if not more important, than having a postsecondary vocational or university education. Many occupations that surpass the income threshold of 70,000 baht a month—such as selling noodles on the street or street-based sex work—are not considered middle class, even if "selling noodles in a shopping mall or being an institutionally based sex worker can command both the income and cultural capital of middle classness" (185n6). Drawing on the work of Jim Ockey (1999), Käng observes that "there is no clear coincidence of class position with education, occupation, or income in Thailand. For example, the lowest status occupation is 'service woman', e.g. masseuse, 'partner' or a sex worker . . . but women in this category may make incomes greater than white collar professionals such as professors. Clearly interrelated issues of education, family wealth, land ownership, and cosmopolitan experience also play a major role in class standing. Furthermore, lifestyle costs vary immensely by region in Thailand, with Phuket, not Bangkok, being the most expensive region" (Käng 2015, 94).

A Homoerotic History of Bangkok's Gay Middle Class

In the early 1980s, Bangkok's largely closeted homosexual culture consisted of a small number of relatively expensive bars and pubs for well-off patrons and an extensive scene of public cruising venues for working- and lower-middle-class men. Thai homosexual men from different social strata explored their sexuality in these largely separate domains. In the 1970s and early 1980s, middle-class gay men found partners in both gay bars and cruising areas, while working-class homosexual men found their sexual partners among members of their extended families and kin groups as well as at cruising areas in public spaces. In the middle decades of the twentieth century, the major cruising sites in Bangkok were Lumphini Park, Wang Saranrom Park, and Sanam Luang, the large open space near the old royal area of the city adjacent to the Grand Palace and the Temple of the Emerald Buddha. Many homosexual men went to these locations in search of the young men who worked there as casual sex workers. In the 1970s and early 1980s, it cost between thirty and one hundred baht for sex with these informal sex workers. Bangkok's public cruising sites were not just places for commercial sex but were also locales where sexual relationships and ongoing friendships were formed. The men who frequented these public cruising areas formed social and sexual networks and coined their own idioms for the spaces in which they fashioned sexual and romantic lives. For example, an octagonal pavilion that is still located in the center of Lumphini Park, which was formerly hidden by thick shrubbery that made it an especially popular cruising spot, was colloquially called "the love nest halo" (*rang rak song klot*) (Narupon 2010b).[3]

Bangkok Gay Bars Before *Mithuna Junior*

Before *Mithuna Junior* was published, most Thai gay men remained in the closet. In this period large numbers of Thai homosexual men continued to enter heterosexual marriages to be seen as normatively masculine (Jackson 1995, 62). Jackson (1995, 2016) has detailed the stresses and issues faced by Thai gay men in the decade before *Mithuna Junior* was published in his study of letters to the gay lonely-hearts columns "Love Problems of Third Gender" (*panha hua-jai phet thi-sam*) and "Sad Gay Lives" (*chiwit sao chao gay*), published from 1975 in the popular magazine *Plaek*, which were responded to by an agony uncle going by the pen name of Uncle Go Paknam. Until the publication of *Mithuna Junior*, Uncle Go's fortnightly column in *Plaek* was the only print media space in which Thailand's homosexual men could find a nonjudgmental listening ear (Jackson 1995, 105). The Thai men who wrote to Uncle Go in the 1970s and early 1980s overwhelmingly described their lives as being characterized by loneliness and frustration and a need to conform to heterosexual norms and male gender expectations. In an interview published in an early issue of *Mithuna Junior*, Pratchaya Phanthathorn, the real name of Uncle Go Paknam, observed that "gays in the past [in the 1970s and earlier] lived in the closet and could not come out. When I interviewed famous gay people, such as [the celebrity hairdresser] Pan Bunnag, they revealed their gay identity. Then, many people came to learn about gay men, and they have become more accepted" (*Mithuna Junior* 1985f, 105). However, the previously private and closeted world of Thai homosexual men changed rapidly with a significant opening of both print media and lived spaces following the publication at the end of 1983 of *Mithuna Junior*, the country's first nationally distributed commercial gay magazine. This was a major turning point in Thai gay history that supported the development of a modern public Thai gay identity.

It was in Thailand's period of rapid economic and sociological transition that the country's gay middle class came to see themselves as masculine-identified men whose prime sexual and emotional attachments were with other masculine-identified men. Starting in the 1960s, this masculine-gendered form of male sexual relationship came to be known as "gay" and was increasingly distinguished from the feminine trans woman *kathoey*, with whom cisgendered masculine homosexual men were often confused in mainstream media and discourses (see Jackson 1989, 1995, 2016; Narupon 2010b). The earliest records of the borrowed English word "gay" being used in Thailand to refer to masculine homosexual men are in Thai newspaper reports of the 1965 murder of Darrell Berrigan, the American-born editor of the *Bangkok World* newspaper (see Jackson 1999). Berrigan was a prominent expatriate figure in Bangkok in the 1960s and his murder by a male sex worker led to exposés of his private homosexual life and the world of Bangkok gay men in this period. In the later 1970s, Thai gay usage came to distinguish between sexually receptive *gay queens* and sexually insertive *gay kings* (see Jackson 2000). The English word "man" was also borrowed to denote masculine presentation by homosexual men. The term *man* was distinguished from the Thai word for "a man," *phu-chai*, which came to have the specific meaning of a heterosexual male. In the 1980s and 1990s, masculine identity categories and descriptors such as *gay king* (top), *man* (masculine presenting), and *mai sadaeng ork* (not expressing [gayness or effeminacy]), became the dominant idioms for masculine presentation among homosexual men (see Jackson 1995, 2016).

The Origins and Early Years of *Mithuna Junior*

Mithuna Junior was not the very first Thai gay magazine. *Cherngchai* ("manly") was published in 1982 but folded after only one issue. Furthermore, *Mithuna Junior* did not exist for long before a swath of competitor magazines was published, capitalizing on the market for gay publications that this pathbreaking magazine had shown to exist. These early competitor magazines and their years of publication included *Boy* (1983), *Neon* (1984–1995), *Morakot* (1985–1998), *Midway* (1986–2001), and *My Way* (1989). However, *Mithuna Junior* (1983–1997) was far and away the most influential of the gay magazines published in the 1980s and 1990s and it is for this reason that we use it as the focus of analysis in this chapter. The pages of *Mithuna Junior* reveal how Bangkok's gay middle class approached homoerotic contents in the print media and how awareness of gay identity first developed in the context of popular culture.

The magazine was initially titled simply *Mithuna* and began publication in December 1983, with its final issue, as *Mithuna Junior*, being published fourteen years later in 1997. The magazine focused on the sexual lives of younger gays and included short stories, interviews, and nude centerfold photos of male models in erotic poses. *Mithuna* is the Thai term for the astrological sign Gemini, represented by a symbol of male twins. Anan Thorngthua, *Mithuna*'s founding editor and executive manager, decided on this name for the magazine because he felt that common representations of Gemini's twins had homoerotic overtones (see Jackson 2016). When Chomphunut Publications launched *Mithuna* magazine in 1983 under the stewardship of gay-identified Anan, it was one of the first mass-circulation Thai publications to include full-color centerfolds of male models. *Mithuna* in fact began as a crossover magazine with its beefcake images of erotically posed Thai male models being oriented toward female readers as well as gay men. This pattern of crossover marketing to both heterosexual female and gay readerships was reproduced by upmarket mainstream fashion magazines such as *Phraeo, Image,* and *Volume* in the 1990s and early 2000s, with these glossy titles often including homoerotically posed male models on their covers. The significant response from gay readers to *Mithuna*'s beefcake-style male centerfolds led Anan to realize that there was an unmet demand for a magazine focusing specifically on the sexual and social interests of gay men. In March 1984, under Anan as executive manager and Sethasak Srithorngthuam as editor, the magazine was reoriented toward a gay readership and renamed *Mithuna Junior* to mark this repositioning. The first issue of *Mithuna Junior* sold for 30 baht with an annual subscription of twelve issues costing 330 baht.

Perhaps reflecting editorial and management concerns about possible reactions against a publication marketed too openly to gay men, early issues still represented *Mithuna Junior* as a magazine for both women and men, with the slogan "For sensitive women and flower men" (*samrap phu-ying thi orn-wai lae phu-chai chao dork-mai*) printed under the title on its cover. The expression *phu-chai chao dork-mai,* "flower men"—often abbreviated to *chao dork-mai* or "flower people"—was a common idiom used in gay circles in the 1970s and 1980s to refer to gay men and *kathoey* in positive terms. In contrast to then-current mainstream discourses that pathologized and stigmatized gay men and trans women as degenerate (*witthan*), perverted (*wiparit*), deviant (*biang-ben*), indecent (*lamok*), abnormal (*phit-pokkati*), unnatural (*phit-thammachat*), and mentally ill (*rok-jit*), the expression *phu-chai chao dork-mai* challenged heteronormative labels by conveying the sense that an expression of "masculinity" (*phu-chai*) could be as beautiful as a flower (*dork-mai*). While the expression *chao dork-mai,* "flower people," was often used to refer to effeminate gay men and *kathoey*, the addition of the word *phu-chai,* "a man," in *Mithuna Junior*'s cover-slogan description of its intended market referenced male same-sex interest in a normatively masculine frame.

After the magazine surveyed its readers and found that 99 percent were men, the editor announced in *Mithuna Junior*'s seventh issue that the column

"Midnight Women" (*phu-ying yi-sip si nor*), which had detailed the nightlife of women seeking male partners in Bangkok's pubs and bars, would be discontinued. From late 1984, *Mithuna Junior* was exclusively targeted at a gay readership, becoming the first nationally distributed commercial publication managed and edited by gay men. It provided Thai gay readers with opportunities to discuss sexual expression and affirmations of gay identity in columns such as "Loving and Understanding Gays" (*rak lae khao-jai gay*), "Gay Dictionary" (*photjananukrom gay*), "Mithuna Window" (*na-tang Mithuna*), and "The Third Way" (*thang sai thi-sam*). These columns presented positive images of gay people as well as encouraging Thai gay men to understand themselves and be more self-accepting.

At the end of 1985, a new editor, Nukul Benchamat, took over the reins at *Mithuna Junior* for a short period after Anan Thorngthua had resigned in December of that year. While the reformation of *Mithuna* into the gay-oriented *Mithuna Junior* had taken place largely because of Anan's initiative, the young and comparatively inexperienced publisher, then in his early twenties and only recently out of university, had confronted a range of problems in operating the pathbreaking magazine. Difficulties included financial issues arising from the corrupt behavior of employees who defrauded some of the magazine's subscribers. The publisher also faced legal problems in guaranteeing distribution, which arose from police classification of some of the magazine's issues as pornographic. Thailand's anti-pornography law is more strictly enforced in the visual domain than in textual accounts, with sexually explicit narratives typically evading censorship while photographic images of sexual organs and sex acts are more stringently controlled. Visual representations of the penis, sexual arousal, and sometimes even exposed male nipples were defined as obscene. In the 1980s and 1990s, many Thai gay magazines, including *Mithuna Junior*, skirted around this law by printing erotic photos of mostly nude male models but avoiding any overt representation of an exposed penis.

In January 1986, Surasarn Publications, owned by Surasak Chakkawanmongkol, took over the publication and a second-generation management team began running *Mithuna Junior*, with Prach Sathana as the new editorial director and Sakkarin Sirirak as editor. In this period, *Mithuna Junior* placed an emphasis on publishing gay fiction, short stories, and poetry that detailed same-sex love, friendship, relationships, and homoerotic experiences. *Mithuna Junior* came under new management and editorship once again at the end of 1986. At that time, Lek Malee and Atthapol Phanbunlert came to work as editors under the new owner, Sitthichai Chavanothai, the founder of Him Studio, which published a range of other publications including photo albums of male models. Under this new ownership and management, the word "Junior" was cut from the magazine's title with it being badged simply as *Mithuna*. Changes included enlarging the format from pocket-size to notebook-size pages and adding more color pages, especially erotic male photos. The price of the magazine was increased to thirty-five baht. Well-known Thai gay media commentator and former Thammasat University lecturer in mass communications Seri Wongmontha (b. 1949) began writing a regular column, "The Bright Light Shining the Way for Gays" (*fai sawang sorng thang gay*). He sought to inform Thai gay men about ways of living a homosexual life in Thailand and solving readers' problems. Under Lek Malee's editorship, *Mithuna* also briefly changed to a general variety and lifestyle magazine with articles on films, music, songs, poetry, books, horoscopes, sports, fashion, health, food, and travel pitched to a wider audience. These articles diluted the gay focus and content of the magazine, which overall assumed a more heterosexual feel that diminished its attraction for gay readers.

However, the flirtation with seeking to attract a wider readership was short-lived, with the magazine once again changing hands for its forty-third issue in September 1987. Chucheep Satitchai became the magazine's fourth editor in its short lifespan. Under Chucheep, the pocket-size format was reinstated, the name reverted to *Mithuna Junior*, and the focus on content for a gay readership was reemphasized. This fourth and final generation of *Mithuna Junior* management included many regular contributions by gay activist Natee Teerarojjanapongs, who contributed columns such as "Before We Became a Gay Association" (*korn ja ma pen samakhom gay*). Natee's significant input to *Mithuna Junior* changed the magazine into a mouthpiece for promoting gay rights and supporting HIV/AIDS prevention and education campaigns. In this period, *Mithuna Junior* included regular interviews with famous personalities speaking on gay issues as well as resource persons working in social welfare and development, human rights, and charity and volunteer activities with a focus on providing support to gay men as well as *kathoey* in a range of areas.

Across its more than a decade of publication, *Mithuna Junior* evolved from a magazine that reported Bangkok's commercial gay scene of bars and pubs, with their emphasis on providing sexual services for a predominantly closeted clientele, to a rights- and health-oriented newsletter that reflected the more activist perspective of Thailand's emerging NGO sector of community organizations. Significantly, through all its changes of ownership and editorship, which reflected the difficulty of establishing a commercially viable gay magazine in Thailand in the 1980s, advertising from gay bars remained *Mithuna Junior*'s financial mainstay.

The four generations of *Mithuna Junior* ownership and editorship each represented different emerging perspectives on gay lives and masculinity in 1980s Bangkok. The transitions in editorial focus also reflected rapid changes in Bangkok's gay society across the decade. From an almost singular focus on bars, pubs,

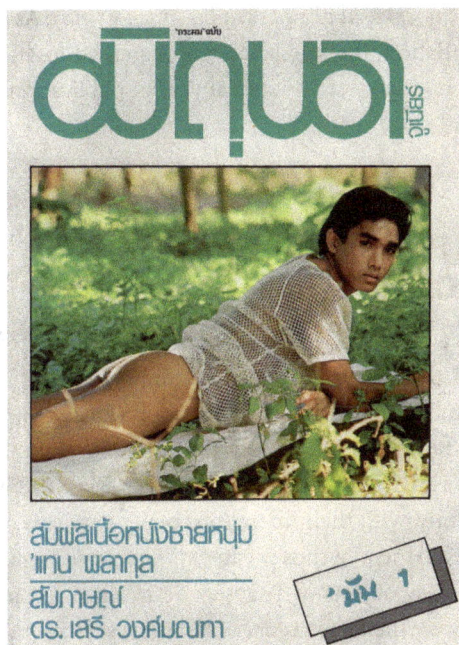

FIGURE 1. Cover of the inaugural issue of *Mithuna Junior* (1984a), Thailand's first commercially successful gay magazine. Text on the cover reads: "Feel the flesh of the young guy Thaen Phalakul [cover model], Interview Dr Seri Wongmontha." Seri is a well-known Bangkok gay academic and media personality.

and male commercial sex workers, the short-lived and ultimately unsuccessful attempt to refashion *Mithuna Junior* into a general interest lifestyle magazine under Lek Malee in 1987 nonetheless paralleled the beginnings of Thailand's economic boom decade, when a rapidly expanding gay middle class with increased purchasing power began to seek out services and products tailored to their lifestyles beyond commercial sex. *Mithuna Junior's* subsequent refocus on rights activism and HIV-related health issues under Chucheep Satitchai and Natee Teerarojjanapongs indicated that, in line with the rise of a more visible gay middle class within Bangkok's booming economy, new forms of homosexual community organization also came into being to confront the existential challenges that HIV posed for the nascent gay community. All the while, the emphasis on advertising from gay bars and commercial sex continued to provide the financial foundation for *Mithuna Junior* through all its changes.

In 1992 *Mithuna Junior* raised its newsstand price to 40 baht, and 450 baht for an annual subscription. At that time, the magazine also adopted a new slogan—printed below its title on the front cover—"The Magazine for Knowledge and

Close Friendship" (*maekkasin pheua sara lae krachap mit*). As the booming Thai economy fueled inflation, the sale price was increased to 40 baht in 1995 and then 50 baht four months later. In its final year of publication in 1996, *Mithuna Junior*'s price was 70 baht.

The Central Place of Male Sex Work in Thai Gay Culture

During more than a decade of publication, *Mithuna Junior* reflected significant social and cultural changes in the gay communities of Bangkok and Thailand. These changes can be divided into two broad periods. The first period, from the mid-1980s to the early 1990s, was a time when the number of gay bars in Bangkok—as well as the tourist centers of Chiang Mai, Pattaya, and Phuket—increased significantly, with their operations being based on offering the sexual services of young Thai men. In those years, *Mithuna Junior* emphasized male sex workers as the primary objects of Thai gay desire. The second period, starting in the mid-1990s, was when gay saunas emerged as sex-on-premises venues that attracted large numbers of urban gay men.[4] At this time, *Mithuna Junior* shifted its focus from idolizing male sex workers to providing advice and guidance on how to seek out other gay men as lovers and boyfriends. For a younger generation of Bangkok gay men, who were increasingly self-confident in their sexual identities and who had benefited from the country's rapid transformation from a developing to a middle-income economy, gay bars came to be seen as somewhat old-fashioned and male sex workers, who were often heterosexual, fell out of favor as sexual partners. Many gay men turned their interest to saunas where they could meet other gay men as sexual partners. The advertisements for gay bars and male sex workers in *Mithuna Junior*—which formed the mainstay of the magazine's advertising income throughout its existence—increasingly failed to interest a new generation of gay men who sought other gay men of similar backgrounds as sexual and romantic partners. *Mithuna Junior* ultimately failed to adapt to the rapidly changing sexual culture that centered around gay venues, continuing to base its advertising primarily on bars with male sex workers even as their importance as the focus of socializing and sexual culture for many middle-class gay men was being eclipsed. These changes were associated with increasingly affirmative and self-confident notions of gay identity among middle-class gay men; a marked growth in the number and diversity of gay venues and businesses, including many new gay magazines; and the transformation of the media landscape with the arrival of email, digital communication platforms, and the internet from the mid-1990s. The impact of digital media on Thai gay culture is considered in later chapters.

In its later years, from 1992 to 1997, the contents of the magazine focused on readers' personal classifieds for finding friends and lovers as well as advertisements for bars, pubs, karaoke halls, and gay saunas. In that period, each issue carried an average of eighteen pages of advertisements for gay bars. In the twilight years of *Mithuna Junior*, the magazine published letters from readers who regularly complained that the male models photographed and profiled for the centerfolds were "low quality," not cute or handsome, and the magazine's contents concentrated too much on sex stories while neglecting social issues and cultural matters. The following two readers' letters were published in 1995. "Some stories are bad. The sex stories are fabricated and ridiculous. *Mithuna* should have an advice column for the younger gay generations to inform them about social behavior and ways of being a good person. *Mithuna* shouldn't have so much sex and should start a good column that introduces careers and skills training" (*Mithuna Junior* 1995b, 118). Another reader wrote: "Does *Mithuna* work for us or for money? When we read *Mithuna*, we are dominated by sexual need rather than understanding social responsibility" (*Mithuna* Junior 1995b, 119). *Mithuna Junior* found it increasingly difficult to survive in the face of many competitor gay magazines that came onto the market during Thailand's economic boom years of the 1990s. The final issue was published in April 1997.

The centerfold models for the fourth generation of *Mithuna Junior* were predominantly male sex workers from gay bars and were introduced to readers as sexual commodities whose services were available from the venues that were profiled. In the 1980s, male sex workers, called *dek bar* or *dek off* in Thai, were a readily available source of models for nude photo shoots as most middle-class gay men in that period would not have wanted to have nude photos of themselves published in a publicly distributed gay magazine. Interviews with the models for *Mithuna Junior*'s covers and centerfolds were published in each issue and the models typically stated that they identified as heterosexual men (*phu-chai*) and often had female partners as well as being male sex workers. A *dek bar* who worked in Alex Bar in Bangkok's Silom area and identified as *phu-chai* explained in an interview for the article "Introducing Gay Bars" (*nae-nam gay bar*): "I've come to work in this bar because I need the money. I don't think that working like this causes any damage [to my heterosexual identity] because I give others happiness and I'm happy too" (*Mithuna Junior* 1985d, 18). The male sex workers photographed for *Mithuna Junior* introduced themselves in the published interviews in the expectation that the magazine's readers were potential customers. Publishing photos of *dek bar* thus served to promote the venue where they worked and the photo exposure of *dek bar* as the models in gay magazines such as *Mithuna Junior* contributed to the expansion of male sex work. Indeed, commercial gay print media promoted the commodification of male sex work and the general expansion in the number of bars with male sex workers or *dek bar* working from them.

In addition to advertising from gay bars, *Mithuna Junior* also derived income from mail order services for pornographic gay videos and nude albums of "secret" pictures of the male centerfold models. Because of Thai censorship laws, full frontal nudity was not possible in the images printed in *Mithuna Junior*. However, the magazine's publishers used this to financial advantage by making nude shots of the cover and centerfold models available for mail order purchase. Historically, pornographic videos have not been available for sale openly in Thailand, leading to an extensive underground market. While the Thai police have periodically rounded up erotic videos and publications sold under the counter from a range of outlets across the country, including occasional raids on mainstream newsstands and bookstores that stocked *Mithuna Junior* and other gay magazines, in general the authorities have not stopped the advertising of otherwise banned materials for sale by mail order. *Mithuna Junior*'s income from these mail order sales was considerably higher than that derived from the sale price of the magazine. In the later 1980s, when the price of the magazine was 40 baht, a gay video cost between 400 and 600 baht, while a set of nude photographs of the male cover and centerfold models cost 100 baht. At that time, the sexual services of a male sex worker working from a gay bar cost between 500 and 1,000 baht. The high prices of these sexual commodities meant that they were only accessible to higher-income gay men.

Mithuna Junior and Bangkok's Gay Bars

In the 1980s, the stratification of Thai gay communities between working-class and middle-class men was most clearly reflected in the large numbers of gay bars that opened in Bangkok and other large cities in that decade. Unlike the case in most Western countries, where gay bars are venues where customers socialize and seek sexual and romantic partners with other customers, Thai gay bars are commercial sex venues where mostly middle-class gay men go to buy sexual services from working-class employees. *Mithuna Junior* reflected the development of Thai gay bars as class-stratified commercial sex venues. In addition to revenue from advertisements for these establishments forming a financial mainstay of the magazine, articles about gay bars and interviews with the male sex workers in these venues were a major part of the content of each issue. In the 1980s, most of the male models for covers and centerfolds were commercial sex workers from the gay bars. A symbiotic relationship developed between *Mithuna Junior* and gay bars as the rise of Thai gay print media contributed to a parallel expansion in commercial sex venues for middle-class homosexual men.

Operating the early gay bars in Bangkok from the late 1960s to the early 1980s had been very difficult, with an ongoing risk of police raids. In the decades before *Mithuna Junior*, there were at most fifteen gay bars in Bangkok. In *Mithuna Junior*'s semiregular gay history column "Digging Up the Hiding Places of Thai Gay Bars" (*khut kru bar gay thai*)—written by a columnist using the pen name Mercedes Benz—it was reported that in the 1970s Bangkok gay men would meet friends at a coffee shop near Wat Pho, the Temple of the Reclining Buddha, in Bangkok's old royal precinct (*Mithuna Junior* 1986c, 36–43). The first generation of Bangkok gay bars in the 1960s and 1970s included Framing House, located near the railway line in the Phloenchit area, and the Sea Hag Bar, which was in the basement of a tourist hotel on Charoen Krung Road. Both bars—which had a jukebox for customers to listen to music—had English names and were secretive places frequented only by well-off customers (*Mithuna Junior* 1986a, 15). After these two bars closed, the second generation of Bangkok gay bars were Ban Than Chai ("the prince's house"), Siamese Bar, and Tulip Bar, which were all located in the Silom area. In 1972 another new gay bar opened in the Patpong red-light precinct. Known as Yosawadi's Bar, named after the flamboyantly cross-dressing Thai gay owner, this became a popular venue for many Western and upper-class Thai gays to meet and party.

In a 1986 interview with *Mithuna Junior*, the owner of the popular 1980s venue Tulip Bar, Niwat Sae Khow, related that in the 1970s gay bars were often seen as dangerous and immoral places and many of the Thai homosexual men who visited them lacked self-confidence (*Mithuna Junior* 1986c, 36). Suthat Chanket, owner of Apollo Bar, which opened in 1973, similarly observed that in the 1970s and early 1980s Thai homosexual men were reluctant to be seen at a gay bar (*Mithuna Junior* 1986c, 36), a situation that was confirmed by Phrompriang Phulphon, manager of Harry's Bar, who said that in the 1970s the vast majority of Thai gay men were largely still in the closet (*Mithuna Junior* 1986c, 38).

While the owners and managers of Bangkok's gay venues were predominantly Thai gay men and *kathoey*, during the 1970s and early 1980s many of the customers at Bangkok's gay bars were Western gay men who had come to the city as tourists and travelers. Because most Thai gay men were too scared to go to gay bars for fear of being outed, Bangkok's early gay bars evolved as sites for entertaining gay tourists (*Midway* 1986, 55–56). According to Apollo Bar owner, Suthat Chanket, the main customers in the 1970s were Western gay tourists and a small number of upper-class Thai gay men, whose social standing gave them a degree of independence from the bourgeois social norms that middle-class gay men felt compelled to conform to. In the 1970s, Bangkok's gay bars were expensive venues that only better-off gay men could afford to patronize. In the early years of that decade, many working-class gay men earned the legal minimum wage of only 25 baht per day, while the average price for a beer in a gay bar was 40 baht, a soft drink was 30 baht, and a cocktail cost 50 baht. In 1975 the Thai government raised the minimum wage to 33.90 baht per day. *Mithuna Junior* columnist Mercedes Benz described the first generation of Bangkok gay bars as follows:

> At the beginning of Bangkok's gay bar scene, Thai gays were still in the closet. Only small groups of Thai gay people visited the gay bars because they felt uneasy in those venues. The most popular gay bars [in the 1970s] were Apollo, Rome Bar, Tulip Bar, Tomboy Bar, and Lonely Boy Bar. In the 1970s, Thai gay bars were often raided by the police, and they were reported negatively in Thai newspapers. However, after *Plaek* magazine [and Uncle Go's column of letters from gay men] was published in the mid-1970s, people came to know more about gay men.[5] Gay bars at that time did not have male sex workers, *dek off*, or cabaret shows for entertainment. There was only a bar for drinks and a dance floor. All the customers coming to the bars would do ballroom dance steps. There was no a-go-go boy dancing. Following the ballroom dance era, the soul step and bump step dances were introduced to gay bars. The Apollo Bar was at its height in the ballroom dance era. Gays at that time dressed like men. But nowadays [in the 1980s], gays dress in expensive and luxurious clothes. Gay people do not act like women and are not feminine. (*Mithuna Junior* 1985a, 98)

Table 2.1 lists gay bars that were established in Bangkok before 1984. The table collates information from early issues of *Mithuna Junior* and details the area of the city where each bar was located and the years it opened or operated. Reports in *Mithuna Junior* identified the venues using the English terms "bar" and "pub."

The Development of Thai Gay Bars as Commercial Sex Venues

In the later 1970s and early 1980s, Bangkok's gay bars were transformed into venues where better-off but closeted Thai gay men, often represented in gay publications as "lonely men" (*chai khi-ngao*) in search of a special male friend, purchased sexual services from younger, working-class heterosexually identified male sex workers (*Mithuna Junior* 1986c, 37). This evolution reflected the class-based

TABLE 2.1   Bangkok gay bars and pubs established before 1984

NAME	CITY LOCATION	YEAR OPENED/OPERATED
Cafe near Wat Pho (pub)	Phra Nakhon	Before 1967
Ban Than Chai (bar)	unknown location	1967–1968
Framing House (bar)	Phloenchit	1967–1968
Sea Hag (bar)	Charoen Krung	1967–1968
Twilight (bar)	Silom	1967
Tulip (bar)	Silom	1969
Siamese (bar)	Silom	1969 (estimated)
Blue Child (bar)	Silom	1970
Yosawadi (bar)	Patpong	1972
Apollo (bar)	Silom	1973
Lonely Boy (bar)	Silom	1973–1974
Rome Club (pub)	Silom	1973–1974
Tom Boy (bar)	Silom	1973–1974
Harry's Bar (bar)	Silom	1978
Barbeiry (bar)	Silom	1982

Source: Information collated from issues of *Mithuna Junior*.

stratification of Thai society as well as the fact that at this time many gay men did not regard other gay men as attractive sexual partners.

Thai gay bars differ from those in Western societies, where gay men meet to socialize and seek sex partners from among other patrons (Chauncey 1985, 1994). At times, gay bars in the West have also been venues for the creation of homosexual identity, instilling political awareness and engendering support for gay rights movements (Carter 2011). In contrast, from the late 1970s, Thai gay bars evolved into commercial venues where young men who were not necessarily gay provided sexual and other services for typically middle-class gay customers. The social and cultural patterns of homoeroticism found in Thai gay bars developed in a frame of patronage and economic relations between men from different class backgrounds and were not related to movements for sexual liberation or advocating for gay political rights. In Thailand venues where gay men go to socialize with other gay men, rather than to buy sex from a male sex worker, came to be called pubs and cocktail lounges rather than bars.

Thai gay bars evolved into commercial sex venues for a middle-class clientele in response to two main factors. First, as noted, in that period many Thai gay men were closeted and were not interested in establishing an ongoing relationship with another man. Thai gay men's lives were often limited to seeking out casual sex. Second, the patron-client structure of middle-class customers paying for sex with working-class men reflected the economic disparities and stratification of

Thai society. This pattern of working-class men providing sexual and other services for middle-class Thai gay consumers continues to this day.

In Thai, the male sex workers at gay bars are variously called *dek bar* ("young bar workers"), *dek off* ("young workers taken *off* premises"), or *dek nang drink* ("young workers who sit and *drink* [with customers]"). In English, these workers are typically called "bar boys" among tourists and expatriates, although they are usually young men in their early twenties. "Bar boy" is a translation of the Thai expression *dek bar*, where the term *dek* can mean either a child or a young service worker in their teens or early twenties. Thai law specifies that bar workers need to be at least eighteen years old. Bangkok gay bars began providing sexual services in the mid-1970s, when Apollo Bar being the first venue to introduce *dek bar* male sex workers (*Mithuna Junior* 1986c, 36). *Dek bar* were usually working-class, rural-urban migrants who had come to find work in Bangkok. One heterosexually identified man from Sakon Nakhon Province in Northeast Thailand, who worked as a male sex worker in the Apollo Bar in Silom Soi 4, stated in a 1985 interview in *Mithuna Junior* that he had worked as a wage laborer before a friend suggested that he try working in a gay bar. At that time, he earned the then considerable sum of between 10,000 and 20,000 baht per month, with gay clients paying him between 1,000 and 2,000 baht for each sexual service. He said the job was good for him as he was able to send money home to his family each month. He stated that he was able to respond to all his gay clients' sexual requests, but he declined clients' invitations to live with them because he said that gay men were not sincere (*Mithuna Junior* 1985a, 29). The owner of Apollo Bar, Suthat Chanket, explained that gay customers who asked bar boys to live with them usually paid them a living allowance of between 3,000 and 5,000 baht per month. However, Suthat said that most bar boys did not live with clients for very long because they preferred the freedom of sex work, with some returning to work in gay bars or changing to work in other jobs after breaking up with a client-boyfriend (*Mithuna Junior* 1985a, 100). Gay bars usually required their bar boys to wear a standard uniform, whether close-cropped shirt, jeans, tuxedo, suit, or simply underwear. Some gay bars required their *dek bar* to dress as sailors, cowboys, or mechanics.

In the 1980s, Bangkok's gay bars developed the pattern of serving drinks and cocktails with songs and music playing in the background while several *dek bar* waited for customers on couches and sofas spread around the venue. Some gay bars had a small platform in a corner for *dek bar* to dance. These spaces were not for customers to dance but rather for *dek bar* wearing only swimwear or underwear with identifying numbers attached to perform erotic moves to slow music and show off their bodies to potential customers. This kind of erotic dance to attract customers is called go-go in Thai, following the English and French usage, and learning to move their bodies in sexually enticing ways was a work skill that a successful *dek bar* needed to acquire. The importance of go-go dancing in Thai gay venues is discussed in detail in chapter 5. Young men between eighteen and twenty-two years old were favored as bar boys, and once a customer had ordered a drink, he would typically choose a *dek bar* by specifying the number on the bar boy's underwear. The system of male sex workers wearing identifying numbers was borrowed from the patterns of female sex work in Thailand, where women in massage parlors also wore numbers to make identification easier for customers. If a *dek bar* provided good service and pleasant conversation, the customer would pay the bar manager a fee, called a "bar fine" in English or in Thai *kha off*, "a fee to take the bar boy *off* premises," typically to a hotel that rented rooms by the hour (*Mithuna Junior* 1986c, 37). Bars provided a set daily rate of pay for bar boys and if they were chosen to go with a client they would receive an additional fee for the sexual services.

The *dek bar* who worked at a venue were bar employees not freelance sex workers and were trained, monitored, and controlled by the senior manager and "captain" (Thai: *kaptan*) in the ways of welcoming customers and the rules of the bar. It was typical for customers to socialize by sitting and drinking with *dek bar* rather than with other patrons and the bar captain was central to the process of arranging for a customer to choose a *dek bar* to take off premises. The captain would introduce and recommend *dek bar* to a customer, be responsible for negotiating the sexual services to be provided, and encourage the customer to rent a bar boy. This kind of recommendation of bar boys to customers is known as *cheer khaek*, "encourage the customer," by which the captain described the penis sizes and sexual abilities of different bar workers.[6] The captain was also responsible for the well-being of *dek bar*, playing the role of an older brother (*phi*) to bar boys, who often lived and worked together like a family. Sometimes a relationship formed between a *dek bar* and a customer, who would invite a particular bar worker to live with them as a lover. However, many *dek bar* felt that living with a gay man was not easy as it might limit their freedom to generate a higher income from sleeping with other gay customers. It was more typical for gay customers who came to like a particular *dek bar* to return to the bar where they worked to rent them again (*Mithuna Junior* 1986c, 38). Käng describes this "off" system of male sex work that developed in Thai gay bars from the second half of the 1970s as having several distinguishing features.

> First, the system ensures safety for the patron. As the workers are employees of a bar, a patron can go to the bar to file a complaint about the worker. This prevents petty theft and ensures that workers will provide a minimally adequate service. Complaints will get a worker fired

and over time will prevent one from working in the industry. Second, prices are not negotiated firmly in advance. That is, though there are standard guidelines, the patron pays the amount he wishes based on his satisfaction and his sense of generosity. Even if a worker has a minimum [fee] in mind, particularly unsatisfied customers will show their disapproval by paying less. Third, is the 'open-ended'. . . nature of the system, where Thais often perform services more like temporary romantic and companionate partners rather than sex workers. This means that a patron might off a worker for a week or two while he is on vacation in Thailand, and travel throughout the country together. The Thai not only provides sex, but also general companionship, and acts as tour guide, translator, and bargainer. (Käng 2015, 103)

The bar manager was often an older *kathoey*—referred to as *Mama*, *Mamasang* (from *mamasan*), or *Mae* ("mother")—who took care of and directed the activities of the *dek bar*, including meting out punishment to workers who broke the bar's rules.[7] In interviews in *Mithuna Junior*, *dek bar* stated that bars usually laid down several rules for workers. Bar boys should not give their telephone number to a customer so as not to encourage the development of an ongoing relationship. *Dek bar* should not flirt with each other because such expressions of affection and/or envy would negatively impact the service provided to customers. And they should not try to influence customers' choices by making themselves too prominent in front of clients. *Dek bar* should also act like a man and not express effeminacy in the bar or on the stage. However, in practice these sorts of rules were often violated. Some *dek bar* gave their telephone number to customers in the hope of establishing an ongoing relationship with a man who would be prepared to support them.

The stage of a gay bar is a space for *dek bar* to make money. Before going onstage, many bar boys honor and pay respect to the venue's protective deity or spirits by raising their hands in the *wai* gesture of respect to the images of deities on the bar's shrine. Like almost all Thai businesses, Thai gay bars have a shrine installed in one corner or on one wall where the bar owner will place images of deities such as the elephant-headed Hindu god Ganesha or other gods. These sacred beings are highly respected by bar workers. Bar boys offer prayers to these deities in the hope of being successful in being chosen to go with a client.

To guarantee a regular income, it was necessary for bar boys to learn to practice both insertive and receptive sexual intercourse. If a *dek bar* was asked by a customer to be the receptive partner, he would usually be paid more money. When comparing male and female customers, bar boys interviewed in *Mithuna Junior* indicated that they tended to get bigger tips from female customers than from gay men. They also indicated that in the 1980s female customers in Bangkok gay bars were most often Chinese and Japanese women tourists.

In the 1980s and 1990s, the majority of *dek bar* in Bangkok's gay bars came from Northeast Thailand. And in the early 2000s, most sex workers in Bangkok's gay bars continued to be young Thai men who had migrated from the country's rural areas. However, in the following years, men from neighboring countries such as Myanmar, Laos, and Cambodia also began working as bar boys. Most gay bars had *dek bar* who represented a range of body types to respond to different customers' views of male sexual attractiveness. Some *dek off* were men who had a good physique developed from regular exercise in a gym and were popular with Thai gay clients. Others were young gay men who had a slim body and were called *gay queen* or *gay sao*. Their customers were usually Western gay men. According to *Mithuna Junior*, Thai gay men usually did not find more feminine *gay sao* bar boys to be sexually attractive, with more feminine male sex workers being popular among Asian gay tourists from Japan, Singapore, and Malaysia as well as among Western gay clients.

In countries with ethnic Caucasian populations, hair color—blond, red, brown, black—can sometimes be a basis for sexual preference or fetishization among gay men. In ethnically diverse Thailand, various skin tones—on a color scale from "black" (*dam*) to "dark/intense" (*khem*) and "fair/white" (*khao*)—are often eroticized in different ways. Skin color is also often coded for socioeconomic class, with darker skin being associated with low-status, unsophisticated men from rural backgrounds and fairer skin being associated with higher status, education, and cosmopolitan urban lifestyles. The differential eroticization of skin tones in Thai sexual cultures has been appropriated within the commercial sex industry, where gay customers of different ethnic and cultural backgrounds are assumed to prefer either darker- or fairer-skinned Thai men. From the 1980s, Bangkok's gay bars began to institute a form of ethnic stereotyping of customers by allocating Thai sex workers of different skin tones and body types to different national clienteles. Gay tourists from Western countries were believed to find darker-skinned Thai men more attractive, while Thai gay customers were assumed to be attracted to fairer-skinned men. A *dek bar* of a particular skin tone, whether dark or fair, would then tend to find the management directing him toward a certain ethnic clientele.

The reports of Bangkok's gay bars published in the *Mithuna Junior* columns that introduced readers to venues did not differentiate between bars that provided services to gay tourists or to Thai gay men. However, it appears that the same procedures outlined above operated in most gay bars whatever the nationality of their customers. Significantly, while many gay bars provided services for tourists and expatriates as well as Thai gay men, *Mithuna Junior* and the other

Thai gay magazines published in the 1980s and 1990s focused exclusively on the local market. While tourists and expatriates have historically been visible presences in Bangkok's downtown gay venues, they are absent from the reports and images published in *Mithuna Junior*. While the magazine often published reports of gay activism and events overseas—such as pride parades in Europe, North America, or Australia—its accounts of Bangkok's gay scene focused exclusively on the world of Thai gay men. This reflected the fact that in the 1970s and 1980s very few expatriates or tourists spoke Thai well enough to participate in the local dimensions of the gay scene, and in these years only a small number of Thais spoke English or other Western languages well. This meant that while tourists and middle-class Thai gay men at times occupied some of the same spaces in the gay scene of bars and pubs, the language barrier led to the two groups existing as distinct social and cultural worlds. As an exclusively Thai-language publication, *Mithuna Junior* provided a record of the Thai gay world of the latter decades of the last century, even as that world existed in proximity to a culture of non-Thai-speaking Western and Asian gay men.

Mithuna Junior and the Expansion of Bangkok's Commercial Gay Scene

Mithuna Junior had diverse influences on Thai gay culture. The magazine reflected the generally closeted middle-class gay culture of the 1980s and to survive commercially in this milieu it took advertising from the gay venues that hosted the *dek bar* who provided sexual services for middle-class men. However, in doing this, *Mithuna Junior* also contributed to the further expansion of male commercial sex work and facilitated a significant growth in the number of gay bars in Bangkok and beyond, being the first media outlet to regularly advertise these venues and their workers. The magazine also provided spaces for the further development of gay culture beyond commercial sex, promoting notions of gay pride and opportunities for gay men to seek long-term sexual and romantic relationships with other gay men rather than with sex workers. *Mithuna Junior* supported the development of a culture of gay relationships by publishing gay classifieds. The fact that in the 1980s many gay men were indeed looking for long-term romantic partners, not merely casual sex, was indicated by the large number who placed advertisements with photos in the magazine's personal classifieds section. *Mithuna Junior* sought out its commercial existence within the limitations of the closeted gay culture of the 1980s while at the same time providing a space for voices that aimed to develop a Thai gay world outside the closet and beyond the bars. Nevertheless, in both its conservative inscription within the closet and the world of commercial sex that it helped spawn, and its more trans-gressive call for an open gay identity, *Mithuna Junior* reflected a middle-class outlook. The sale price of one issue was roughly equivalent to the daily income of a manual laborer. In 1984, the year that *Mithuna Junior* began publication, the legal minimum wage of Thai laborers was sixty-six baht per day (Phorphan 1999, 96), which placed the magazine, at thirty baht per issue, beyond the reach of working-class men.

In the years immediately following *Mithuna Junior*'s publication, many new gay bars and venues opened around Bangkok and in the nearby resort city of Pattaya. While only 15 gay bars had existed in the entire period until 1984, many of which were only short-lived, in 1984 and 1985 a total of 21 gay bars oper-ated in the capital. In 1986 alone, 13 new gay bars and venues opened. Over the three-year period 1984 to 1986, more new bars opened than had existed in all previous years combined. All these new bar openings were reported in *Mithuna Junior* (see table 2.2). In 1986 *Mithuna Junior* undertook a survey of Bangkok gay venues and found that there were 29 gay bars in the city. This rapid growth in the number of gay bars contrasted with the generally flat economy in the years leading to the takeoff of Thailand's economic boom in 1987. In 1984 and 1985, Thailand experienced 6 percent annual GDP growth (Nikom 2007, 33), much the same as in previous decades. However, in these two years alone the number of gay bars almost doubled in comparison with earlier years. This suggests that the growth of Bangkok gay businesses in these years was not driven by economic growth alone. The arrival of nationally distributed magazines that were oriented specifically toward gay readers, which extensively reported and advertised gay bars, was the major factor that facilitated the rapid expansion of gay venues. The new gay magazines and gay bars formed a symbiotic commercial relationship. Gay bars were the main advertisers in the magazines, and the gay print media included extensive reports of new bars, special bar events, and interviews with bar workers.

In the early 1990s, *Mithuna Junior* carried an average of 15 or 16 pages of advertisements of gay bars, out of a total of 120 pages in each issue. The only other advertisers in *Mithuna Junior* during its first decade were gay saunas, which were much fewer in number than gay bars, and the Domon brand of men's underwear. A color advertisement of a man wearing Domon briefs often appeared on the back cover of *Mithuna Junior*. Unlike the situation in the early twenty-first cen-tury, when many mainstream brands of products and services seek to reach a gay market by advertising in gay media, in this early period only a very small number of businesses were prepared to place advertisements in an openly gay publication.

Perhaps even more important in the evolution of relations between Thai gay magazines and gay bars was the fact that models for the covers and male

FIGURE 2. Cover of an early issue of *Morakot* (1987), one of the early gay magazine competitors of *Mithuna Junior* that began publication in the 1980s. *Morakot* became known for younger-looking cover and centerfold models.

centerfolds that were prime features of each issue were almost always *dek bar* sex workers, who were also interviewed and profiled. In a period when most gay-identified men were closeted, posing nude or near-nude for a magazine cover and centerfold photo would have been a source of shame in the bourgeois culture of the country's middle-class gay men. In Bangkok's middle-class gay culture of the 1970s and 1980s, even taking off one's shirt or wearing revealing shorts or briefs in public, other than when going swimming, was seen as low class and uncouth. Nevertheless, *Mithuna Junior* and other early gay magazines such as *Neon*, *Morakot*, and *Midway* soon discovered that there was a massive market among middle-class gay men for images of exposed male flesh. As a result, it was typically lower-class men and male sex workers who needed the money from posing for a centerfold who were photographed in the gay magazines of this period.

The focus on gay bars in the contents and advertising in the new magazines, and the photographic representation of scantily dressed *dek bar* as the dominant images of desirable masculinity, worked together to create the impression that gay men should visit gay bars and that consuming the sexual services provided in these venues represented what it meant to be a gay man in 1980s Thailand.

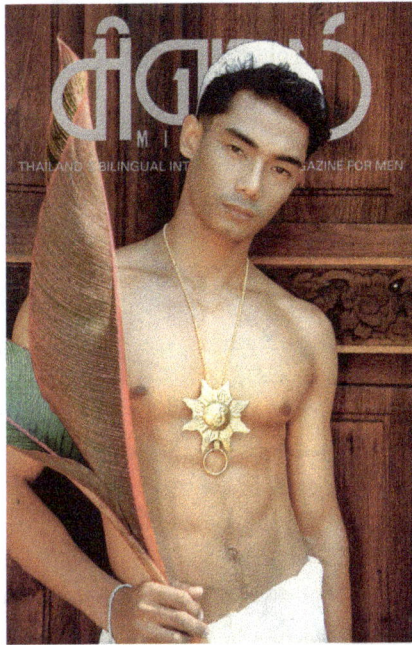

FIGURE 3. Cover of *Midway* (1991a), one of the most successful of the first generation of Thai gay magazines of the late 1980s and early 1990s. *Midway* included several pages in English in each issue and had the subtitle *Thailand's Bilingual International Magazine for Men*. The magazine was popular because of its handsome centerfold models who often dressed in exotic, Thai-style costumes.

The message the magazines repeatedly conveyed, both in text and images, was that the modern, middle-class Thai gay man found sex and romance with *dek bar* commercial sex workers.

So many new gay venues opened in 1984 and 1985 that *Mithuna Junior* initiated regular monthly columns that reported on new bars, cocktail lounges, and saunas in Bangkok and Pattaya. The titles of some of these columns were "Gay Bar News" (*khao-khrao gay*), "Favorite Gay Bars" (*gay bar thi na-thiao*; literally, "gay bars worth visiting") and "Tiptoeing Out for Fun at Gay Bars" (*yorng pai he thi gay bar*). The title of the last-mentioned column alluded to closeted gay men sneaking out of the heteronormative family to visit gay bars. These columns provided details of a highlighted bar's location, owner, manager, decoration, the *dek bar* available for customers, and bar services provided as well as special activities such as birthday parties, handsome man contests, and other celebrations. In the 1980s, these columns dedicated to reporting new bars were the primary guides for urban gay life that were offered to readers.

All the first generation of Thai gay magazines that began publication in the 1980s and early 1990s included columns that profiled *dek bar* and relied on male sex workers as the main source of their models. *Violet* was another early magazine that promoted male sex workers at gay bars. Here is a typical account of a *dek bar* featured in this magazine. "Joon is a small guy who has smooth white skin. He was born in Bangkok and studied to be a mechanic in college. His friends often call him Big Dick Joon because his cock is seven inches long.[8] When you see his secret photo, you'll feel horny. Joon is very proud of his big treasure [*sombat*]" (*Violet* 1993, 23).

Morakot magazine also had a regular column introducing young men who worked in gay bars. This column, "Before Becoming a Star" (*kwa-ja pen dao*), informed gay clients about the personalities and masculine qualities of male sex workers, always emphasizing the size of the sex worker's penis. For example: "Piyawat has a big cock ("weapon," *awut*) that is really appreciated by the owner of the bar where he works. He's become an especially popular man because of his big sexual organ. Num is also attractive. He's a handsome sportsman with a perfect body. What's more, Num also has a big weapon. Certainly, both guys earn more money from lots of gay clients who want to have sex with men with big dicks" (*Morakot* 1991, 92). Some readers wanted younger male models, especially teenage boys. However, it was not easy to persuade Thai teenagers to pose nude for a gay magazine. *Morakot* was the first magazine to feature teen models in its column "Admiring Teenagers" (*pleum wai-run*). For example: "Tae is 17 years old. He loves to play skateboard. This sport is very popular among Thai teenagers because it helps them to be strong. Tae has a beautiful backside and a firm body. Particularly, he has a perfect big dick ("weapon," *awut*). Everyone will be surprised when they see his weapon" (*Morakot* 1995, 54).

Midway was another magazine that introduced male models who worked in gay bars, with their sexual experiences and the size of their penis also being emphasized. Here are two examples:

> Kawi is a guy from Thailand's south. He's a Muslim and has passed the ritual of circumcision. Every part of his sexy body is covered by hair. He's a really nice guy and lots of people love him because he's a five-star (*ha dao*) fucker. (*Midway* 1995, 63)

> Kuladet comes from the south of Thailand and has been a sailor. He's slept with gay guys in the navy. It's usual for him to have sex every day and he has to masturbate twice a day. With his big cock, everyone will certainly love his sexual action. (*Midway* 1997, 81)

In 1985 the editor of *Mithuna Junior* acknowledged that gay bars and gay magazines were good partners because readers wanted to see erotic content in

TABLE 2.2   New gay bars and other venues in Bangkok opened during 1984–1986

LOCATION	1984	1985	1986
Saphan Khwai area	Adam (cocktail lounge)	Back Door (bar) Laguszo (bar) Paradise (cocktail lounge) Stax (cocktail lounge)	Arcadia (cocktail lounge)
Silom area	Super Lex (bar)	Garden Bar (bar) Khrua Silom (pub) My Way (bar) Zero Bar (bar)	Buddy (cocktail lounge) Jasmin (cocktail lounge) Super A (bar) The Genesis (bar)
Sukhumvit area	Inter Mustache House (bar)	Big Boy (bar) Boss (sauna) Studio 982 (bar)	City Men (pub) The Log Cabin (bar)
Petchburi area		Poppy (cocktail lounge)	Cottage (bar)
Pratunam area		David (bar)	Second Tip (bar)
Ramkhamhaeng area		Alex (bar)	
Ratchadamri area		Happy Boy (bar)	Kor Kaew (bar)
Bangrak area			Big Apple (bar)

Source: Information collated from issues of *Mithuna Junior*.

the magazine, which was provided by the photos and interviews with the *dek bar* working at these venues (*Mithuna Junior* 1985b, 22). The importance of these reports and images for promoting the business of gay bars was noted when *Mithuna Junior* reported that after the Adam Cocktail Lounge had been detailed in a previous issue, so many new customers visited the venue that the manager had a hard time keeping up with welcoming all the guests who came all night long (*Mithuna Junior* 1985b, 22).

During the 1960s and 1970s, Bangkok's gay community life had been limited to a small number of mostly secretive gay bars patronized by predominantly upper-class gay men. However, by the later 1980s and early 1990s, the gay scene had expanded considerably with concentrations of bars in several locations across the city, including the downtown Silom, Surawong, and Sukhumvit areas; Pratunam in the inner north; and the Suthisarn and Saphan Khwai areas further north. These areas all became known for their gay nightlife.

While significant numbers of bars had English names, this did not mean that they were necessarily oriented toward Western customers. For example, the bars in the Saphan Khwai area in the north of Bangkok were almost solely patronized by Thai customers, often middle-class men who lived in the many upmarket gated housing estates that had been built on the city's fringes since the early 1980s. The popularity of English names for Thai gay bars paralleled the influence of English on the coining of many new terms in Thai gay discourse at this time.

FIGURE 4. Advertisements for gay bars in *Mithuna Junior* (1991a) including photos of *dek bar* male sex workers at the venues. The "Adam Group" of bars (*left image*) lists two bars in Bangkok and one in Chiang Mai. The Moon Struck bar (*right image*) was in the Sukhumvit area of Bangkok. Gay bars were *Mithuna Junior*'s largest source of advertising revenue.

Mithuna Junior, Masculinity, and Male Erotica

Nude photographs of male models have an important place in the history of Thailand's gay culture. Included from the first issue, full-color images of models in erotic poses were crucial to the success of *Mithuna Junior*. It was its erotic visual content that first attracted the attention of many readers. As one reader wrote in an early issue,

> I couldn't believe it when I found *Mithuna* at a sidewalk store. At first, I didn't know what *Mithuna* was, but the handsome young man pictured on the cover made me feel so horny. I decided to buy it on the spot and rushed home. When I was in my room, I locked the door and tore open the plastic wrapping. I can't say how glad I was. I was so excited my hands shook. I wanted to scream out loud that I've met my friend. I've found my beloved magazine. I concentrated on slowly reading each page, every page and every word in your magazine. (*Mithuna Junior* 1984e, 123)

Another reader expressed similar sentiments in a letter published in 1985.

> I've read *Mithuna Junior* since the first issue. I'm always very satisfied
> and willing to buy *Mithuna*, although I'm very embarrassed and uneasy
> when I buy it [from the newsstand]. I really appreciate the male nudes
> in *Mithuna*, especially those in Issues 7 and 10. I'd also like *Mithuna* to
> present the art of the world's great artists, such as David sculpted by
> Michelangelo. (*Mithuna Junior* 1985c, 142–43)

In 1987 the magazine surveyed one thousand readers on their attitudes toward
images of nude models and found that 90 percent wanted more nude pictures to
be included (*Mithuna Junior* 1987a, 116). Several *Mithuna Junior* columns were
dedicated to profiling and interviewing the male models, such as "Tapping the
Handsome Guy on the Shoulder" (*krathaek lai num lor*), which introduced good-
looking young men working as models or actors together with their photos. The
photo essay column "Handsome Personality" (*lor bukkhalik*) presented male
models working in fashion, while the column "Naked Young Guy" (*nude chai-
num*) included shots of the magazine's cover model for each issue. Models were
also interviewed about their life, work, family, love, and sexual experiences. The
erotic photos of male models included in each issue and the explicit full-frontal
"secret" photos of each month's centerfold model available by mail order were
especially popular, as reflected in the following excerpts of letters to the editor.

> I like many things in *Mithuna*, particularly the erotic photos *(phap
> po)* of young men. I love nudity and pictures of naked men. I'd like to
> be a naked model in *Mithuna* and I hope that *Mithuna*'s editor might
> consider me. I think that the male body is beautiful. (*Mithuna Junior*
> 1984b, 141)

> I'd like *Mithuna* to have working-class laborers (*kammakorn*) as models.
> I don't like models who have effeminate characteristics. I love to see the
> bodies of men who work as construction laborers. It's not necessary to
> be handsome but he should have a tough, masculine body. (*Mithuna
> Junior* 1984c, 141)

> Why doesn't the guy [in the centerfold] take off all his clothes? I want to
> see his naked body. It's very sexy. *Mithuna* should have nude photos of
> male models in every issue. (*Mithuna Junior* 1984f, 138)

The photos of the cover and centerfold models were so popular that *Mithuna
Junior* published special volumes that collated images of its models. To celebrate
its first anniversary in 1985 the magazine published a special mail order album of

nude photos of its cover models. In the same year, *Mithuna Junior* also produced its first gay video, "On the Way," which was based on a story about a relationship between university students. Also in 1985, the magazine invited young men to send in nude photos of themselves to compete in the "Mr. June" model contest, with the winner being awarded a prize of ten thousand baht and being signed up as a model for the Mr. Media PR company for one year.[9]

As mentioned earlier, the back cover of most early issues of *Mithuna Junior* also included a color photo of a male model wearing Domon brand underwear briefs. The Domon company was founded in Bangkok in 1978 to market a range of male fashions but had not been particularly successful in its first few years. However, Domon achieved commercial success after advertising in *Mithuna Junior*. From 1986 Domon collaborated with *Mithuna Junior* to sponsor Domon Man (*num Domon*) contests at which attractive male models wearing Domon underwear competed for prizes at events held in gay bars and other venues. These events were among the first in Thailand to provide public recognition of the importance of images of masculine male bodies for the local fashion industry. Domon's advertisements in *Mithuna Junior* and its cosponsorship of the Domon Man underwear fashion competitions also reflected an acknowledgment of the importance of visual references to homoerotic desire in male fashion marketing. Domon was the first mainstream Thai company to find that partnership with gay media provided an avenue to commercial success by tapping new markets among Thailand's emerging gay middle class.[10]

Under its second-generation editorial and management team, *Mithuna Junior* published even more erotic images of male models in an increasing number of columns that operated as advertisements for the rapidly expanding number of gay bars in Bangkok. The columns that profiled *dek bar* sex workers were variously called "69 Guy" (*num 69*), "88 Guy" (*num 88*), and "Guy on the Last Page" (*num na sut-thai*). Readers' demand for erotic images of male models was such that from 1987 *Mithuna Junior* needed to locate an additional source of models beyond the bars that were the mainstay of its advertising revenue, so they invited readers to apply to be models by sending in nude photos of themselves.

The images published in *Mithuna Junior* reflected a range of masculine images and male body types. However, most male models in *Mithuna Junior* had slim physiques, with a general absence of images of muscular men with bodybuilder physiques. The body types of *Mithuna Junior*'s models were like those of the lean, athletic coyote boy performers (detailed in chapter 5) who were a key feature of many of Bangkok's gay bars and pubs in the early 2010s.

Homoeroticism and soft-core porn were not only characteristic of the images included in *Mithuna Junior*; they were also features of many of the texts published in the magazine. The "Sexual Experiences" (*prasopkan thang-phet*) column published readers' accounts of their sex lives, with those who had their story published

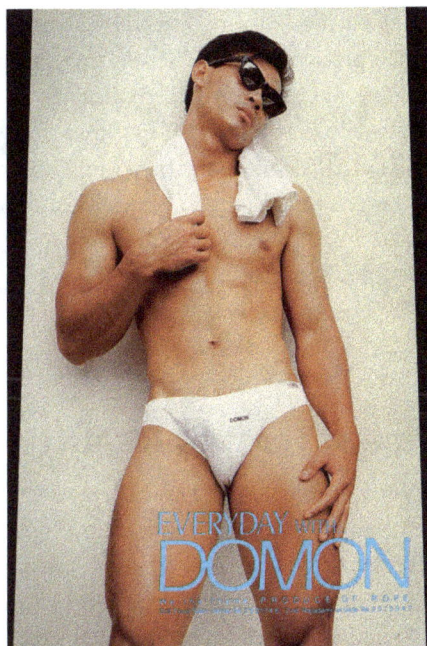

FIGURE 5. Advertisement for Domon brand men's underwear on the back cover of an early issue of *Mithuna Junior* (1985e). Thai menswear brand Domon was the first mainstream business to advertise regularly in a gay magazine, a commercial relationship that significantly boosted the company's sales in the second half of the 1980s. Domon also regularly sponsored events, such as the Domon handsome man contests, at Bangkok gay venues.

receiving a five-month subscription to the magazine. These stories were almost always sexually explicit, using terms and idioms generally considered obscene, such as "blowing cock" (*om khuay*), "sucking dick" (*dut khuay*), "licking cock" (*lia khuay*), "licking nipples" (*lia nom*), "fluffing cock" (*pan khuay*), and "fucking ass" (*yet tut*). While Thai censorship laws strictly, if erratically, monitored visual erotica and pornography, explicit discourse and texts often evaded monitoring and censorship. Readers' stories of their sexual experiences were so popular that in 1985 *Mithuna Junior* published a special booklet book called *Gaysorn Prasopkan* that compiled previously published sexual experiences stories in one volume.

After 1987 *Mithuna Junior* also marketed Western gay porn videos, introducing American and European gay porn stars to the Thai gay community. These videos were available by mail order for between four hundred and five hundred baht. In the early 1990s, Japanese pornographic gay videos were also advertised in *Mithuna Junior*, with increasing emphasis placed on images of attractive Asian men. In this period, some of *Mithuna Junior*'s cover and centerfold models imitated Japanese styles, such as wearing a fabric headband. Gay bars, saunas, and escort agencies also presented their Thai *dek bar* in Japanese fashions or placed images of Japanese men in their advertisements. At the same time, an increasing number of locally produced Thai erotic videos were also made for the local market. As HIV/AIDS infection spread in Thailand, *Mithuna Junior* advertised its diverse range of multiethnic American, European, Japanese, and Thai pornographic videos by advising readers that they could stay safe from HIV infection by masturbating to the images of video porn stars: "Find happiness at home; you won't risk contracting AIDS" (*Mithuna Junior* 1994, 61).

Mithuna Junior and Thai Gay Identity

The publication of *Mithuna Junior* had a transformative impact on Thai gay culture and for the thirteen years of its publication the magazine was widely regarded in the gay community as a good friend of Thai gay men. At a time when Thailand's mainstream press consistently represented homosexual and transgender people in stigmatizing and pathologizing ways, *Mithuna Junior* was the first major print medium to represent gay and *kathoey* lives and loves using nondiscriminatory language. *Mithuna Junior* contributed to constructing a sense of pride in gay identity. In the magazine's fourth issue in 1984, the anonymous author of the column "The Third Way" (*thang sai thi-sam*) explained.

> Being gay is not bad because gay people do not harm society. From the past to the present, many gays have created better things for this world. In every generation some gay people have created artistic masterpieces, such as Leonardo Da Vinci, Oscar Wilde, and Yukio Mishima. Even today time, famous people are coming out as gay, such as Elton John. . . . Don't be afraid to accept yourself as gay, because you can learn to love and understand yourself. (*Mithuna Junior* 1984g, 45)

Before the publication of *Mithuna Junior*, few Thai homosexual men had access to sources that would enable them to come to a positive understanding of gay identity. In the 1970s, Uncle Go Paknam's fortnightly gay lonely-hearts column "The Sad Lives of Gays" (*Chiwit Sao Chao Gay*) had been available in the nationally distributed magazine *Plaek*. However, this column focused on homosexual people's unhappy romantic and sex lives and, while accepting of same-sex preference, was penned by an avowedly heterosexual man whose sometimes idiosyncratic attitudes pervaded his replies to the problems related in the letters mailed in by his gay "nephews" (see Jackson 2016). Uncle Go Paknam's column provided little by way of help for Thai homosexual men to understand their sexual identity in affirmative terms and as a basis for a happy life.

The sense of connection that *Mithuna Junior* engendered is clearly expressed in the following letter from one reader upon coming across the first incarnation of the magazine as *Mithuna* in late 1983. "I can't tell you how I felt when I first saw *Mithuna*. It filled me with warm delight. Reading *Mithuna* is like having a friend standing by my side. I'm not lonely or confused anymore. It's the magazine that I've dreamed of. I'd like to send my love and my heart to everyone at *Mithuna*" (*Mithuna Junior* 1984a, 142). Letters to the editor expressed sentiments that *Mithuna Junior* was like a gay "friend" who readers had never been able to find before. Although many in the wider society, including the Thai police, often saw *Mithuna Junior* as obscene, the magazine and its erotic images instilled a sense of self-confidence in Thai gay men that they were worthy of human dignity. *Mithuna Junior* helped change Thai gay men's attitudes toward their homosexuality, to see themselves in positive terms, not as someone who was mentally disordered or morally corrupt. As one reader wrote in a letter published in the magazine's second issue, "We need *Mithuna* to be a mediator for us and tell people that we aren't aliens like E.T. They shouldn't hate us. If *Mithuna* helps us, we'll find more social acceptance" (*Mithuna Junior* 1984b, 144).

Mithuna Junior and Socializing the Thai Gay Middle Class

Publishing a gay magazine in Thailand in the 1980s was not an easy undertaking. Editors and publishers confronted a raft of problems, from the high cost of printing to the ongoing threat of having the contents classified as pornographic by the police and having issues seized from sales outlets. It was out of financial necessity that *Mithuna Junior* cooperated with gay bars, with advertisements from bars coming to provide the most reliable source of income. However, *Mithuna Junior* did not just promote commercial sex at gay bars; it also organized activities that helped readers meet new gay friends. In its first year of publication in 1984, the magazine's management organized a "Men friends meeting men friends" (*pheuan chai phop pheuan chai*) party at the Super Star discotheque in Bangkok's Patpong district, which many middle-class gays attended to see the evening highlights of "Handsome Guy" (*num lor*) and "Beautiful Guy" (*num suay*) competitions. Also in 1984, Mithuna Club was established as a focus for social activities for readers, with the following announcement published in the magazine's sixth issue.

> For your intimate enjoyment, forget about cruising the bars, saunas, and discos. Through 'Mithuna Club', the first gay social organization in Thailand, you can meet someone special one-to-one or through exciting parties, dinners, theatre outings, weekend trips, etc. Find out

how *Mithuna Club* can add a new dimension to your life. Call now for more information at 2824244–9 (contact Khun Nukul or Khun Anan) or write to 573/21 Samsen Rd. Dusit, Bangkok 10300. (*Mithuna Junior* 1984d, 105)

Mithuna Club's first organized event was called "Meeting Friends Along the Way" (*nat phop pheuan ruam thang*) and involved twenty-five readers who joined a holiday trip to Samaesan Island in Chonburi Province a couple of hours east of Bangkok. The second organized event was a trip to Khao Yai National Park northeast of the capital in May 1985, attended by twenty-two readers for a cost of two hundred baht per person. Mithuna Club's third members' trip was to Kanchanaburi west of Bangkok in June 1985, with a fourth trip being organized to Koh Lan Island east of Bangkok in December 1985. In 1985, the magazine reported that the Mithuna Club social organization had three hundred registered members. In April 1987, Mithuna Club organized a trip to Koh Mun Nok Island in Rayong Province east of Bangkok for a price of one thousand baht, which some of *Mithuna Junior*'s male models joined. Mithuna Club members also met at several places in Bangkok, including at "*Mithuna* House," which was the name for the magazine's office on Nakhon Sawan Road. For a membership fee they received discounts on *Mithuna Junior* as well as at gay bars and venues that had deals with the magazine. Mithuna Club's members came from both Bangkok and other provinces, and included teachers, civil servants, businessmen, actors, and students.

On April 5, 1985, *Mithuna Junior* held its first anniversary party at Bangkok's Indra Hotel, which was attended by a range of famous gay people, such as the hairdresser and media personality Pan Bunnag, as well as the editor of the competitor gay magazine *Neon*, which began publication in late 1984. As had become the custom at many gay celebratory events in Bangkok in the 1980s, the anniversary party included a handsome man competition, with a prize awarded to the attendee judged to be the favorite handsome guy. On August 18, 1988, *Mithuna Junior* held a fifth anniversary party called "*Mithuna* Night" (*ratri mithuna*) on the Oriental Queen dinner cruise ship along the Chao Phraya River in Bangkok. Participants paid five hundred baht to attend the party, which also included some of the magazine's cover and centerfold male models (*Mithuna Junior* 1988b, 109).

Personal Classifieds in *Mithuna Junior*

Mithuna Junior also included a personal classifieds section to enable readers to advertise to meet friends and lovers. In the publication's early years, it was called Gemini Club; it was later renamed *Samosorn Mithuna* ("Mithuna Club").

These small notices included each advertiser's name, nickname, age, address, telephone number, personal photo, and a short message describing themself and their sexual preferences. Unlike some competitor gay magazines that began publication later in the 1980s, which charged readers a fee to place classified advertisements, the Gemini Club and *Samosorn Mithuna* notices in *Mithuna Junior* were free. Readers lauded this as an exemplary social service (*Mithuna Junior* 1988b, 125). The classifieds were an especially popular part of the magazine, with the *Samosorn Mithuna* column publishing an average of eighty personal advertisements in each issue. In 1991 *Mithuna Junior* added more pages as demand increased and in 1996 it published a special issue made up solely of *Samosorn Mithuna* notices from more than two hundred gay men.

The profiles published in the *Samosorn Mithuna* column exemplified Thai gay men's felt need to represent themselves in masculine terms to attract other gay men as sexual and romantic partners. The predominantly closeted middle-class gay men who were *Mithuna Junior*'s main readership typically identified in masculine terms and did not want to be associated with the feminine

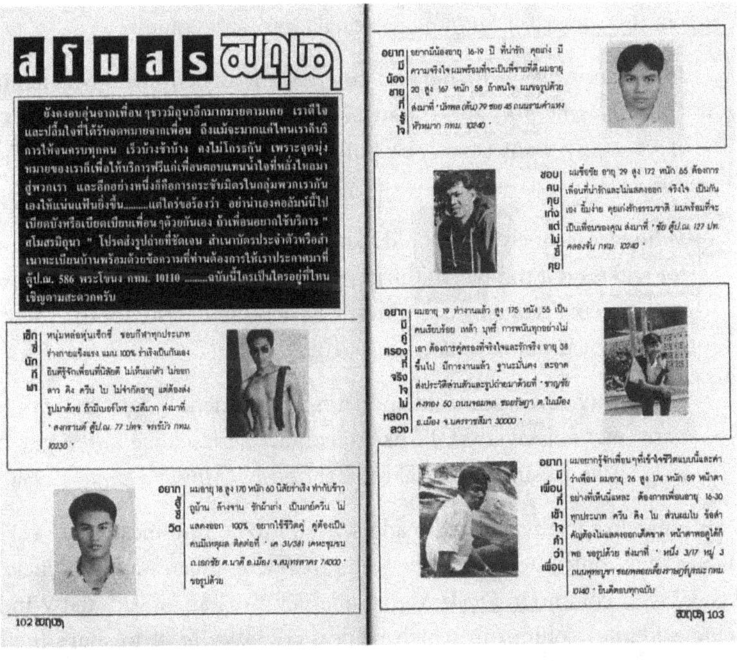

FIGURE 6. Sample pages of the "Mithuna Club" (*Samosorn Mithuna*) personal classifieds pages of *Mithuna Junior* (1992). The personal classifieds were among the most popular sections in the magazine for readers interested in contacting other gay men.

characteristics of the trans woman *kathoey*. Advertisers in the *Samosorn Mit-huna* personal classifieds column generally described themselves as looking for a partner who was a *man* or *gay king* (i.e., taking the insertive role) and who did not exhibit feminine characteristics, described by the idiom *mai sadaeng ork,* "not showing or expressing (gayness or femininity)." As detailed in the previous chapter, *mai sadaeng ork* denotes behaving in a masculine way, as a *man*, and not expressing feminine mannerisms that might identify a man as gay in public. This discourse of *mai sadaeng ork* was intimately associated with the rise of Thailand's urban gay middle class and reflected Thai gay men's conformity to dominant male gender norms.

In surveying 500 advertisements from gay men in *Mithuna Junior*'s personal classifieds columns published between 1984 and 1997 we found that 280 of the advertisers lived in Bangkok and 220 were from other provinces. The gay men who sought partners through *Mithuna Junior*'s classified advertisements usually had good careers and higher levels of education. Most were between eighteen and thirty years old and had either completed high school or university. The majority worked in the public sector and state enterprises, including schoolteachers, university lecturers, soldiers, and government officers. Here are some typical advertisements in the *Samosorn Mithuna* personal classifieds column.

> I'm twenty-five years old and *king*. I want a friend who isn't feminine (*mai sadaeng ork*) and is between eighteen and thirty-five years old. If you only want sex, don't bother contacting me. (*Mithuna Junior* 1987d, 101)

> Whoever is lonely and would like to get to know me, please write a letter and send it to me. I'm thirty years old, 170 cms tall. I don't show my gayness (*mai sadaeng ork*). I want a friend who also doesn't show that he is gay. (*Mithuna Junior* 1991b, 105)

> I'm twenty-seven years old and I'm self-confident. I don't show my gayness (*mai sadaeng ork*). I'd like to contact a masculine top *bi* guy (*man king bi*) who is sincere and takes life seriously. (*Mithuna Junior* 1995a, 102)

As a response to socially isolated readers' desire to communicate the problems and issues they confronted as gay men, and following the example of Uncle Go's "Sad Gay Lives" column in *Plaek*, *Mithuna Junior* also had a "Mithuna Window" (*na-tang mithuna*) column in which readers could write in to share their life experiences. Here is one example of the types of letters published in this column.

> I'm nineteen years old and gay. But I can't be open, and I've never told anybody. I've struggled with my feeling of intense anguish. Now, I'm tired of fighting my own feelings. I know that I'm a very sensitive person,

because I was so scared to be seen socially in the lovely gay community. I tried to find myself, who I am. Then, I finally knew that I'm gay and I don't hate myself anymore. (*Mithuna Junior* 1985c, 101)

In addition, the "White Room" (*horng si-khao*) column provided a venue for readers to express their thoughts, emotions, and feelings in more extended essays of two to three pages. *Mithuna Junior* also included articles explaining gay rights activism and the gay liberation movement in the West and provided background information summarizing research on homosexuality and homosexual behavior. Issue 46 in 1987 included the article "If you want to be a good gay" written by gay rights and HIV/AIDS activist Natee Teerarojjanapongs. Natee introduced his notion of *kunla-gay*, "the good gay man," who he described as embodying the good practices and personality that would lead to Thai gays being accepted socially. According to Natee, the *kunla-gay* or "good gay" should embody seven sets of characteristics: (1) trust, respect, and honor yourself; (2) be modest; (3) avoid envy and recrimination; (4) be a friend of heterosexual people; (5) do not tolerate homophobia in others; (6) know your limitations and capabilities; and (7) avoid being dominated by your sexual desire (*Mithuna Junior* 1987c, 132–33). Natee also argued that Thai gay men should seek out masculine partners as lovers because feminine gays, whom he called *gay sao*, were regarded as inferior by the wider community. He argued that if gay men expressed feminine characteristics, they would not be accepted by society and also would not be able to find a lover. Natee's critique of effeminate gay men reflected the editorial policy of *Mithuna Junior*, which was to discourage Thai gay men from acting in a feminine way like a *kathoey* and to assume a more masculine presentation so they could be more readily accepted in Thai society (*Mithuna Junior* 1987c, 132).

Mithuna Junior, Homonormativity, and Thai Middle-Class Gay Culture

Lisa Duggan (2003) coined the term "homonormativity" to describe the privileging of heteronormative ideals and values within LGBTQI+ cultures and identities.[11] This concept refers to forms of power that sustain the social regulations and structural ideas of heterosexuality within queer cultures. It emerges from the often-implicit assumption that the norms and values of heterosexuality should be replicated and performed among homosexual people (Schmiedgen 2007) and can be understood as emerging from gay men's survival strategies in a nonaccepting society. The heterosexually inflected forms of homonormativity also reflect a liberal ideology in which gay men's individual liberty and collective lifestyles are dominated by the production of commodities in the consumer culture of late capitalism (Hin 2008, 11). Mary Louise Adams (1997) contends that the heterosexual patterns of gay identity and lifestyles are normalized by consumerism and commodification, which while assuming an apparent form of individual autonomy characterized by consumer choice in a market of diverse options, in fact operates as a form of control in which the norms of heterosexuality are internalized in the constitution of queer subjects as consumers. Under the dual influences of both heterosexuality and capitalism, homonormative gay culture continues to reproduce forms of discrimination and domination that previously regulated and stigmatized homosexual people, even as gay culture is represented as a domain of tolerance and sexual liberation (Agathangelou et al. 2008, 124).

These analyses provide perspectives for considering the place of *Mithuna Junior* in the formation of the homonormativity of Thailand's modern middle-class gay culture. The magazine positioned itself as representing the Thai gay mainstream and played a leading role in fashioning the country's urban gay culture in relation to sexual commodities and consumption. *Mithuna Junior's* commercial foundation on, and promotion of, the sexual commodification of working-class men also reflected how same-sex sexual relationships in the 1980s were patterned by the class stratification of Thai society. It is true that without *Mithuna Junior* and the competitor gay publications that soon emerged in the media space pioneered by this pathbreaking magazine there would have been no direct connection between the nascent gay community that was forming in Bangkok's gay bars and the large numbers of homosexual men who at that time still lived isolated and separated from one another. The magazine played an important role in the formation of modern urban Thai gay identity and community. Nevertheless, this promotion of affirmative notions of gay identity and community was based on a commercial foundation. And the homonormative character of the commodified sexual culture of middle-class gay men perpetuated forms of inequality and discrimination within Thai gay communities even as it provided a delimited space of liberty within which forms of same-sex community became possible.

In the 1980s and 1990s, public discussions about gay culture in Thailand were typically framed in terms of heteronormative stereotypes that gay men were promiscuous and only interested in sex. Critical accounts in mainstream media also claimed that gay cultural influences from the West were contributing to the destruction of Buddhist morality and traditional Thai norms. These stigmatizing discourses led to many gay men staying in the closet and remaining confused about their sexual identity and behavior. In this setting, *Mithuna Junior* fostered the understanding that gay people could create their own distinctive cultural forms and social life free from social discrimination. However, the path to escaping social stigma was defined in terms of looking to consumer culture to provide opportunities for creating an autonomous sexual life.

The Continuing Influence of *Mithuna Junior*

A market in cheaper, secondhand copies of *Mithuna Junior* and other gay magazines developed across Thailand soon after these publications went on sale. Since the middle decades of the twentieth century, markets across Thailand have often included stalls selling secondhand books and magazines. From the later years of the 1980s, these book stalls often stocked older issues of gay magazines that lower-income gay men could afford. *Mithuna Junior* thus had a life beyond the years it was published and an influence beyond the predominantly middle-class men who could afford to buy its latest issues. Old issues of the magazine continued to circulate across the country for many years after they were first published, with their contents continuing to echo and extend their influence beyond the urban middle-class.

However, while large numbers of men undoubtedly had access to *Mithuna Junior* and its message of gay pride, not all could afford the consumerist lifestyles offered by the gay bars and venues whose advertisements and promotional columns made up a significant portion of the magazine's contents. Working-class gay men had to content themselves with imagining visiting the bars profiled in *Mithuna Junior*, or perhaps by themselves becoming a *dek bar* male sex worker at one of these venues. As a mediatized playground of Thailand's gay middle class, *Mithuna Junior* supported the social and sexual stratification of the country's gay community between working-class sexual service providers and middle-class sexual consumers. It conveyed middle-class gay lifestyles as the implicit norm of what it meant to be gay in 1980s Bangkok, and over time these class-based standards came to dominate urban gay culture in Thailand. The middle-class expectations and patterns reflected in *Mithuna Junior* fall into three main categories: (1) the commodification of masculinity; (2) masculine images and the discourse of "straight acting" (*mai sadaeng ork*) in gay sexual relations; and (3) homoeroticism as a Bangkok gay lifestyle. We consider each of these themes in turn.

Mithuna Junior and the Commodification of Masculinity

Richard Dyer (2002) contends that while commercial gay magazines in the West reveal the experiences of gay men, who have historically been marginalized and discriminated against in mainstream society, the contents of these commercial gay media do not reflect all aspects of gay culture but rather depict sexualized commodities for sale in gay markets. Michael Bronski (1998) argues that life-styles based on the consumption of commodities in everyday life are not merely a manifestation of popular culture but also constitute forms of social control. In the 1980s and 1990s, *Mithuna Junior* reflected urban middle-class gay cul-ture and lifestyles centered around consumption. Through this magazine and the increasing number of competitor gay publications, Thai gay men came to understand their sexual identity and lifestyles as being mediated through sexual products and services. The products and services advertised in *Mithuna Junior*, typically located in gay bars and other commercial venues, were represented in overtly masculine terms, as illustrated by eroticized images of nude and semi-nude male centerfold models. However, unlike the case in many Western societ-ies, this commodified and eroticized mode of realizing and affirming Thai gay identity in masculine terms was not related to a social movement or a political agenda of activism calling for same-sex or transgender rights. While Thai gay men were historically minoritized, their sexuality was not criminalized under Thai legal codes. And as consensual homosexual practices had not suffered direct legal prohibition, Thai gay men had no need to mobilize politically to overturn homophobic laws in order to create social spaces for sexual contact, friendship, or love. In the absence of a gay rights political movement or a need to mobilize collective action to agitate for the repeal of anti-sodomy laws, the Thai gay communities that emerged in the 1980s and 1990s were fashioned by commercial forces and the commodification of sex to an even greater extent than was the case in Western countries. Ironically, Thailand's less overtly homopho-bic culture—when compared to the historical situation in many Western and other societies—meant that the market and consumerism assumed singular dominance in fashioning the country's modern gay culture, which until the early twenty-first century had lacked parallel formative influences from politics and community-based activism.

The erotic male nudes in *Mithuna Junior* provided mirrors for Thai gay men to imagine same-sex relations in masculine terms and escape the stereotyping of homosexual men as effeminate. However, the images of masculine male models came with a price. Not only did *Mithuna Junior*'s gay readers have to pay higher prices to order the special nude photos of the models but the images of masculine bodies were also central elements of the advertisements for gay businesses where bar boys were available as sexual commodities. The pervasive images of mascu-linity in *Mithuna Junior* affirmed modern Thai gay identity as being distinct from the feminine *kathoey* while simultaneously regulating gay masculinity within the bounds of a middle-class consumer culture that created class-based exclusions which limited this new form of sexually autonomous existence to those with incomes to afford it.

The Straight-Acting Discourse of *Mai Sadaeng Ork* in *Mithuna Junior*

Mithuna Junior provided space for finding and making friends in personal classifieds columns such as "Mithuna Window" (*na-tang Mithuna*) and "Mithuna Club" (*Samosorn Mithuna*), to which readers contributed their profiles and photos. They overwhelmingly presented themselves as masculine men who sought friends and partners who were also masculine and did not publicly reveal their gay identity—referred to in Thai gayspeak as *mai sadaeng ork*. The masculine, or not visibly gay, habitus of *mai sadaeng ork* was pivotal to the imagining of gay sexual and romantic relationships, and hence of public gay existence, in Thailand in the 1980s and 1990s.

Most men who placed personal classified advertisements in *Mithuna Junior* typically stated that they sought a masculine partner who was an active top, known in the Thai gay parlance of the period as a *gay king*. In the Thai gay community in the 1980s, the binary sexual roles of active *king* and receptive *queen* were complementary sexual positions that were defined by an implicit gendering in which men taking the sexually insertive role were considered to be more masculine, while those taking the receptive role were seen as effeminate and less sexually attractive. Masculine *gay kings* did not want to associate with *kathoey* or feminine gay men (*gay sao*) because they feared that their femininity would reveal (*sadaeng ork*) their same-sex interest to a critical public gaze. Under the dominance of the straight-acting discourse of *mai sadaeng ork*, masculine characteristics were central to the structuring of sexual relations between gay men. The straight-acting norms of *mai sadaeng ork* also dominated *Mithuna Junior*'s personal classifieds. Men who failed to conform to the homonormative expectations of this form of masculine presentation may have found it difficult to establish sexual and romantic relationships. At times, more feminine gay men were also labeled as presenting negative images of gay identity to Thai society. The privileging of normative forms of masculine gendering in the representations of gay sexual and romantic partnering in *Mithuna Junior*'s classifieds established a gender-based hierarchy of sexual desirability that worked to exclude those regarded as failing the *mai sadaeng ork* test of masculinity. *Mithuna Junior* sustained the homonormative forms of 1980s Thai gay consumer culture within a gender hierarchy that valorized masculinity as the basis of both gay identity and gay sexual relations and minoritized effeminate gay men.

Mithuna Junior and the Emergence of Homoeroticism as a Bangkok Gay Lifestyle

Before the 1980s, gay social life in Thailand had been severely restricted. The transition from the pre–*Mithuna Junior* period to what some gay men now nostalgically remember as a golden age of Bangkok's gay scene—from the mid-1980s to the later 1990s—saw dramatic changes in the forms of homosexual desire and activity as gay identity and lifestyles became increasingly prominent in major urban areas. Thailand's gay scene also expanded beyond Bangkok to Pattaya, east of the capital, and subsequently to Chiang Mai in the north and Phuket in the south. As a nationally distributed magazine, *Mithuna Junior* was a medium that communicated ideas, outlooks, and practices from the metropole of Bangkok to middle-class gay men in urban provincial centers around the country, where gay lifestyles like those forged in the capital became increasingly visible from the later years of the 1980s.

Mithuna Junior fostered ideas of gay love, friendship, sex, and eroticism as they could be found in gay bars and nightclubs and as expressed in columns illustrated with images of naked male models. This urban gay lifestyle, centered on forms of sexual desire and eroticism that could be found in the company of male sex workers and as represented in homosexual pornography, quickly expanded in the second half of the 1980s as the Thai economy boomed and the number of gay bars and other commercial venues increased. *Mithuna Junior* was both a witness and a contributor to the rapid changes in gay lifestyles in Thailand over this period.

Mithuna Junior opened print media spaces for representing homosexual desires expressed through gay commodities and contributed to the creation of social spaces where a new generation of younger urban gay men could meet friends, lovers, and partners. This led to the establishment of networks and groups with shared cultural understandings of gay identity. However, this modern gay social formation was based on the experiences of Thailand's urban gay middle class, whose lives and aspirations were forged in the consumer culture of late capitalism. Modern Thai gay lifestyles and culture are not reflections of traditional Thai society. Rather, they are creations of consumer spaces formed by gay bars and commercial gay magazines that first became major influences in the 1980s.

Mithuna Junior manifested the relationship between commercial spaces of bars with commercial sex workers and saunas, on the one hand, and the evolution of the ideals of masculinity that embody normative understandings of what it means to be a gay man in modern Thailand, on the other. Gay print media such as *Mithuna Junior* were formative influences in the coeval evolution of these dual, intersecting processes of sexual consumer lifestyles and masculine gender culture. Thai gay print capitalism (Jackson 2009) brought together gay men from various places and statuses into a virtual community in which the sexualization of masculinity formed the basis of identity as well as the means to establish relations of sexual connection, intimacy, and friendship. Although later issues of *Mithuna Junior* under the editorial guidance of HIV/AIDS and gay rights activist Natee Teerarojjanapongs supported notions of the *kunla gay*, "the good gay man," this idea never gained traction or influence among Thai gay men. Being gay in Thailand's consumer culture has not stressed notions of sexual morality but rather the eroticization of masculine body images. In Thailand's gay consumer culture of commercial venues, a large number of gay men came to understand their masculinity and sexual feelings without any anxiety about whether they were a "good gay person."

While *Mithuna Junior* began with an emphasis on commercial sex between middle-class and working-class men, the magazine nonetheless also prefigured the transformation of gay sexual relations from commercial transactions between men from different classes to noncommercial sexual and romantic relations between men from the same class background. *Mithuna Junior* also supported the rise of a culture of egalitarian gay relationships outside the bars and beyond commercial transactions. The magazine provided space for supporting friendship and romantic relations beyond commercial transactions in gay bars by sponsoring social activities for readers and including a considerable number of personal classifieds. While commercial sex in gay bars has not disappeared from Thailand's commercial gay scene, from the 1990s, egalitarian relations between men of largely similar backgrounds emerged as the prime focus for middle-class gay social life and partnering.

The emergence of egalitarian sexual and social relationships was also paralleled by a growing emphasis on masculine self-presentation. When sexual relations transitioned from commercial transactions with heterosexual sex workers to interactions and relationships with other gay men, gay men sought to make themselves attractive to potential lovers and partners, which required conforming to norms of masculine sexual attractiveness. With the shift from commercial sex to egalitarian relationships, gay men not only sought out masculine sexual partners but also aimed to embody norms of masculine attractiveness themselves.

The culture of masculinity became central to Thai gay culture in the 1990s as gay men turned to fitness to make themselves attractive to sexual partners. At the same time that Thai gay men embraced the masculine regimens of modern fitness culture, the gendering of gay relations between a masculine *gay king* top and a feminine *gay queen* bottom was also replaced by a masculinization of gay sex, with both top and bottom being redefined as masculine sexual positions and respectively relabeled as *ruk* and *rap*, terms borrowed from the masculine martial art of Muay Thai. Nevertheless, this rise of a culture of gay masculine gendering took place within a class structure in which distinct middle-class and working-class norms of masculine attractiveness emerged. The new culture of middle-class gay masculinity is detailed in chapter 4 while the new culture of working-class masculinity is discussed in chapter 5.

Even as the content in its later issues came to reflect emerging notions of gay community, *Mithuna Junior* continued to reflect a Thai middle-class gay culture based on commercial sex. It did not adapt its financial base to the new patterns of egalitarian relationships. Given *Mithuna Junior*'s financial dependence on advertising by gay bars with male sex workers, the rise of noncommercial egalitarian sexual relationships between gay men undermined the financial basis of the magazine, leading to its eventual demise in 1997, the year of the onset of the Asian financial crisis. Indeed, the 1997 economic crisis saw the end of almost all the first generation of Thai gay magazines. Nevertheless, the comparatively rapid economic recovery at the turn of the new century would see the publication of a new generation of much more sexually explicit magazines, which are considered in chapter 3.

3

THE STRAIGHT MALE NUDE AND THAI GAY MASCULINITIES

In this chapter we detail the masculine imaging of the male models who posed nude for the homoerotic photos that were published in Thai gay magazines from the 1980s to the early 2010s, analyzing how forms of visual representation reflected changing patterns of male homosexual desire. We consider how Thai gay men perceived these masculine images and how the representation of male nudity responded to and sustained Thai gay men's sexual imaginations. It is not just the textual forms of discourse in Thai gay magazines that tell us about the country's gay culture and history. The photographs of the men in these magazines also reveal much about the culture of masculinity in Thailand and the roles of the media and the market in the formation and evolution of Thai gay culture. Drawing on visual sources, we investigate the relationships between representations of male nudity, homoeroticism, and gay men as they were linked in the consumer culture that formed the matrix within which modern Thai gay identity evolved. Several body types are identified in the photographs of men in Thai gay magazines across this period: the natural body; the muscular body; the metrosexual body; and the male body decorated with tattoos and earrings. Notable changes in the styles of masculinity in Thai gay magazines over the decades are transitions from the style of Thai boxers and sportsmen to the metrosexual and, since the late 1990s, to that of the bodybuilder. We explore the cultural and social contexts behind the changing representations of the masculinity of the Thai male body, Thai gay desire for masculine sexual partners, and the types of masculinity that Thai gay men have regarded as sexually desirable.

The full-color male centerfolds that were a mainstay of Thai gay magazines from their inception in the early 1980s tell us much about ideals of masculinity in the country. The most notable finding is that there are multiple valorized modes of being a man in Thailand, not one single hegemonic form of manhood. These various ideals are related to class—in particular, working class versus middle class—and ethnicity, particularly Thai versus Chinese as well as Asian in contrast with Caucasian. Idealized forms of masculinity have also changed over time in response to the diverse influences of both Western and Asian cinematic media in Thailand, such as the muscular, gym-developed Caucasian male body typified by Arnold Schwarzenegger, and the lithe East Asian male body on display in the movies of Bruce Lee and Jackie Chan. Further factors influencing changes in masculine expression have been evolving fashions following in the wake of economic development, such as the rise of the metrosexual style and the increasing popularity of tattoos and body art.

Evolving Patterns of Homoeroticism in Thai Gay Magazines

As masculine ideals evolved across the decades, older images of the sexually attractive male body were not superseded but rather remained as alternatives in an increasingly complex gender culture of multiple masculinities that came to exist as options and matters of taste and preference for gay men. Different ideals and modes of Thai masculinity also came to be marked as indicators of social class and ethnicity. In Thailand's highly class-stratified society—characterized by widely divergent income levels between working-class, middle-class, and upper-class gay men—older forms of masculinity that reflected premodern, indigenous ideals of manhood are now often stigmatized as working-class and rural, while newer forms of masculinity influenced by trends from both the West and East Asia are viewed positively as indicators of middle-class status and cosmopolitan lifestyles. As outlined in the previous chapter, the homosexual desires and imaginations of gay-identified Thai men have been formed within a consumer culture of sexual commodities. Western gay culture has not been directly reproduced in Thailand, and under the capitalist consumer culture that has dominated the formation of modern Thai gay identities no single model of gay masculinity has emerged. Rather, Thai gay men now negotiate and create their body images from different patterns and urban Thai gender culture is characterized by a complex of masculinities in which different ideals of male sexual attractiveness coexist.

The history of changes in the sourcing of male models in Thai gay magazines is also informative about the developing patterns of the commercial gay scene in the country. In the first Thai gay magazines in the early 1980s, the male models were mostly sportsmen while in the second half of that decade most models were male sex workers from gay bars. As discussed in the previous chapter, in the 1980s, male centerfolds in gay magazines were important for the development of gay bars by providing images that advertised the male sex workers at these venues. In the 1990s, the models for gay magazine centerfolds were men who came from the evolving middle-class fitness and gym culture, while in the early 2000s commercial modeling and advertising agencies became major sources of the magazines' models. Male centerfolds were important to the commercial viability of Thai gay magazines and there was strong competition for attractive models among the many publications that were on sale in the later 1980s. From the 1990s, and especially from the early 2000s, there was a notable trend toward more sexually explicit images. The male centerfolds were also the basis for a parallel production of mail-order nude photographs and pornographic videos, VCDs, and DVDs, which were comparatively expensive and provided significant additional revenue for the magazines.

Homosexual desire and homoerotic images of the male body are intimately connected. Like gay men around the world, large numbers of Thai gay men have come to understand their homosexual feelings from their response to viewing eroticized images of the male body. From the 1980s to the 2010s, the photographs of men pictured in the large number of gay magazines that competed in the Thai marketplace were the primary source of the sexualized materials from which Thai gay men came to understand their homosexual desires and in relation to which they fashioned both their sexual identity as gay and their gendered identity as masculine. Thai homosexual men have also molded their gay identities through seeking out and aiming to embody masculine characteristics observed in straight and bisexual men. Many of the male models in Thai gay magazines were represented as being straight, which was reflected in the interviews and articles that accompanied the photographic images. The heterosexuality of the models in Thai gay magazines was not hidden or obscured. On the contrary, it was often highlighted and emphasized. The masculinities of Thai gay and heterosexual men are thus closely related, and the masculine bodies represented in gay magazines are not merely photographs of individual men but rather reflect cultural notions of the ideal male body. Changing patterns in the sculpting of the male physique through exercise and its photographic imaging embody shifting cultural understandings of masculinity.

Our research is based on data obtained from almost two dozen gay magazines that were published from the mid-1980s to the early 2010s. The selected magazines include *Mithuna Junior, Morakot, Midway, Neon, Male, Weekend Men, GR Male, Male Mini, Grace Male, Door, Door Dek, Heat, H, K-Mag, Body, Need+,*

Step, Stage, Born, Hey, Firm, KFM, and *Full.* Notes from magazine editors, interviews with male models, and readers' letters are also considered.

Changing Ideals of Thai Masculinity

The multiplicity of masculinities and body images represented across the decades in which gay magazines were the dominant media form in Thai gay culture reflect social and cultural transformations and the changing lifestyles of Thai gay men. A notable trend in the evolution of Thai cultures of masculinity has been the marking of characteristics that, in the premodern era, were general features of manhood across all social classes as now representing only the masculine cultures of urban working-class and rural agricultural laborers. In the past, the exposed male body, male tattooing, and penis enhancement were common across all classes. However, since the early twentieth century, these practices have largely been restricted to working-class men. This means that early twenty-first-century Thai working-class masculine culture has greater continuity with the country's premodern patterns of male gendering than the contemporary gender culture of middle-class Thai men, which by comparison has undergone dramatic changes since the beginning of the twentieth century.

In the nineteenth century, the exposed male body was commonplace in Siam and was not in itself viewed as a source of erotic interest or fetishized as a sexual object. In Thailand's tropical climate, men of all classes, including ruling elites, were typically naked above the waist in everyday life. Buddhist monks were among the few men whose clothing of monastic robes covered the whole body. Historically, working men wore few clothes, often only loose Chinese trousers or a sarong tugged around their waist while the chest and upper body were left uncovered. It was also common for young boys to go about naked until the age of seven or eight. The exposure of the male torso was not seen as erotic but rather as a simple expression of normative manhood.

Indeed, nineteenth-century Western visitors to Siam were often shocked by what they regarded as the "nakedness" of the Siamese populace (Jackson 2003). However, with the adoption of Western dress codes from the later nineteenth century and the clothing of the "naked" Siamese body, the exposure of the male torso came to be more marked by both class and by erotic connotations. The borrowing of Victorian-era attitudes that equated the covering of the body with civilizational status has meant that Thais today often regard exposing the body in everyday situations as demeaning. Even into the latter decades of the twentieth century, men's underwear advertisements in Thai newspapers and magazines typically used Caucasian not Thai male models because it was regarded as demeaning for a respectable man, even a model, to be photographed posing in his underwear. However, this situation has changed dramatically since the early 2000s, as seminude Thai male models have come to grace the covers and pages of increasing numbers of mainstream fashion magazines.

Key terms in Thai discourses of normative heterosexual masculinity are "strength" (*khwam-khaeng-kraeng*) and "endurance" (*khwam-ot-thon*). To be considered a "man" (*phu-chai*), a male must be brave and courageous (*kla-han*) and not show weakness. In the premodern period, Thai men's bodies were not characterized by highly developed musculature. Nevertheless, the ideal man was regarded as being strong (Khetara 2007, 6) and toughened from manual labor (Tuay 2003, 47). Historically, Thai men have had smaller physiques than Caucasian men but were regarded as embodying strength, power, and agility—characteristics that are emphasized in training for the Thai martial art of Muay Thai. A key principle of Muay Thai is skill in movement, using every part of the body—hands, arms, and legs—for kicking, hitting, striking, and pushing (Khetara 2007, 12). In the past, preliminary training in Muay Thai involved strengthening the body by carrying buckets of water, pounding rice into flour, and chopping firewood. These manual tasks developed strength in the arms and shoulders, the parts the body that are especially central to Muay Thai combat, and it was only after young men had developed sufficient strength that they were permitted to begin formal training (Khetara 2007, 39).

However, with the development of the Thai economy and a comparative decline of agricultural labor as the primary occupation of working-class men, fewer men now undertake the heavy manual labor that produced the classic Muay Thai–style male physique. The contemporary jobs of working-class male service workers—such as waiters, bartenders, and sex workers—mean that these men typically have a less developed, if more natural, masculine figure, perhaps trained by exercise from playing sports such as football, badminton, and sepak takraw. In their free time, many young urban working-class men participate in informal games of these sports in public parks, sports centers, and community playgrounds. In the earliest issues of Thai gay magazines, young men who had trained in sports and had been school athletes were common male models. The images of attractive Thai sportsmen found in these early Thai gay magazines—such as a lithe Muay Thai boxer or sepak takraw player—contrasted with the more developed physiques of Caucasian sportsmen who were often photographed in early Western male erotic publications. In the 1980s, the ideal masculine image was of a Thai sportsman whose body had been trained to develop agility and the ability to move and respond quickly. This contrasted with the more solid physique of the bodybuilder that became popular in the following decades.

Representation and Transformation of the Penis in Thai Masculine Culture

The importance of the male sexual organ in Thai cultures of masculinity is reflected in a large number of terms for the penis, listed in the glossary, and in forms of penis enhancement. Historically, many Thai men have engaged in practices of transforming and enhancing the penis. Young men who want a larger penis may rub skink oil (*nam-man jing-len*), made from the tails of small lizards, or inject olive oil into their sex organ. While it has no scientific basis, many working-class men, especially from Northeast Thailand, believe that skink oil helps enlarge the penis. Another practice is to enhance the width and appearance of the male organ by inserting glass or plastic beads beneath the skin of the penis. This practice was once common across mainland Southeast Asia (see D. Brown et al. 1988). In Thailand it is known as *fang muk*, "inserting pearls." *Fang muk* is popular among some heterosexual working-class men, who believe that the practice will make them better lovers by increasing their female partners' sexual pleasure. However, it is not clear whether *fang muk* genuinely increases women's sexual pleasure, as some complain that the glass beads cause painful scratching of the vagina. Discussion of the penis and its enlargement was common in Thai gay magazines across the decades that they were published, as indicated in the following excerpts from interviews with male sex workers.

> I had to enlarge my penis (*khorng*) by using skink oil. I started using it when I was fourteen years old. It has to be used every morning, because the penis (*khorng*) needs to be erect. I rub my penis with this oil to make it bigger. I think my penis is bigger from rubbing with skink oil, but it takes a long time to work. (*Midway* 1990a, 89)

> My gay clients say my penis (*khreuang*) is beautiful: big, and strong. Most of them like it a lot. (*Midway* 1990b, 29)

> I think that I've a big cock (*khorng*) because I've got my father's genes. Every man in my family has a big cock. I saw my brother's cock when we were bathing together. He's got a big cock (*khorng*) like me. Also, I have to masturbate every day: maybe three times a day. If I read a pornographic magazine, I'll wank. I'm a sex addict. (*K-Mag* 2001, 48)

Crossover Marketing and the Male Nude in Thai Women's Magazines

Before the first Thai gay magazines were published in the 1980s, some women's fashion magazines had included photographs of nude male models. The short-lived *PG* (Playgirl) magazine, founded in 1974, was the first magazine targeted toward a Thai female readership that included beefcake images of bare-chested male models in underwear. *BR* magazine, founded in 1971, also included photographs of male nudes in issues later in that decade. The Thai men who posed for these nude photos were typically well-known movie stars and singers of the period, such as Suriya Chinnapan, Kraisorn Saenganan, Asawin Rattanapra-cha, and Thun Hiranyasab. Suriya Chinnapan (1952–2022) was born in Udon Thani Province in Northeast Thailand and was a singer and actor in many TV series and movies. In his later years, he also directed several television series, the most famous of which was the 1988 Channel 3 series "Son of the Wolf" (*Orot Ma Pa*). He was married and has two children. Kraisorn Saenganan (born 1957) is a movie actor who began his career in Thai film in 1979. He is also well-known as having been the husband of the famous Thai *luk-thung* country-style singer, Pumpuang Duangchan (1961–1992). Asawin Rattanapracha (1946–2021) was born in Chanthaburi Province east of Bangkok and started his acting career in 1971. The work that made him famous was the 1971 TV version of the period drama "Conqueror of the Ten Directions" (*Phu-chana Sip Thit*). Thun Hiran-yasab graduated from an Australian university and began working as a model in 1980. He later acted in several movies, often paired with the famous leading actress Jarunee Suksawat. He is married and has three children.

Num-sao ("young man, young woman") was an early-1980s lifestyle magazine with a crossover market among both men and women. *Num-sao*'s first issues published photos of scantily clad female models. However, in 1983 this magazine published a photo album of sexy men that showcased Yuttana Saensanae as a male nude model. Yuttana was born in the southern Thai province of Songkhla in 1964 and started working as a model when he was in vocational college. After the *Num-sao* album was published, Yuttana became a rising star in Thai movies and fashion modeling. The handsome Yuttana subsequently became well-known in the gay community, later working as a nude male model with several gay magazines. Though he had become famous in the 1980s, Yuttana retired from the entertainment industry in the early 1990s.

In parallel with the rise of gay publishing, in the 1980s mainstream fashion magazines also became prominent trendsetting features of Thai popular culture. Oriented primarily toward a middle-class female readership, these publications often included fashion shoots of attractive young male models. Some of the most popular magazines that included photos of male models, and their first year of publication, were *Priao* ("slender," 1981); *Thoe Kap Chan* ("you and me," 1983); *Hello* (1985); *Sai* (1987); and *Image* (1988). The male models in these glossy, full-color publications were often photographed in provocative erotic poses that led to these publications becoming popular with both gay and female readers.

From the 1990s, Thai women's magazines increasingly targeted a crossover gay market by regularly including erotic covers and "fashion" shoots of male models. While the models for early gay magazines were often working-class men, including male sex workers from gay bars, the models for women's fashion magazines were often well-known male personalities from film, television, or sports. While gay print media declined across the 2010s, going online and being replaced by digital media, glossy fashion magazines continued to publish often-homoerotic images on their covers and in men's fashion sections until the end of that decade. Many fashion titles have now also ceased publishing, ultimately succumbing to the financial pressures that online media presented to all forms of print media. The not so subtle, but nonetheless still implicit, marketing of glossy women's fashion magazines to gay as well as female readers reflected the increasing mainstreaming of gay men within urban Thai society in the early 2000s.

The Aestheticism of the Natural Male Body in the 1980s

During the 1980s, Thai gay magazines often represented their cover and centerfold models in artistic settings in combination with poetic stanzas praising the male body and masculine beauty. These poems invoked loneliness, quietness, and calmness as dominant themes in providing a discursive context that sought to guide viewer-readers' interpretations of the feelings of the photographed model. Models were often posed with natural landscapes—such as forests, mountains, rivers, lakes, seashores, and rice fields—as backdrops. To add interest, the models were also often dressed in outfits such as Thai traditional costumes, cowboy hats, boots, and sportswear. These costumes constituted a visual narrative for an implied story within which the model was a presumed actor.

According to the interviews published in the first issues of the gay magazines, the models were typically young straight men the magazine editors had met by chance—when commuting on the bus, eating at streetside food stalls, shopping in a mall, or walking along the street—and had been invited to be amateur models. Some models were contacts of the magazines' house photographers, who invited men they met while jogging and exercising in public parks and at swimming pools. In addition to finding male models by happenstance encounters, some magazines also invited readers to apply to become models by sending in a nude photo and profile.

As more gay magazines were published in the second half of the 1980s, demand for male models increased and the editors who competed for sales found it difficult to rely on chance encounters to find their models. As the number of gay bars with *dek bar* boys grew in Bangkok in this decade, commercial sex workers became a convenient source of straight-identified models for the gay magazines. Competition for male models was an important factor that drove the shift toward gay magazines' increasingly close commercial relationship with gay bars, as described in chapter 2. The photographic and interview profiles given to these *dek bar* sex workers helped the venues they worked for to attract more customers and may also have contributed to the model himself gaining more customers. These *dek bar* sex worker models were usually young straight men who identified as *phu-chai* or *phu-chai thae*, "real men."

Straight Working-Class Male Models and Middle-Class Thai Gay Men

In the 1980s, interviews accompanying magazines' photospreads of their cover and centerfold models revealed that the men were typically from lower-income working-class backgrounds, eighteen to twenty-five years old, and predominantly identified as bisexual (*bi*) or straight (*phu-chai*) (Narupon 2003). A 1988 issue of *Mithuna Junior* provided the following introduction to one of its *dek bar* cover and centerfold models.

> My name is Tum. I'm working at Adam Bar in Soi Rong Nang Pradiphat. It seems like I'm a twentieth century Adam. I don't have any lover as my Eve, but actually that doesn't worry me. My Eve could be anybody, and not necessarily a woman. You, gay people, could be my lover. If you feel the same way, come talk with me at Adam Bar. I'll take you to Eden, the heavenly garden where Adam and Eve made love. (*Mithuna Junior* 1988a, 98)

In the 1970s and into the early 1980s, Thai gay culture was dominated by attitudes and notions of effeminacy, with many gay men identifying in feminine terms. The fact that many gay men viewed all homosexual men in feminine terms meant that they did not regard other gay men as attractive sexual partners. At a time when notions of gay masculinity had yet to consolidate, gay men's desires for masculine sexual partners were fulfilled by commercially mediated relations with heterosexually identified men. It was because many gay men excluded other gay men as possible sexual partners that heterosexual men were a main source of sexually attractive male models in Thai gay magazines in the 1980s. The fact that the models were not gay, or even primarily sexually interested in men, did not detract from their attractiveness to gay men in this period. On the contrary, it was the fact that the models were not gay that contributed to their perceived masculine status and made them sexually attractive.

The shift toward using *dek bar* as models was a convenient option for the magazines for several reasons. First, there was a large number of young men working in gay bars to choose from. In 1989 there were sixty gay bars in Bangkok, with each bar having from fifteen to twenty *dek bar* sex workers (*Midway* 1989, 112). Second, the young male sex workers needed to promote themselves to get more customers. And third, many gay bars needed to advertise and were more than happy for gay magazines to profile their workers and market their services.

In addition to using *dek bar* as models, the early gay magazines *Mithuna Junior, Neon, Morakot,* and *Midway* also included regular columns that profiled young male sex workers from different bars. *Mithuna Junior* had two regular columns, "Young Guy 69" (*num 69*) and "Young Guy 88" (*num 88*), which published a color photo of the profiled *dek bar* together with the name and telephone number of the bar where he worked. *Midway* also had two columns profiling *dek bar*, "The Owl's Shadow" (*ngao nok-huk*) and "Five Star Guy" (*num ha dao*). *Neon* had one column, "Neon Discovery," and *Morakot* also had one column "Morakot Guy" (*num Morakot*), which included color photos of two male sex workers in each issue. In addition to representing *dek bar* as sexually attractive, these columns also detailed the young men's sexual qualifications by describing their diverse sexual encounters with women, gay men, and *kathoey*.

Voices of Straight Men in Thai Gay Magazines

Thai gay magazines often included interviews with their straight male models, especially in the early years of gay publishing in the 1980s and 1990s. The attitudes toward homosexual behavior and gay men that models expressed in these interviews reflected a Thai male culture defined more in terms of masculine gendering than sexual object choice. The straight men photographed and interviewed in the magazines typically expressed open-minded attitudes about gay people and homosexuality, such as in the following interview published in *Mithuna Junior* in 1988s.

> I'm twenty years old. I've had sex with a gay guy, but I took the insertive role (*king*). I don't hate gay people, because they're human beings. I don't have any reason to discriminate against them. I can talk to everybody. It's good to have lots of friends of various genders (*phet*) and ages. At present, I'm single and working as an artist in a private company. I come from Nakhon Sawan Province [in mid-north Thailand] and moved to live in Bangkok many years ago. This is the first time that I've been a model in a gay magazine. (*Mithuna Junior* 1988a, 60–61)

The straight men who posed as models for gay magazines often thought that doing a nude photo shoot would be an exciting experience that they should try once in their life (*Midway* 1987b, 141), observing that being naked in front of other men would not be as shameful as taking off their clothes in front of women. When they became accustomed to being with the magazine staff, the models reported that they relaxed and enjoyed the work, as reflected in the following observations by another model for *Mithuna Junior* in 1988.

> When I took off my clothes, I felt exposed and empty. I was ashamed to have so many people standing around me. But I thought that I had to be brave, especially when shooting the secret photo [cum shot]. Fortunately, the place where the magazine photo shoot took place was a private beach where some foreign tourists come to have sex. This made me feel horny and it got me excited. It was easy to masturbate behind a rock at the beach. (*Mithuna Junior* 1988c, 59)

Because they viewed getting naked and masturbating as bringing in money, the models thought of it as work and not as ethically problematic.

> When I was contacted by a gay magazine to pose for a nude photo shoot, I went to talk with my friends. My friends told me that it wouldn't cause problems for anyone. Don't worry about anybody. So, I decided to do this without any hesitation. (*Midway* 1987a, 88, 139)

> I've had sex with gay guys. I wanted to know what it feels like to make love with a gay guy. I know that it's not wrong or a sin. It's a normal practice. (*Mithuna Junior* 1984f, 102)

In their interviews, several of the straight male models indicated that they were ready to try new sexual experiences, including homosexual activity. This is like Jackson's (2016) finding in his study of the letters sent to the gay lonely-hearts columnist Uncle Go Paknam in the late 1970s and early 1980s, with some self-declared heterosexual letter writers saying that they had experimented with having sex with a gay man or *kathoey* out of interest in exploring what it would be like. Some models stated that having sex with a gay man or a *kathoey* would be an exciting form of sexual release that could be pleasurable and enjoyable. However, they usually observed that having sex with a gay man could not compare with making love to a woman.

> I've had sex with a gay man. It made me feel happy, but it wasn't any better than with a woman. I think that trying to have sex with a gay guy is an exciting experience. A man should try to do lots of things. (*Midway* 1989, 107)

A *kathoey* at a gay bar taught me about having sex. I've been fucked by gay men, and I learned to fuck gay men. I know that there are different types of gay people. Some don't make me feel happy, but others give me more pleasure than fucking with a woman. (*Midway* 1987a, 107)

I've had sex with a handsome gay guy. He looked like a man. When we were drunk, we started to make love. He sucked my cock and licked my ass. It was the first time that I'd been rimmed by a man. I was very happy and excited. (*K-Mag* 2001, 49)

In the 1980s, Thai gay magazines also often included articles that described the story behind the photo shoots with their male models. These photo shoots usually involved traveling to exotic locations such as a beach, national park, waterfall, or an island and involved overnight stays in a hotel or resort, with the behind-the-scenes articles doubling as travel reports to advertise gay-friendly tourist accommodations. In *Midway* magazine this regular column was called "For You and You" (*samrap khun lae khun*). The columns detailing the photo sessions included accounts of the straight male models staying and working with the magazine's gay staff. These columns typically eulogized the attractiveness of the model's body, and the paeans to a model's physical attributes encouraged readers to buy the mail order "secret photos." Before the arrival of hardcore magazines in the early 2000s, these secret photos were one of the few regular sources of print media pornography in Thailand. *Neon* magazine often promoted the secret photos of its models with vivid descriptions, as in the following examples.

This man often walked by our *Neon* magazine office, and every time he passed his masculine body attracted us. We wanted to take his clothes off and see his big muscles. His tanned skin and regular Thai face might not be so enchanting, but his big dick would amaze you. We caught our breath when we saw the size of it. We'll present this attractive man, Chut, to you, who has an extraordinary sexual appeal. He's beyond your expectation and imagination. If you don't want to keep your desire all pent up inside, please send in your order for his special photos. (*Neon* 1985, 73)

Our model is a straight man who used to be a soldier and later came to live as a civilian. He really knows what life is about and his masculine toughness comes from a life of hard work. But behind his hardiness, he's tender and has sentimental feelings. He's open to new experiences in life. His masculinity flows in his blood, and expands across his chest, muscles, legs, and other parts of his body, which will be kept for your sexual imagination. We always expect that someone could touch the secret parts of his body. (*Neon* 1986, 50)

Some readers asked to join the photo shoot trips, as in the following letter to the editor published in *Midway* magazine.

> If it's possible, I'd like you to arrange a trip to travel with your photography team. It'd be a good chance for me to see your work and see the male model as well. I'd like to take a photo with the male model when he's naked. This would really help my imagination and my sexual fantasies. (*Midway* 1991b, 6)

When readers ordered the magazines' secret photos, they wanted to see the male model's penis and cum shot. However, readers sometimes complained that the mail order secret photos were not sexy, and the printing was low quality.

> I've got some recommendations about the secret male pictures. I think the pictures were taken without a properly focused lens that resulted in a blurred picture. It's not satisfying to look at these pictures, especially when the male model isn't handsome. Also, there wasn't any picture of the model cumming. What happened to your male model? (*Neon* 1991, 8)

> I recommend that your magazine should have pictures of men having an orgasm and cumming. It would help improve my sexual mood. I'd be happy if I could see a cum shot *(nam taek)* of a handsome man. (*Male* 1995, 97)

> Looking at pictures of naked guys makes me feel horny. I imagine his secret male organ under his underwear. But the pictures of guys in your magazine don't show any sexy cocks *(khorng lap)*. Most of the pics are of guys' bodies without showing the male genitals clearly. If I want to see the male secret organ, I have to order the secret photos from your magazine. (*Mithuna Junior* 1985d, 138)

Ethnicized and Class-Based Images of Ideal Thai Masculinity

Thailand's multiethnic society includes groups and communities with diverse skin tones, ranging from dark tan, called "black" *(dam)* or "intense" *(khem)* in Thai, to fair, called "white" *(khao)*. Thai men from the south of the country are regarded as having dark or tan skin tones, while Chinese men as well as ethnic Thai men from the north are described as having "white" skin. In Thai "white" is used to describe the skin tone of East Asian peoples, including Chinese, Koreans, and Japanese as well as Caucasians. Käng (2015) uses the expression "white Asian" to describe Thai perceptions of fair East Asian skin tones. While a person's skin tone may reflect their ethnic heritage, Thai attitudes toward skin color typically relate more to notions of class, status, and beauty than to race. Brown skin, which is often described as "black," is stereotypically regarded as being less attractive and as symbolizing lower-class or uneducated people. In contrast, "white" skin is seen as being sexually attractive. Nevertheless, among Thai gay men these stereotypical attitudes toward the presumed attractiveness of different shades of skin tone may be counterbalanced by other aspects of a male model's appearance, such as his face, physique, and the size of his penis. Darker-complexioned models who were handsome and had a big penis were still admired as being sexually desirable. Thai gay attitudes regarding ideal forms of masculinity and male attractiveness are thus complexly negotiated through multiple factors and dimensions.

Skin tone is a common topic of conversation in Thailand, and in a society where men's complexions extend across a wide range from dark to fair particular skin tones can also become objects of sexual preference for some Thai gay men. As the number of Thai gay magazines increased in the second half of the 1980s, some magazines established market niches by emphasizing models with a

FIGURE 7. Contrasting "dark intense" (*dam khem*) and "white" (*khao*) varieties of Thai masculinity on the covers of gay magazines. In multiethnic and socioeconomically stratified Thailand, different skin tones are associated with distinct ethnic and class groups and are commodified as discrete forms of masculinity. Left: Cover of *Neon* (1990). Right: Cover of *Lap Chaphor: Chao Si-muang* (Top Secret: Lavender People) (2001).

particular ethnic look or skin tone, whether dark Thai or fair Chinese. *Midway* tended to choose darker-looking men as their models. They were often from southern Thailand, a region known for men having "sharp intense" (*khom-khem*) facial features, similar to ethnic Malay men from neighboring Malaysia. By contrast, *Morakot* tended to select fair-complexioned, younger-looking men who often exemplified the ethnic Chinese look that in Thai is called *ti*, a Chinese dialectical term for a boy or youth.

Mithuna, *Morakot*, and *Midway* usually relied on *dek bar* sex workers as their models. The brown skin and slim bodies of these young men marked their Thai and Thai-Lao ethnicity, with many coming from poorer farming and wage labor families in the country's northeast. In contrast, the models in *Male* magazine often were of Thai-Chinese heritage, with their fair skin marking them as middle-class urbanites with good jobs. *Male* also emphasized the metrosexual style of urban men whose care for their image was complemented by having fair skin. *Neon* and *Weekend Men* magazines often presented muscular male models whose gym-toned bodies reflected the masculinity of men whose lives emphasized sports and health within the expanding consumer culture that proliferated in Bangkok in the 1990s, which we discuss in more detail in the next chapter.

FIGURE 8. Cover of *Weekend Men* (1992), one of the growing number of gay magazines that began publication in the 1990s and competed for market share among Thailand's increasingly wealthy gay middle class.

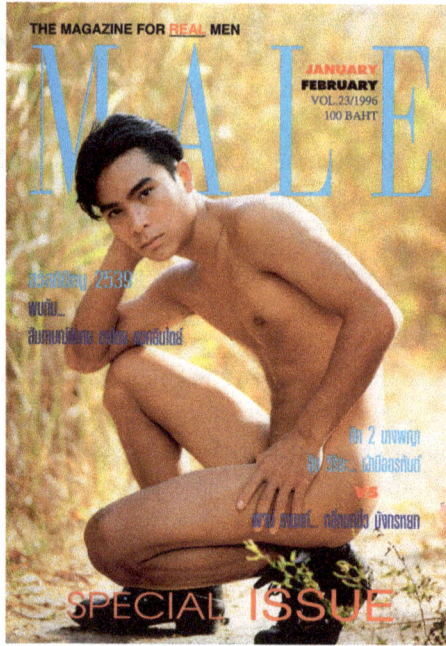

FIGURE 9.   Cover of *Male* magazine (1996b), one of the most successful of the second generation of Thai gay magazines that began publication in the 1990s. *Male* became known for attractive cover and centerfold models.

Mid-1990s: The Arrival of Muscular Male Models

As the Thai economic boom continued into the first half of the 1990s, a rapidly growing number of gay magazines were published and competed for market share in the country's increasingly well-off gay communities. A prime indicator of a successful magazine was having consistently handsome models. The magazines with the most attractive models on their covers sold the most copies. During the later 1980s, *Midway* gained a reputation among middle-class gay men as being the magazine that consistently included photos of the most handsome men. *Midway* also featured men who had won prizes at "handsome man" male model contests. In the 1980s, male model contests were organized by gay bars as activities to promote business. The contestants were usually working-class men, not necessarily *dek bar*, who needed the additional income that could be won from the prizes that were awarded. The winners of these contests were also approached by gay magazines such as *Midway* to be models. Because of its success in engaging the winners of gay bar handsome man contests as its models, *Midway* became the best-selling gay magazine in the early 1990s, with the editor proudly reporting his magazine's leading market share in the editorial of one issue in 1991 (*Midway* 1991b, 8).

Cover and centerfold models were crucial to the economic success of Thailand's gay magazines. Readers indicated that male models were important for the magazines because gay men would always look at the cover before deciding whether to buy one, as noted in the following letter to the editor published in *Mithuna Junior* in 1987.

> Gay magazines always have pictures of naked male models. It's very important. Usually, I look at the pictures of the male model before reading the columns. If a gay magazine has a handsome man in every issue, then it will be a real benefit for that magazine. Many readers will buy a magazine that has nude pictures of a sexy man. (*Mithuna Junior* 1987b, 119)

However, if a magazine did not have a handsome male model, gay men would turn away. Some readers of *Mithuna Junior* complained that later issues of the magazine did not have handsome men on the cover.

> Perfect male models should be chosen to be photographed in your magazine. The editor should pay more attention and be careful in selecting models. Some men pictured on the cover aren't attractive. It deflates the reader's satisfaction. If you put an effeminate guy on the cover, I won't want to open the magazine. The important thing is that the male model should be photographed naked. You aren't a male fashion magazine that only shows clothes and shirts. (*Mithuna Junior* 1988d, 124)

> None of the male models photographed in any of your issues are attractive. Most of them are unpleasant to look at. Nobody would be happy to walk next to them. Even though your magazine is aimed at giving the reader more substantial content, the male models are still very important. When the reader finds the magazine in the book shop, the first thing they see is the male model on the cover. If the man on the cover isn't attractive, the reader won't buy it. (*Mithuna Junior* 1993, 117)

Some of the first generation of gay magazines, such as *Neon*, adapted to the increasingly competitive environment by approaching muscular bodybuilders (*nak-klam*) to pose nude for its centerfolds. Including images of muscular, fully naked men was an innovation for Thai gay magazines in this period and differed from earlier centerfold images of more lean-bodied men who, while fit, had an athletic musculature developed from playing sports rather than bodybuilding. The new look of more muscular Thai male bodies followed from Western bodybuilding practices of gym training and weightlifting and in the early 1990s male models also began to talk more of their interest in bodybuilding in their interviews. The following is an excerpt from an interview with a model in a 1991 issue of *Midway*: "I love to exercise and go to the body building club at university every day. Actually, I have a slim, tall body. My muscles aren't any bigger than guys who have a shorter, broader physique. While I've been exercising doing weight training, I haven't got big muscles yet, so I'll need to keep training for a longer period" (*Midway* 1991c, 91). Some gay bars also began organizing muscleman contests in the 1990s, with men with gym-developed physiques wearing bikini briefs also performing go-go dancing. Most of the contestants in these competitions were *dek bar* boys who had developed their physiques by working out in the fitness rooms that increasing numbers of gay bars installed on site. One male model interviewed by *Neon* magazine in 1990 related that he wanted to have muscles like Arnold Schwarzenegger. Hollywood movies were highly popular among Thai audiences and stars like Schwarzenegger—whose movies *Total Recall* (1990) and *Terminator 2: Judgment Day* (1991) were high-grossing releases in Thailand—had a major influence on Thai men's masculine images. Schwarzenegger was a significant inspiration for bodybuilding (*phor-kai*) in Thailand, and in the early 1990s many Thai men viewed him as a masculine idol.

Bangkok gay men's growing interest in developing muscular bodies found expression in a rapid expansion in the number of gay saunas in the city. Saunas became highly popular in the first half of the 1990s, being much sought out venues where gay men could meet for sex and explore their sexual fantasies. Nine gay saunas opened in 1992 alone, including GG, Boss, Volt, Babylon, Adonis, Harrie's Gym, Colour, Otoko, and Colossus. Another new sauna, Colony, opened in 1993 followed by Obelisk in 1994. In advertisements in gay magazines these saunas were represented as men's health clubs and they introduced gyms and workout exercises to increasing numbers of Thai gay men beyond the older and much smaller community of Thai bodybuilders. We describe the history of bodybuilding in Thailand in more detail in chapter 4. All the new gay saunas included exercise and fitness rooms where gay patrons could work out and do weight training. The gyms in gay saunas were also venues where desirable muscular bodies were on display, becoming sites where gay men could perform a new, more robust image of Thai masculinity and where a big chest and a six-pack abdomen became commodities in affirming gay men's sexual attractiveness.

In addition to saunas with gyms, the Tawan Bar on Surawong Road became the first Bangkok gay venue where muscular men worked as *dek off* male sex workers. The male sex workers at Tawan Bar developed their bodies by regularly working out and doing weight training, often spending their days before going to work at the bar training in the open-air public gym in nearby Lumphini Park.

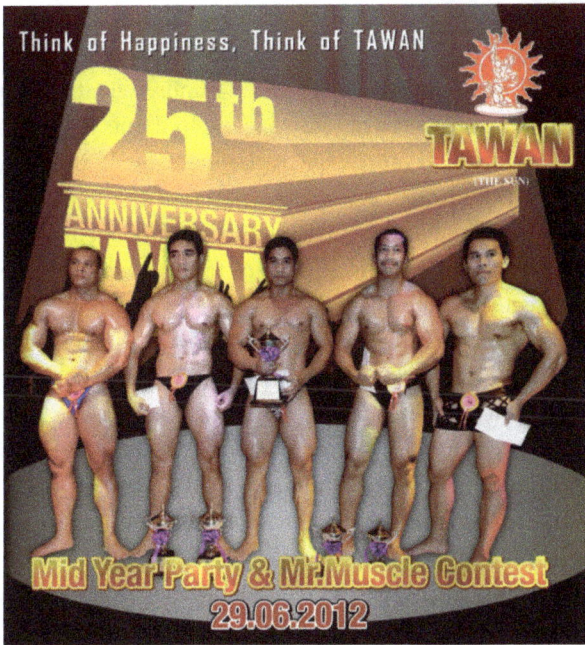

FIGURE 10. Advertisement for "Mr. Muscle" muscleman contest at the Tawan Bar in Bangkok in mid-2012. This long-running gay bar has been known for its muscleman male sex workers since the 1990s and regularly sponsors special events to attract customers.

This gym in Bangkok's oldest public park was free and had already been a focus for working-class bodybuilders in the city for several decades. Some of the *dek off* at the Tawan Bar, which became known colloquially as *bar nak-klam* or "the muscle-man bar," were pictured as models in gay magazines.

Another new trend in the early 1990s was for gay magazines to sell videotapes that gave a behind-the-scenes look at the photo shoot for the centerfold model for each issue. These videos typically showed the model naked and included masturbation and a "money shot" ejaculation scene. While Thai censorship laws restricted images that could be published in magazines sold from newsstands and bookstores, there was comparatively little police monitoring of pornographic materials sold by mail order and there are no reports of the Thai post office intercepting pornography sent through the mail. The sexually explicit mail order products that complemented the printed beefcake erotica sold across the counter were comparatively expensive, often several times the cover price of the magazines themselves. In the early 1990s, the nude models were only filmed alone, and at that time the videos of photo shoots did not include any oral or anal sexual intercourse between male models. *Midway* called its videos "Sneaking a Look at the Male Model" (*aep du nai-baep*), which sold for six hundred baht, while *Male* magazine's photo shoot videos sold for seven hundred baht. As the decade of the 1990s progressed, the videos of magazine photo shoots of individual models evolved into a local form of more explicit pornography. In the late 1990s, Thai gay magazines' videos showed two or three male models having both oral and anal sex. And as the technology of video production developed in the early 2000s, Thai gay magazines often sold video discs of the production photo shoots for their cover and centerfold models.

Along with booming economic growth in East and Southeast Asian countries such as Hong Kong, Taiwan, and Singapore, came new fashions in sports and health that accentuated increasingly muscular male bodies. In the 1990s, having gym-built musculature became central to notions of attractive masculinity. In addition to American body culture influences via Hollywood, Thai male fashion also changed in response to Asian influences and styles epitomized by Hong Kong movie stars such as Jackie Chan (known in Thailand by his Chinese name Chern Long) and Simon Yam (known in Thailand as Yern Ta Hoa). These actors had muscular bodies trained in Kung Fu and Chinese martial arts. Another Hong Kong movie star who was influential in Thailand was the Chinese-American Michael Wong, who worked in the country in 1993 and 1994. The handsome Wong was a sex idol of many Thai women and gay men, and in 1994 the Domon men's underwear company, which had advertised in *Mithuna Junior* from that magazine's inception, published a special magazine of its male models in the nude, including Wong. Wong's masculine body was also on show in a series of music videos, movies, advertising, and fashion magazines in the mid-1990s. In the popular 1994 Thai heterosexual soft-core porn movie "Chaophraya Dragon" (*Mangkorn Chaophraya*), he played a nude love scene with Thai sex symbol actress Morakot Maneechai. Wong's masculine image had an impact on the style of many Thai men, who became increasingly interested in taking care of their bodies and learning to build up their muscle mass.

Later 1990s: The Rise of the Thai Metrosexual Man

In the second half of the 1990s, the style of the male nude centerfolds in Thai gay magazines was increasingly influenced by a sense of a trendy, middle-class Thai metrosexual man who was interested in fashion, personal grooming, and beauty. The metrosexual look was a new trend in urban male lifestyles that was reflected in clothes, personal grooming, and healthy food as well as cosmopolitan tastes in music, movies, entertainment, and travel. This kind of urban lifestyle was also reflected in the characteristics of the male models photographed in gay magazines in this period. Information about fashion and lifestyles expanded rapidly with new communication technologies as the use of pagers, mobile phones, and the internet increased in Thailand. The first commercial internet service in Thailand was initiated in March 1995 by Internet Thailand Public Company Limited, now known as INET. This media transition reflected the changing ways that Thai gay men received and responded to an expanding variety of sources of information. Moreover, the internet also allowed foreign gay men from the West and from East and Southeast Asia to learn about gay culture and entertainment in Thailand.

Darker-complexioned models had often appeared in Thai gay magazines in the 1980s. However, from the mid-1990s, these local men were increasingly marginalized within Thai gay print media as no longer being seen as sexually attractive in terms of the new urban lifestyle of the metrosexual gay man. Within Bangkok's middle-class gay culture, darker-complexioned men came to be discriminated against because of stereotypes that they were poor, uneducated rural men who made a living from sex work for gay tourists (see Käng 2015). Many of the *dek bar* male sex workers in Bangkok's gay bars came from Northeast Thailand and had darker tan skin tones, a body image that, rightly or wrongly, was widely believed to be appreciated by and attractive to Western gay men. With the rise of the metrosexual look, fairer-skinned men came to be perceived as more sexually attractive because they symbolized more sophisticated urban middle-class lifestyles. Darker-complexioned men came to be seen as old-fashioned and were looked down on as fairer-complexioned models became more popular as reflecting a more highly educated gay man with good taste.

The second half of the 1990s was also characterized by a declining interest among Bangkok gay men in socializing in gay bars, which had been the main venues of Thai gay social life for middle-class gay men in the previous decade. Gay bars and *dek bar* sex workers were increasingly viewed as outdated and catering primarily to gay tourists, with the new preferred sites of Bangkok gay social life being the growing number of saunas where younger gay men could meet other gay men as sexual partners. Socializing in saunas—many of which included restaurants, gyms, and specially organized events—came to be perceived as a defining characteristic of the Thai gay metrosexual lifestyle in which urban homosexual men could present their sexual identity and meet fairer-complexioned, educated gay friends and partners. Gay university students and higher-income professional gay men socialized in the saunas, which became sites for embodying a new set of masculine images. Many gay magazines in this period published images of fairer-complexioned male models in accordance with this changed sense of masculinity and sexual attractiveness.

Grace Male was one of several new magazines that began publishing in the mid-1990s and became known for its Eurasian or *luk-khreung* models of Thai-Caucasian heritage, whose fairer complexions reflected the increasingly popular metrosexual look. Chinese-looking male models also became popular in gay magazines in this period, being viewed as attractive and symbolizing international recognition. Magazines such as *Male* and *Grace Male* included Chinese male models from Singapore and Hong Kong among their centerfolds. The stable of gay magazines published by Male Company, which included *Male*, *Male Mini*, *GR*, and *Grace Male*, were all prominent in selecting models who represented the Eurasian metrosexual look. Tony Sandstrom—who is of mixed Norwegian and North American Indigenous heritage and worked as a model in Bangkok and other Asian metropolises—exemplified the metrosexual man who was a Thai gay ideal of the 1990s. Sandstrom was a highly popular model among Thai gay audiences in the mid-1990s because of his fair complexion, Eurasian looks, and gym-toned body. Publication of his nude pictures in issues of *Male* and *Grace Male* led to issues of these magazines selling out quickly.

The Male group of magazines introduced a new sense of the Thai gay man as someone who keeps in touch with novel trends and evolving urban lifestyles. Metrosexual men's fair complexions were seen as clean and this new masculine ideal was of a man of good taste with a higher education, a healthy body, more money, and who worked in a professional job in the city. This model of gay manhood was deemed appropriate for a 1990s urban gay lifestyle that was no longer based on paying for sex with *dek bar* at gay bars but rather was centered on socializing in saunas, discotheques, karaoke cafes, fitness centers, and other venues where one could look for metrosexual men with similar backgrounds as sexual partners. *Male* magazine also reported that metrosexual gay men wanted to see more mature-looking male models who were of working age, a style that contrasted with the younger-looking bar boys who had dominated the centerfolds of Thai gay magazines in the previous decade (*Male* 1996a, 32).

Male magazine broke the pattern set by the gay magazines established in the 1980s that had presented models from working-class backgrounds and gay bars. *Male* and its sibling gay magazines responded to the era of the internet and the information society, with their models presented in trendsetting fashions that reflected the consumer culture of Thailand's booming economy in the first half of the 1990s. In this decade, an increasing array of sexy underwear, an expensive product that only middle-class men could afford, was also advertised in gay magazines. Fashionable underwear, swimwear, bikini briefs, G-strings, and short pants were a dimension of metrosexual gay men's erotic lives that symbolized a self-confident sexually attractive male body. Selling for at least two hundred baht per item, more than the legal minimum daily income of manual laborers, these

FIGURE 11.   The American model Tony Sandstrom on the cover of *Grace Mini* magazine (c. 1996). Sandstrom's fair-complexioned, Eurasian-looking appearance reflected the international metrosexual look that became an ideal of Thai middle-class gay masculine attractiveness in the later 1990s and early 2000s. Sandstrom also appeared on the cover of *Male* magazine (1996c), a sister publication of *Grace Mini*.

metrosexual fashion accessories were well beyond the price range of working-class men.

Some of the older gay magazines did not adapt well to the new metrosexual environment and the shift of middle-class Thai gay life from bars to saunas, consequently finding themselves with progressively declining market shares. *Neon*, *Mithuna Junior*, *Midway*, and *Morakot* had all ceased publication by the turn of the millennium. In addition to maintaining their original focus on gay bars, these magazines were also the first victims of print media's confrontation with the information technologies of the internet and online communications. As reported in the final issue of *Midway*, gay websites—which operated at a much lower cost and created new channels for younger gay men to chat with other gays and to find sex partners much more easily—presented new challenges to print media (*Midway* 2000, 146).

Yet even successful print magazines faced financial pressures. It cost a significant amount to pay professional, metrosexual-looking models to pose for centerfolds, even more if the model was famous like Tony Sandstrom. In the 1980s,
male sex worker bar boys had been a comparatively low-cost source of models.
However, in the 1990s bar boys' smaller, slimmer physiques and tan skin meant
they were no longer regarded as being as attractive as Eurasian male models,
who were taller and had fair complexions. Also, in the 1990s, Thai gay readers
were more interested in seeing national athletes and the winners of the increasingly popular male model contests as centerfold models (*Male* 1996c, 20). In
this decade, the "dream man" contest of the Thai version of *Cleo* magazine for
women was also very popular among the younger generation of Thai gay men.
As reported by *K-Mag*, sexy men in this contest were most definitely attractive to
Thai gay men (*K-Mag* 2002, 14). From the 1990s, male body images in Thai gay
magazines came to be categorized in two different types. The first was the "local
body," sometimes called *dek ban*, or the look of a "local village guy" that typified
working-class men found in gay bars. The terms *num ban* and *num ban ban*, "young
local guy," or *phu-chai ban* and *phu-chai ban ban*, "local man," refer to a man who
looks like an agricultural laborer from a rural village or *mu-ban*. The second body
type was the styled metrosexual physique of trend-conscious middle-class men.

In the later 1990s, gay magazines increasingly turned to modeling agencies to
supply models for their covers and centerfolds. The new metrosexual look called
for men with fair skin tones and modeling agencies sought out men with "white"
(*khao*) skin who had a "clean" (*sa-at*) look and a firm body, preferably including a well-developed six-pack. Local working-class men could not enter the new
modeling business because their styles and physiques were judged as no longer
matching the metrosexual ideal of male attractiveness. This left local men with
darker tan skin tones to find jobs in gay bars and massage parlors rather than
with modeling agencies, although they could still find work as nude male models
in some of the hardcore gay magazines that began publication in the early 2000s,
which included photos of erections, cum shots, and sex. Many local men also
adapted to the new image of the sexually attractive male body, taking up exercise
and wearing new men's fashion accessories including earrings and tattoos.

As noted in chapter 2, from the 1980s, sexy man contests were held in many
gay bars and other venues. These contests were often associated with special
events such as fashion shows and celebrations. Male modeling contests were also
very popular and became a new source of models for gay magazines. In contrast
to the more closeted gay culture of the 1980s, when few middle-class gay men
felt comfortable being photographed for a gay magazine, by the early 2000s an
increasing number of men applied to compete in gay bars' sexy man contests in
order to have a better chance of landing a career in professional modeling or roles
in Thai TV dramas or movies (*K-Mag* 2001, 18). Many men looking to break into

the movies competed in multiple male beauty contests in different gay bars to increase their chances of being discovered by talent scouts.

The modeling agencies and their talent scouts—who came to play an increasingly important role in the Thai entertainment industry in the early 2000s—often had a large number of male models on their books, many of whom were available to pose for photo shoots for gay magazines. Indeed, modeling businesses found a ready market for their stables of models among the large number of gay magazines that competed to find attractive new models for their copy (*Man* 2010). Most of the magazines in this period sold for between 150 and 250 baht, with male models typically being paid about 10,000 baht for a photo shoot. Handsome models with good physiques often landed modeling or media jobs after being photographed in gay magazines.

These male models were not sex workers per se. Nonetheless, the possibility of sexual contact between male models and gay clients was often hinted at. Models working for agencies often found work in fashion shows organized as special events by gay pubs and discos, with some being hired as male entertainers at private gay parties and celebrations. Käng reports that by the early 2010s models or *nai baep* had become featured entertainment at many middle-class gay venues.

> [These men] work in gay clubs that are not focused on sex work, they are an added feature and eye candy. Unlike the coyote boy [see chapter 5], a model is not expected to dance. Rather, he must feature his model-like attractiveness, which means that he must be muscular, preferably light-skinned, and have modern, classy features such as colorful Japanese-style rather than monochromatic, religious Thai tattoos. Model shows also embody catwalk respectability. There is no vulgarity. The limit is what would be acceptable to print in a mainstream fashion magazine. (Käng 2015, 105)

Käng also notes that "high end" freelance models often offered massage or escort services via gay websites. "This is more specialized and requires both the capital investment to be online, either at home or at an internet café, and sufficient English language skills to be able to communicate with their primarily foreign clients. Some online freelancers specifically state in their profiles that they are not money boys, which they use as a tactic to negotiate higher prices" (Käng 2015, 98).

Early to Mid-2000s: Full-Frontal Nudity of Gay Magazine Male Models

The Asian economic crisis that began in Bangkok in July 1997 and continued into 1998 and 1999 severely impacted the Thai economy, with the currency losing

50 percent of its value and leading to the closure of many of the gay magazines that had begun publication in the previous decade. However, the Thai economy rebounded from the crisis comparatively quickly and a large number of new publications oriented to the gay market were released in the first years of the new century. In the early 2000s, many of them became increasingly explicit in their depiction of the male body and sexual expression. The new publications— *Door, Door Dek, H, K-Mag, Dik, Body,* and *Heat*—all challenged Thai censorship laws by publishing images of full-frontal nudity and, for the first time, including sex scenes. It was revolutionary for Thai gay magazines to include full-frontal nude photographs of the erect penis and ejaculation, and this new generation of publications represented the emergence of mass-marketed gay pornography. In addition to showing models' penises, these glossy monthly magazines also used explicit language in articles about the male libido and sexual relations; terms such as *khuay* ("cock"), *yet* ("to fuck"), *tut* ("ass"), and *ru tut* ("asshole") were common.

The trend of this new wave of gay magazines was to emphasize sexual arousal. *H* magazine included a column, "The Way They Were," publishing the explicit stories of men who had had hot sexual experiences. Photos of kissing, masturbation, oral sex, and anal sex were included to illustrate these erotic stories. In the first issue of *Heat*, the magazine's editor, Tawan Songklot, wrote that he wanted to bring happiness to gay men by presenting more sexually exciting stories. He wanted it to be as if semen flowed from the magazine (*Heat* 2002, 3, 69), with an increasing number of photos of the penis as well as of male models fucking. In the published interview, the model for the first issue of *Heat* said that he had not been shy when doing the sex scene with another man, that he had felt especially horny when performing in front of the camera. He also related that after the magazine was published, he expected to be contacted by rich gay men wanting to have sex with him, but he would tell them that he had a girlfriend. While stating that he had a female partner, the magazine nonetheless also reported that the model lived with a gay friend he had fallen in love with (*Heat* 2002, 17). While male models in this period may have been photographed engaging in homosexual activity and exhibiting same-sex desire, they were often still represented as having complex identities that merged straight, bisexual, and gay.

In an early issue of *Door*, the editor wrote that his magazine promised to bring new sexual excitement to Thai gay men, stating that sex is enjoyable and everyone should have access to the pleasures of good sex, sexual attractiveness, and intimacy in responding to their sexual needs. Human beings should seek out new, arousing sexual feelings. He proclaimed that reading an erotic story was not a sign of sexual addiction or obsession, as claimed by moral conservatives, but rather a source of sexual pleasure and satisfaction (*Door* 2005, 4). The title of the magazine *Door* is an abbreviated form of *krador*, a crude term for the penis. *Door*

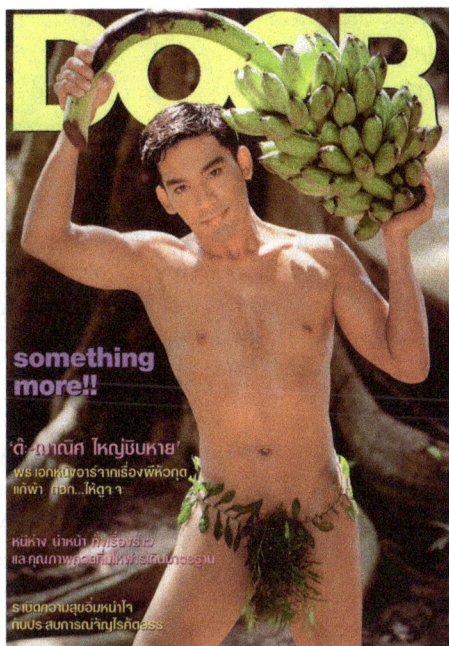

FIGURE 12. Cover of November 2002 issue of *Door*, which in the early 2000s pushed the boundaries of Thai censorship laws with images of full-frontal nudity and erections. *Door* also gave its models sexually explicit stage names. When read aloud, the exotically spelled name of this cover model, Chanit Yaichiphai, is a Thai homonym for the phrase "an extremely huge type" in colloquial Thai.

is also a play on words, being an English translation of the Thai terms *pratu* and *thawan*, both of which mean "door" but also have the sense of an orifice of the body. The compounds *pratu lang* ("back door") and *thawan nak* ("heavy door or orifice") are respectively colloquial and formal terms for "anus." *Door* thus had a double meaning in both Thai and English, simultaneously referring both to the cock and the anus.

The editor of *K-Mag*, Khom Khetkan, said that the "Body Shot" and "Big Cock Club" columns in his publication were intended as venues where readers could send in photos of their penis (*K-Mag* 2001, 48). The name of this magazine includes the first letter of the romanized spelling of the Thai word *khuay*, "cock"; many gay men playfully evaded the heavy sanctions against using this word in public by using the English letter *K* to refer to the penis. The men who had a photo of their penis published in the magazine were interviewed about their sexual experiences and, while their cock was revealed, the faces of these amateur models were usually concealed. *K-Mag* was marketed to the Thai gay community with the slogan "underground sex" (*sek tai-din*).

In the more explicit magazines—such as *Heat*, *Door*, and *K-Mag*—male models were younger-looking men with attractive bodies. They were usually young men from bars or off the street rather than models from agencies, who rarely posed nude. A muscular, hunky body was not necessary, but models usually needed to have a pleasant face and somewhat developed chest, legs, and arms. Importantly, the models in these magazines were photographed with an erection as well masturbating (*chak wao*), including a cum shot (*nam taek*) to the camera. The cum-shot scenes became increasingly important selling points for the new generation of sexually explicit gay print media.

The images in different generations of Thai gay magazines not only reflected changing ideals of sexually attractive masculinity; they also represented changes in the forms of male sex work and middle-class gay sexual culture in Bangkok. In the first generation of gay publications in the 1980s, the cover and centerfold models were often darker-complexioned men from the rural northeast because poorer youths from this region were the largest group of sex workers in the city's gay bars at that time. In the 1990s, the popularity of fairer-complexioned male models followed from the rise of saunas as sites where urban gay men could live out their aspirational middle-class dreams informed by a metrosexual imaginary. A new sexual service that developed in Bangkok in the 1990s was the male escort. About twenty male escort companies were operating in Bangkok in 1997, with escorts being available by landline telephone, mobile phone, and pager. Gay clients no longer needed to go to a bar to select and pay for the services of a bar boy but could call an escort service and request a man to come to their home or other location. This kind of service was available twenty-four hours a day and was an indication of how new communication technologies were quickly employed in helping gay men meet their sexual needs.

In the early 2000s, the explicit images of magazine models showing their penis and ejaculating responded to the sexual activities found in the expensive spas and massage parlors that opened in these years. These venues typically employed handsome masseurs and were marketed as having a clean, aesthetically pleasing decor with the aim of promoting clients' health while also providing sexual services. Some of the men who worked as masseurs had high levels of education and also worked in other jobs as music video actors and fashion models (*Midway* 2000, 131). While they also provided sexual services, male masseurs were regarded as being of a higher social status than the working-class bar boys in gay bars and their services were more expensive. The men who worked in these establishments needed to be skilled in Thai massage, and preferably have a metrosexual look. The spa and massage services also took place in more luxurious surroundings than a typical Bangkok gay bar and were marketed to well-off gay men who were often called "high-status gays" (*gay mi radap*) (*Midway* 2001, 19).

The Decorated Male Body in Gay Magazines in the Later 2000s

A wide range of new gay magazines started publication in the second half of the 2000s. These were often photo-album format publications that focused on male nudes and had significantly less written content compared to the magazines published in earlier decades. These new magazines and their first year of publication were: *Stage* (2006), *Menthol* (2006), *I Am Guy* (2006), *Dude* (2007), *Step* (2007), *Need+* (2007), *VZmen* (2007), *Real* (2007), *Hey!* (2008), *The Boy Models Story* (2008), *DGuy* (2008), *Born* (2009), *Dark* (2010), *Firm* (2010), *Fresh Boy* (2010), *Hero* (2010), *G Story* (2011), *Up* (2011), *Full* (2012), *KFM* (2012), and *Dophuchai* (2012). Most of these publications were soft-core porn magazines that represented attractive male models in arousing homoerotic poses. A smaller number of new magazines were hardcore publications that included images of erect penises and oral and anal sex. Among the new hardcore magazines, with their first year of publication, were *D Day* (2010), *Janraem* (2011), *Norngmon* (2012), *Nam Phrik Num* ("spicy guys," 2012) and *Reuang Khorng Rao* ("our stories," 2012). Some of the magazines published in the period 2006 to 2012 were sold with an accompanying video compact disc or VCD with additional sexually explicit content that could be played on home computers or on TVs via VCD players. These VCDs included a behind-the-scenes video of the modeling photo shoot that usually showed full frontal nudity and ejaculation. While of a lower visual resolution quality than DVDs, VCD discs and players were much cheaper than DVD technology and in the 2000s this format was the dominant video technology in Thailand, only superseded by the rise of online visual content in the following decade. The male models who appeared in most of the softcore and hardcore magazines of this era could be contacted by gay clients, with the phone number of the agency the models worked for often being published or included on the accompanying VCD. Readers were informed that the models were available to provide sexual services, and the hardcore magazines were especially upfront in promoting the sexual services of their models.

Perceptions and understandings of tattoos among Thai men have changed over time. In the past, tattooed men were regarded as being strong, and different regions of the country had distinctive local tattoo patterns. Black tattoos were found among the Tai Yai ethnic group in northern Thailand; abdomen and leg tattoos were worn by the Lanna people in the north; and full-body tattoos were found in parts of the northeast (Prathern 1991, 34). Among the Thai Phuan ethnic group, men liked to have animal figure tattoos on their bodies; in the northeast leg tattoos, called *kha lai* or "leg lines," were regarded as making men persons of value and were thought of as being sexually attractive to women.

Historically, only men were tattooed. For many, tattooing the body was considered a ritual of masculine empowerment and protection undertaken by Buddhist monks and men who were formerly ordained in the Buddhist monkhood. In the central region of Thailand, tattoos inked by monks and other religious figures were regarded as magical sources of sacred protective power (Nattaphat 1978). Ritually empowered tattoos in the context of Buddhism are related to a gender culture of masculine status and authority. In the contemporary setting, some men continue to believe in the esoteric power of tattoos with magical designs, called *sak yan*, and it is still common to have this type of tattoo on the back of the neck and central upper part of the back. The most popular magical tattoo design is "the nine pinnacles" (*kao yort*), which symbolically refers to the ethical pinnacle of nine virtues of the Lord Buddha. It is believed that men who get the nine pinnacles tattoo will be rendered invulnerable and protected from attack by weapons.[1] The protection conferred by magical tattoos is known as *khong-kraphan chatri*, "warrior invulnerability." Premodern Thai warriors always had this type of tattoo as it was believed that it helped them survive in combat, and this type of body decoration continues to be popular among working-class Thai men to this day.

Sacred *sak yan* tattooing is carried out by a Buddhist monk or a lay adept called a *keji* or *keji ajan*, who is learned in empowering incantations and magical designs. After being tattooed with a sacred design, a man is required to respect Buddhist ethical precepts and control his behavior. In ancient times, a man without a tattoo would be seen as a weakling, labeled in Thai as *khon orn-ae* (Prathern 1991, 35). Thai men were tattooed to give them the appearance of strength and potency (Rat 2003, 19).

Following international fashion trends in the West, ear piercing and tattooing became fashionable among young Thai men in the early 2000s as part of a broad transformation of images of the sexually attractive male. Some middle- and upper-class Thais regard these protective and empowering tattoos as reflecting the bad-boy attitudes of hoodlums and prisoners (Rat 2003, 19), sometimes being labeled as unattractive and "not clean" (*mai sa-at*). However, tattoos are increasingly coming to be regarded as cool fashion additions when men show off their exposed decorated bodies. Tattooing is now widely regarded as a form of body art that anyone skilled in design can do, without training in ritual traditions or Buddhist ethical practices (Salinee 2015). Tattoos on the chest, arms, and shoulders are especially popular among men who want to show off their muscles and six-packs when they go shirtless or wear a revealing vest. Graphic design tattoos are now increasingly popular among young urban men, who regard this art form as helping them become more sexually attractive. Increasingly, Thai male models, actors, and singers seek to enhance their masculine image with tattoos.

In the early 2010s, tattoos and earrings became popular fashion accessories among young straight men. Many young working-class Thai men, especially laborers and vocational students, adopted the fashion of wearing decorative tattoos and having their ears pierced. This contrasted with the smooth, clean, middle-class metrosexual look that had been the ideal male body image in the final years of the twentieth century. Rather than offering ritual protection, the newer tattoo designs, along with body painting and earrings, are regarded as aesthetic enhancements that accentuate a man's masculine appeal and attractiveness. Tattoos on the upper arm or chest and black stud earrings have become signs of masculine sexual appeal for many Thai gay men. This type of male body fashion is especially common among the coyote boys whose erotic dance performances in gay bars and nightclubs are detailed in chapter 5. Young men who sport this trendy, cool (*the*) look of male attractiveness are called *dek naeo*.

There are thus two types of class- and region-based forms of tattoo culture among Thai men today. The magical protective types of tattoos that in the past were characteristic of all Thai men have largely come to be regarded as signs of working-class masculinity. In contrast, middle-class men, and increasingly younger men from all class backgrounds, sport tattoos for aesthetic purposes. These tattoos are applied in tattoo parlors by commercial tattoo artists rather than in Buddhist monasteries or shrines by monks or ex-monks who are masters in the rituals of magically empowering tattoo designs. Käng notes that the kind of tattoo a Thai man sports now makes a class statement. Older *sak-yan* magical religious tattoos, although currently undergoing something of a revival, are generally considered déclassé and are associated with older rural men, especially when the body is covered in symbolic figures of tigers, monkeys, temple motifs, cosmological designs, and religious texts. As talismans that offer protection from harm, these tattoos are viewed by many middle-class Thais as signs of a superstitious, and hence unmodern, working-class culture. As Käng explains, "These tattoos are considered backward, their bearers either undesirable or desirable precisely for those who eroticize a rugged working-class masculinity" (Käng 2021, 285).

Tribal tattoos derived from Polynesian designs or simple, monochromatic patterns—which have been in favor in the West and among gay men in East Asia following Euro-American trends—are becoming increasingly popular among middle-class Thai men. Also well-liked in Thailand are so-called "Japanese" tattoos that take inspiration from the vivid colors and orientalist motifs

FIGURE 13. Model on the cover of *I Am Guy* (2007) with the type of stylized tattoo that became common among Thai gay men from both working-class and middle-class backgrounds. *I Am Guy* was one of several glossy gay lifestyle magazines published in the 2000s but was not successful in the highly competitive gay magazine market, shutting down after only ten issues.

of dragons, carp, cherry blossoms, and other Japanese symbols. Käng observes that "ironically, while Japanese tattoos have become popular among middle-class gay men in Thailand, they continue to have strong associations with criminality and degeneracy in Japan and to a lesser extent Korea. Thus, the practice of 'Japanese' tattooing in Thailand is associated with Japanese stylistic forms that do not actually exist or have a drastically different symbolic association in Japan" (Käng 2021, 286). Male sex workers in gay bars fit within this classed schema of tattooing. Working-class sex workers in gay bars are more likely to sport magical *sak-yan* tattoos while higher-end "models," who tend to be light-skinned and muscular, have aesthetic tribal or Japanese-style tattoos. Class distinctions thus influence the styles and practices of body modification among male sex workers as well as among Thai gay men more broadly (Käng 2021, 286).

Having a tattoo now increasingly symbolizes a masculine culture of revealing the body for public display. Famous Thai male models, singers, and actors typically present themselves with aesthetically attractive tattoos. Paranyu (Tack)

Rojanawuttitham, born in 1984 in the northern city of Chiang Mai and an actor in TV soap operas and the films of famous gay director Poj Arnon, has tattoos on his arm and in the early 2010s appeared on the covers of the upmarket women's fashion magazines *Volume* and *Image* as well as gay magazines. Another especially popular male model in the early 2010s was Peerawich Phandeang, whose muscular tattooed physique appeared on the covers of several gay magazines. Well-known in the Bangkok gay community as a sexy gay idol (*khwan-jai gay*), he also appeared in many sexy fashion shows and at parties held in gay bars and discotheques.

The Male Nude in the West and Thailand

In studying the history of the male nude in Western art and literature, Pierre Borhan (2007) observes that the first generation of male nude photography in the early twentieth century was not oriented toward sexual arousal but rather was represented in terms of artistic expression. Early photographers of the male nude such as Wilhelm von Gloeden in Europe and Fred Holland Day in the United States highlighted artistic style in representing male attractiveness. Von Gloeden and Holland Day's photographic styles were of "erotic estheticism" and represented the male nude in relation to classical Greek sculpture (Borhan 2007, 48).

Valentine Hooven (2002) argues that there were no openly erotic male images in the West until the middle of the twentieth century. Prior to that, photography of the male body had either been in relation to classical references or in the context of physical culture, sports, and health (Hooven 2002, 20). Erick Alvarez (2008) contends that magazines representing physical culture redefined the modern male image. At the end of nineteenth century, the magazine *Physical Culture* was published in the UK by the Prussian bodybuilder and showman Eugen Sandow for the purposes of self-promotion. This magazine promoted fitness and body-building and supported bodybuilder competitions in which musclemen posed in front of audiences. It featured near-nude photographs of bodybuilders and was one of the first venues where images of men were represented for the aesthetic appreciation of other men, becoming early sexual material for homosexual men.

After World War II, fitness culture and physique development became increasingly common mainstream practices in the United States, especially among former soldiers who had practiced weight-lifting training during their time in the armed forces. A range of new magazines emerged in the United States to respond to the popularization of gym culture. *Physique Pictorial*, first published in 1951, was one of the most influential of these magazines. Published by Bob Mizer, who founded the Athletic Model Guild, *Physique Pictorial* presented muscular male seminudes in poses that reflected classical Greek art and sculpture. While ostensibly presented as a male health magazine, it was especially popular among American homosexual men at a time when same-sex relations were still illegal (Cagle 2000; Ibson 2002; Escoffier 2009; Poirier-Poulin 2021; Waugh 1996). The success of *Physique Pictorial* inspired other magazines, which followed during the 1950s. Western gay magazines emerged in the following decades from the context of the bodybuilding culture and beefcake images that represented and celebrated the beauty of musclemen (Alvarez 2008, 64).

In parallel with the physique magazines, an underground business in photographs of male nudes also developed. In the 1960s and 1970s, the nude photographs of musclemen models for the physique magazines evolved into gay porn when sexual representation became more prominent than artistic images (Alvarez 2008, 70). This transformation emerged with a new sense of gay identity and liberation in which homosexual men began to create their own communities based on a shared sexual identity. In this period, male pornography was a key element that contributed to the development of the homosexual imagination as a basis of both individual identity and collective community formation. According to Alvarez, the beefcake images of musclemen in physique magazines were foundational to the emergence of Western gay pornography as male musculature evolved over the decades toward increasingly well-developed physiques (2008, 72). It was in this context that the stereotype of the "sissy" homosexual man also began to be challenged as Western men who identified as gay came to appreciate that they could develop muscles through physical culture training. Being muscular also provided support for coming out of the closet as many gay men began to appreciate that they could be both homosexual and masculine (95).

In mid-twentieth-century Western gay cultures, bodybuilding and muscular male physiques became central to the imaging of homoerotic desire. Many homosexual men looked to the muscular male models in physique magazines as inspiration for the idea that they could be gay and also conform to mainstream masculine norms. For a gay man, to develop a muscled body not only reflected a desire to be healthy but also represented a claim for public recognition as a masculine male. This emphasis on physical development was closely related to the gay liberation movement and identity politics that emerged in the 1970s, as many gay men gathered around gyms as social centers that redefined homosexuality in relation to masculinity (Alvarez 2008, 98). Hooven argues that in publishing male nude images, the pioneer publishers and editors of the first gay magazines in America were also social activists whose commercial ventures supported coming out and making a better life for homosexual men (Hooven 2002, 58).

Similar to the situation in the West, Thai gay magazines emerged as a print medium that helped Thai gay men understand their identity in positive terms and in relation to building communities with other gay men. In addition to engendering a sense of pride in gay identity, the imaging of the male nude in Thai gay magazines came to play an increasingly central role in the country's gay communities, with sexual emancipation in Thailand taking place in relation to print media that focused on male nude photographs and increasingly explicit images. However, the history of homoerotic images of male nudity in Thai gay magazines presents a contrast with the situation in the West. In Western societies, and especially in the United States, the dominant masculinity found in gay porn magazines and movies has typically been represented through the big-muscled male body. This type of hypermasculinity reflects the idea that it is the muscular male body that is most seductive and sexually attractive. However, the male models represented in Thai gay magazines have not focused solely on large muscles or bodybuilders. Rather, they have emphasized forms of masculinity based on notions of being good-looking and charming.

Also, in contrast to the West, the men who were photographed in Thai gay magazines were overwhelmingly represented as being heterosexual, not gay. As such, the male nude in Thai gay magazines was not directly related to confirmations of gay masculinity and was not part of a politics of coming out to increase homosexual visibility or challenge effeminization. In being represented as straight, these men may have been sexually attractive but did not necessarily function as role models for gay men. Unlike in the West, the Thai male nude did not evolve from a desire to promote male health, physical culture, or pride in gay identity but rather functioned primarily as a commodity for gay men's sexual pleasure. This history continues the pattern of Thailand's first commercially successful gay magazine, *Mithuna Junior*. As detailed in the previous chapter, *Mithuna Junior* survived by promoting commercial sex with predominantly heterosexual sex workers. This pattern set by *Mithuna Junior* was perpetuated in later generations of gay magazines and continues to this day. Even the popular entertainment of handsome man contests in Thai gay bars have not been displays of pride in gay identity but rather have constituted opportunities for heterosexual men to be presented as sexual commodities to the gaze of Thai gay men. Modern Thai gay culture has been built on the commodification of heterosexual men's bodies, both physically in sex work and visually in erotic and pornographic images.

In Thailand homosexual men have not had their sex lives controlled by antigay legal statutes or religious threats of divine punishment for sinful practices. Rather, Thai gay men have lived in a society dominated by cultural ideas of gender norms that men and women should conform their sexual behavior to their biological sex. A lower presence of overt homophobia among Thai heterosexual men compared to the historical situation in many Western societies has also meant that heterosexual men have not resisted being objectified by gay men or declined to work with gay men, provided their own masculine gender identity has been confirmed. Indeed, many of the men featured in Thai gay magazines identified more in terms of masculine gender than a particular sexual preference. We return to this point in discussing the participation of *bi*-identified men in Thai gay cybersex chat rooms in chapter 6. The commodification of straight men for Thai gay consumers has taken place in a culture where masculine gendering has been more important for men's identity construction than their sexual activity.

This relationship between heterosexual men as commodified sexual objects and gay men as consumers developed in a class-structured society with a rapidly expanding market of sexual commodities that induced middle-class Thai gay men to identify their same-sex desire in terms of consuming eroticized heterosexual male bodies. Thai gay magazines did not use their cover models to represent notions of gay or queer pride, and the male models in these magazines were not positioned as icons with whom gay readers might identify in affirming their own sexual identities. Rather, a politics of the closet dominated Thai gay magazines. While gay men were the target audience of these publications, they were often relatively invisible in the imaging that was included. The male nudes in Thai gay magazines were not part of a politics of homosexual identity but rather elements of a gay-straight sexual economy.

Diverse Male Body Images and Multiple Thai Masculinities

The historical periods of Thai gay magazines and the different images and styles of masculinity they represented across the decades from the 1980s do not present a singular model of masculine body images. Rather, they reflect a set of changes as Thai men appropriated new forms of masculine presentation while older-style masculine images persisted. Furthermore, the image of the attractive Thai man diversified in relation to the complex ethnicity and class structure of Thai society. Older masculine body images developed and combined with the new ones in a dynamic process in which Thai men learned to embody and practice masculine styles in their own experiences. Table 3.1 summarizes the dominant styles of masculinity represented in Thai gay magazines in different decades, which intersected with the evolving lifestyles of urban gay men and their appropriation of different imaginings of masculinity.

Through the changes reflected in table 3.1, older forms of masculine body imaging were not fully replaced by the newer ones. All persisted and coexisted, with each style coming to signify the tastes and notions of masculine

TABLE 3.1   Comparison of male body images in gay magazines in different periods

PERIOD	MAIN CHARACTERISTICS OF MALE BODY IMAGES IN GAY MAGAZINES	REPRESENTATIVE GAY MAGAZINES	THAI GAY LIFE IN THIS PERIOD
Mid- to late 1980s	Natural body of local straight men and rent boys	*Mithuna, Morakot, Midway, Neon*	Booming of gay bars and gay magazines
Early to mid-1990s	Muscular body of men who work out in gyms	*Male, Weekend Men, GR*	Rise of saunas, men's health clubs, and video pornography
Mid- to late 1990s	Metrosexual body of urban men	*Male, Male Mini, Grace Male*	Arrival of escort services and gay websites
Early to mid-2000s	Full-frontal nudity of male models	*Door, Door Dek, Heat, H, K, Body*	Massage and spa services, booming of gay chat and websites
Mid-2000s to early 2010s	The painted male body, tattoos and earrings	*Need+, Step, Stage, Born, Hey, Firm, KFM, Full*	Sexy online video clips, naked sauna nights, coyote boys

attractiveness of different groups of gay men. In the early 2010s, one could find the natural, slim body of young local men represented in one gay magazine, while muscular sportsmen were represented in other publications. Different masculine body images appeared across the decades from the 1980s on and were visual indicators of the social and cultural transformations and the changing lifestyles of each era. Since the 2010s, Bangkok's gay scene has been characterized by multiple masculinities and diverse body images that are embodied and practiced by gay men of different ages, classes, ethnicities, and social and economic backgrounds. The way that these body types and styles of masculinity have become associated with different classes of Thai gay men is considered in detail in the following chapters. In chapter 4 we consider the muscular, gym-developed bodies of middle-class gay men sometimes mockingly called *kam pu*, "crab claws," because of their overdeveloped upper arms, while in chapter 5 we discuss coyote boy dance performers as typifying the lithe, slim physiques of working-class gay men in the early twenty-first century.

Part II

MIDDLE-CLASS AND WORKING-CLASS GAY MASCULINITIES

FITNESS CULTURE, MASCULINITY, AND THAILAND'S GAY MIDDLE CLASS

This chapter and chapter 5 present case studies of the distinctive urban middle-class and working-class masculinities that respectively came to characterize Thailand's diverse gay cultures in the 1990s and early 2000s. Thailand's gay magazines both reflected and supported the development of these two class-based forms of gay masculinity. In this chapter we detail the experiences of middle-class Thai gay men who worked out in fitness centers in the early 2010s. In chapter 5 we consider the slim model of working-class masculinity typified by the coyote boy dance troupes that were a popular form of entertainment in many Bangkok gay pubs in the same period.

In the early 2000s, fitness centers emerged as gay spaces where middle-class men came to find friends and sexual partners in Bangkok's cosmopolitan consumer culture. The common mainstream perception of fitness centers in Thailand now is that they are gay spaces where homosexual men exercise to build up their muscle mass and enhance their masculine profile in order to become more sexually attractive. Although urban Thai gay men share some characteristics with gay men in other parts of the world, homosexual men in the country experience the spaces of fitness centers in terms of their own distinctive sets of cultural meanings. There are differences among Thai, East Asian, and Western gay body images in terms of perceptions of the beautiful male physique. Among Western and predominantly ethnic Chinese East Asian gay men from Singapore, Malaysia, Hong Kong, and Taiwan, well-built muscles around the arms, shoulders, back, torso, and legs are all very important. However, Thai gay men often only train to develop their upper body, particularly the chest and shoulders. Furthermore, in contrast to the situation in some Western countries, gay physical exercise in Thailand has not developed in the context of a modern gay rights movement but rather solely for the purpose of becoming sexually attractive to other gay men.

The analyses in this chapter are based on in-depth interviews with six gay-identified men living in Bangkok who were twenty-five to thirty-five years old, had high incomes and good educations, and whose social lives revolved around interactions with other gay men in Bangkok's gay communities. The interviews were conducted from December 2011 to February 2012 and are supplemented with information gained from studying public online conversations about gay men's experiences in gyms that were posted on the popular webboards men.mthai. com and pantip.com between November 2011 and January 2012. The messages posted on these publicly accessible webboards reveal attitudes about the forms of masculinity that gay men aspired to in the early 2010s, which were regulated by imaginings of the ideal homoerotically attractive male body. The gay men we interviewed were of both ethnic Thai and Sino-Thai (*luk jin*) heritage and their social networks were characterized by urban lifestyles that accentuated maintaining a healthy, attractive appearance. They regarded physical training in fitness centers as not only helping them to develop a healthy body and a masculine image but also making them sexually attractive and enhancing self-confidence.

The History of Male Fitness Culture in Thailand

Before modern physical culture came to the country in the 1930s, Thai men trained and strengthened their bodies through martial arts, especially Muay Thai or kickboxing, fighting with swords and staffs (*krabi-kraborng*), and swordsmanship (*fan dap*). These traditional male martial arts involved physical training as well as self-regulation through moral control and self-discipline. Thai men who trained in Muay Thai and *krabi-kraborng* sword combat undertook both mental and physical training to attain masculine strength and power. These martial arts were not merely bodybuilding exercises but rather involved the regulation of both mind and body (Tuay 2003; Khetara 2007). In addition to developing strength and skilled control of movement, Thai martial arts also trained men in techniques of controlling their minds through rituals of showing respect to sacred objects. These sacred objects included *mongkhon*, magically empowered rope coils worn on the head by Muay Thai boxers; *yan*, magical symbols often inscribed on the body in tattoos; and *pha prajiat*, ritually sacralized pieces of cloth worn on the body. These objects symbolized the sacred power that controls the male body and mind and were sacralized by Buddhist monks and other ritual specialists. In Thailand's premodern agricultural culture, the powerful masculine body was forged by physical training in combination with supernatural ritual invoked in Buddhist and other forms of sanctified practice. While Buddhist monks and specialists in Brahmanical lore and ritual did not themselves engage in physical combat, they were often involved in training laymen in martial arts and the skills of warfare.

The Thai men who underwent this type of combined physical, mental, and ethical training were required to abide by moral guidelines to sustain and pre-serve the potency of the sacred objects that were regarded as guarantors of the masculine power they developed through physical exercise. Lapses in self-control and failure to abide by the Buddhist-inspired moral order were regarded as undermining their physical strength and potentially threatening their mascu-line power. The training of Muay Thai and *krabi-kraborng* were not just forms of physical exercise but were also modes of moral regulation and mental control in which male trainees were instructed in a culture that linked masculine strength and physical discipline with notions of goodness and virtue.

In the culture of the Ayutthaya period from the fourteenth to eighteenth cen-turies CE, Thai men interested in physical culture attended Muay Thai schools that were overseen by a boxing teacher called a *khru muay*, "a Muay guru or teacher." Every Muay Thai school had a talented *khru muay* who taught and dis-ciplined his male trainees, called *luk-sit*, "disciple-students"—the same term that is used to describe the followers of a religious teacher or ritual specialist. The relationship between Muay Thai *luk-sit* trainees and their *khru muay* guru or teacher was a form of male bonding in which the preceptor instructed his *luk-sit* disciples in both moral discipline and physical training, two inseparable elements that together represented the ideal of manliness or being a *luk phu-chai*, "a he-man," that was at the heart of Muay Thai and other Thai martial arts.

Many Thai Buddhist temples had a monk who was knowledgeable in Muay Thai and instructed laymen in the physical and ethical training of martial arts, reflecting the close association of Thai religious culture with the male arts of physical training and masculine empowerment. During temple festivals and on religious holidays, Thai men who were trained in Muay Thai often participated in competitions to demonstrate their strength and masculine prowess. Even today, Muay Thai trainees must demonstrate respect toward their boxing preceptor-teacher. Before each boxing match they perform a *wai khru* ritual of paying respect to their teacher and the lineage of teacher-gurus of which he is a part. The performance of the *wai khru* ritual before a Muay Thai boxing match involves a set of physical warm-up movements of stretching the arms and legs combined with raising the hands over the head in a ritual gesture honoring the boxing teacher-guru. In the later decades of the nineteenth century, as Siam introduced modernizing reforms during the reign of King Chulalongkorn (r. 1868–1910),

Muay Thai was promoted as an element of national culture. The modernizing monarch Chulalongkorn sponsored many Muay Thai competitions, and the prestige of the sport was enhanced by the awards he handed out to competitors and by his inclusion of Muay Thai as part of the school curriculum in the foundations of the modern national education system.

In 1934 the Department of Physical Education was established and this government agency contributed significantly to the introduction of modern concepts of bodybuilding and fitness to Thai society. Physical exercise and notions of good health were popularized during the 1930s and 1940s under the regime of Prime Minister Plaek Phibunsongkhram (Kongsakon 2002). Under his fascist-inspired nationalist policies, Phibunsongkhram sought to improve the Thai citizenry by directing and regulating ideas of good health, which were expressed in a series of edicts that aimed to control and develop the bodies of the populace.

In the period leading up to and during World War II, the Thai state sought to develop a healthy citizenry as a testimony to the nation's strength and civilizational status in the international order. Physical training was promoted not merely for the health of individual citizens but as a symbol of the country's independent status in the international order of civilized nations. In this period, every school instituted health education and exercise programs for students and physical discipline was popularized by health policies that sought to regulate the people's daily activities. A radio program that aired each morning was central to the government's policy of encouraging the populace to take up structured forms of exercise, and as part of this nationalist policy the populace was directed to set aside Wednesdays as regular days for sporting activities. This state media radio programming was based on ideas that the strength of the body symbolized the power of the nation (Kongsakon 2002, 106) and encouraged public awareness of physical exercise to transform the populace into a healthy citizenry that could develop the country into a powerful modern society. The government-encouraged sports for men included Muay Thai, *krabi-kraborng* combat with swords and staffs, athletics, football (soccer), rugby, tennis, badminton, ping pong, and sepak takraw. These manly sports were associated with social expectations that the Thai man should concentrate on developing his physique. Under this regime, the ideal masculine body was defined as being tough, tall, and strong, as these qualities were believed to be necessary for heterosexual men to reproduce a healthy new generation (Kongsakon 2002, 111).

In 1941 the *Srikrung* daily newspaper published a new column titled "Lightning-fast ways to build muscles" (*len klam baep sai-fa-laep*), written by Sawat Tanthasoot. In a series of twenty articles, he explained the biology of the muscular system and techniques that helped men train to build up their muscles (Kongsakon 2002, 105). This was the first time that the Thai press had published information about building the musculature of the male body in what became known as *len klam*, "to build muscles," which is now the most widely used Thai expression for bodybuilding. During this period, increasing numbers of Thai men received information through the print media about what was described as *song ngam*, "the physically attractive body image or physique," and learned how to build up their muscles. The new concepts of the masculine body that stressed muscle size represented a change from traditional perceptions of the Thai male physique developed through Muay Thai training. The lithe but strong body of the Muay Thai boxer was toughened by a combination of physical and Buddhist moral training to be impenetrable to both an opponent's blows and evil external forces. This contrasted with Western ideas of large muscles as a sign of a man's good health. It was no longer enough to possess a strengthened body as a frame for masculine potency and authority. New understandings of the Thai man as embodying ideals of modern civilization and symbolizing national wealth and prosperity were based on images of the ideal man as having large muscles developed through intensive physical exercise. The notion of the "civilized" Thai man required men to develop their musculature. In accord with government policy, mainstream newspapers and magazines campaigned to introduce bodybuilding and encouraged Thai men to exercise and develop their physique. These print media campaigns in both articles and advertisements were illustrated with photos of big-armed Western, mostly American, musclemen, with the clear implication that Thai men should follow the American model and aim to become *nak-klam*, "musclemen" or bodybuilders (Kongsakon 2002, 194).

To promote the new ideal of the modern, civilized, muscled Thai man, the Phibunsongkhram regime arranged regular bodybuilding competitions known as *chai chakan* contests. *Chai chakan* denotes a strong, brave man between twenty and thirty years old who is in the prime of life. *Chai Chakan* was the name chosen for a Thai gay magazine in the 1990s and is also the name of an upmarket Bangkok gay sauna in the north of the city that opened in the mid-1990s.[1] This term now resonates with images of masculine young men that many gay men find sexually attractive. In the years immediately following World War II, *chai chakan* or "beautiful man" (*chai ngam*) contests were popular events at temple fairs and in festivities for celebrating Songkran Thai New Year in mid-April and international New Year. These male contests were framed by health science notions that defined the male body in terms of physical and biological knowledge rather than religious notions of male invulnerability. In the *chai chakan* contests, panels of judges assessed the male contestants based on the development of their upper-body muscles, weight, and height.

In the 1940s and 1950s, the state-sponsored *chai chakan* contests and the physical training spaces of gymnasiums were strongly associated with official efforts

to encourage Thai men to conform to heteronormative forms of social regulation. In this period, bodybuilding and working out were promoted as a public
service and provincial and municipal sports centers were established across the
country as places for men to gather to exercise and play sports. Upmarket hotels
also began including gyms, called "fitness rooms" (*horng fitnet*), as facilities for
guests. The Royal Bangkok Sports Club, founded with a grant from King Chulalongkorn in 1901 (Warren 2001), is one of the oldest Thai elite sporting centers.

The first modern Western-style gymnasium for bodybuilding, known in Thai
as *sathan kai borihan* or "Physical Training Institute," was founded in 1947 by
Jeua Jaksurak. It was located in the center of Bangkok near the Thepsirin School
(Kongsakon 2002, 106). From the late 1940s onward, this Physical Training Institute influenced perceptions of the attractive male body as it became increasingly
well-known among urban Thai people and offered training courses in a range
of sports such as Muay Thai, international boxing (*muay sakon*), wrestling, and
judo. The institute's motto was "A man must be worthy of manhood" ("*Phu-chai
torng pen chai hai som chai*"), which reflected the way in which Thai men now
came to regulate themselves by training in the physical culture that had been
popularized by state radio and educational programs.

State Fitness Culture, Public Parks, and Gay Cruising Areas

In the 1940s and 1950s, the government built large numbers of sports stadiums
and facilities to encourage civil servants and the public to take up playing sports
such as football, badminton, rugby, tennis, and boxing. These stadiums were built
in accessible public areas where people could meet every day. The emergence of
exercise areas in public parks across the country also reflected a cultural change
in understandings of Thai male sexual identity and eroticism. Every man who
trained and played sports in these public areas displayed his muscles and strong
physique, which nationalist discourses took as being emblematic of the modern
man defined as the "fertile male" (*phor phan*) (Kongsakon 2002, 110). The characteristics of the "fertile male" signified a nationalist heteronormative ideology
that constructed the modern Thai man within a sexual and gender binary in
which the virile male body was promoted in terms of notions of sexual fitness
regarded as being necessary for reproduction.

However, the state encouragement of public displays of the virile male body
also unintentionally provided opportunities for images of the healthy man to
be eroticized as the object of the gaze of homosexual men. Popular places of
male exercise in public parks and sports stadiums across the country also became

well-known as gay cruising areas. The first Bangkok cruising areas were in public spaces at Wang Saranrom Park in the old area of the city near the royal precinct and Wat Phra Kaew and in Lumphini Park near the Silom area of modern gay venues. In later decades, the Huamak sports complex, Khlong Chan Park, Jatujak Park, and Rotfai Park also became popular gay cruising areas in the city. Some came to the parks to watch men playing sports and doing bodybuilding training at the free outdoor gymnasiums provided by local authorities. Since the middle decades of the twentieth century, this dual relationship between men's public exercise spaces and homosexual contact has been a significant component of the sex lives of many Thai gay men.[2] While exercise spaces in public parks have been sites for gay cruising for several decades and are open to men from all socioeconomic backgrounds, the rise of members-only fitness centers in the early 2000s provided a new set of venues where male exercise and gay cruising intersected. However, in this case the new venues were restricted to well-off men who could afford the significant membership fees.

The changing meanings of Thai men's fitness activities, from premodern ethical and religious culture to mid-twentieth-century nationalist state policies and, since the 1980s, to commercial discourses, demonstrates how contemporary Thai male body images have been molded by a historical succession of religious, state-centered, and market-based discourses. Consumer culture and new commercial perceptions of masculinity have now become increasingly dominant forms of masculine gender regulation. By the early twenty-first century, bodybuilding and working out had largely become sports and leisure activities for well-off middle- and upper-class men who could afford fitness center membership fees. Commercial fitness centers symbolized the high quality of life aspired to by trend-conscious metrosexual Thai men who view going to the gym as central to both their gender and social identities, with fitness centers functioning as sites that confirm the high social and economic statuses of their members.

The first physical training centers established by state agencies in the 1930s and 1940s were normative spaces that encouraged men to develop their bodies to affirm a modern, strong, and healthy heterosexual male identity. However, in the early 2000s, fitness activities were subsumed by capitalist market forces and became private businesses, with the older state programs of physical training being restricted to health and physical education in schools. In contrast, the new spaces of commercial fitness centers emerged as one dimension of metrosexual lifestyles, with middle-class men paying for the privilege of membership to exercise in private spaces with others from the same class background. In these private-sector fitness centers, better-off gay men did not develop their physiques to conform to nationalist ideals of heterosexual manhood but rather to enhance the masculine homoerotic appeal of their bodies.

Fitness Centers: Services, Facilities, and Physical Environment

Fitness activities have been available to Bangkok's gay communities since the late 1980s (Narupon 2010a), when the first gay saunas provided gym rooms for customers. However, at that time only a relatively small number of gay men took advantage of these facilities to engage in regular exercise, with most customers using saunas solely to find sexual partners. Since the early 2000s, fitness centers and health clubs have become increasingly widespread in Bangkok and other major cities, and many fitness companies now operate across Thailand. The first Western-style fitness company to be established in Bangkok was the Hong Kong–based California Fitness, which opened its first branch in the city in 2002. When California Fitness opened in Bangkok's downtown Silom area, within walking distance of the city's main clusters of gay bars, it advertised its services in campaigns that promoted exercise as entertaining and fun (*sanuk*). Members could enjoy exercising in time with dance music in tastefully decorated spaces. This style of modern fitness center was especially attractive to the new generation living in Bangkok and became increasingly popular among young professionals. This entertainment-oriented exercise contrasted markedly with the older, state-sponsored physical culture that located exercise and bodybuilding within a serious frame of nationalist propaganda and educational indoctrination. While the older idiom *len klam* denotes bodybuilding in the context of state policies, with the arrival of private, members-only gyms a new expression *len fitnet*, from "fitness," came into widespread use to signify exercising to get fit but not necessarily to build up muscle mass.

In 2009 the Kasikorn Thai Research Center of Kasikorn Bank, one of the country's leading financial institutions, estimated that fitness businesses had expanded 9 percent in that one year, with forty-eight new branches of fitness centers and health clubs opening in Bangkok alone.[3] Among these, the Fitness First Company opened twenty-three new branches around Thailand in 2009. In this period, the fitness business in Thailand had the highest growth in Asia, with the three major players being Fitness First, California Wow Experience, and True Fitness.[4] The membership fees varied according to the services provided, with membership types being broadly classified into lifetime and short-term varieties. Lifetime membership was very expensive, so most salaried members opted to pay for short-term membership, either by the month or yearly. Table 4.1 lists the most popular Thai fitness companies in 2011, with their monthly membership fees and number of registered members.

According to the Department of Business Development, in 2019 there were 816 fitness centers in Thailand. Bangkok had 340 gyms, the most of any city in the country (Department of Business Development 2019).

TABLE 4.1 Comparison of Thailand's top three fitness companies in 2011

COMPANY	MEMBERSHIP FEE (BAHT/MONTH)	NUMBER OF MEMBERS IN 2011
California Wow	1,000–1,100	150,000
Fitness First	1,900–2,800	55,000
True Fitness	1,600–1,700	23,000

Source: Siam Thurakit 2011.

Fitness centers and sports clubs provide facilities for exercise, bodybuilding, and weight training as well as relaxing. Activities available at most fitness centers include dancing, group exercise, aerobics, cycling, spas, and yoga training. In most venues male and female trainers are present to guide members in correct ways to work out and to lead exercise lessons and programs. Typically, branches of major chains of fitness centers include different types of exercise equipment such as treadmills and weights in common areas, with lockers, steam rooms, dry saunas, and bathrooms being separated between male and female spaces. Apart from the exercise and workout areas, a relaxation lounge and cafe are also usually available for members. Some of the larger fitness centers have swimming pools. Additional fitness services are also promoted by sales officers, who approach members with at times aggressive sales pitches. Many customers indicated that trainers often came to talk with them while they were exercising with a sales pitch to induce them to buy additional services. In 2010 the members of most fitness centers needed to pay around 1,300 baht per hour or 12,000 baht for eight hours for the services of a personal trainer on site.

The Rise of the Thai Metrosexual Man

In the era of the Thai economic boom from the mid-1980s to the late 1990s, rapid economic growth, new media, globalization, and the rise of the middle class had dramatic impacts on all aspects of Thai society and culture, including gender culture and notions of masculinity. Chalermpong Kongcharoen (2010) notes that from 1987 to 1995 the Thai economy grew at an average annual rate of 9.9 percent. While 32.6 percent of the population was classified as living below the poverty line in 1989, this had fallen to 11.4 percent by 1996. This rapid economic transformation provided large numbers of Thai people with significantly higher incomes and saw an explosion in the availability of new consumer products and services across the country. In the second half of the 1980s and especially in the 1990s, an increasing range of commercial gay magazines and services for gay men were among these new commodities. And as incomes grew, more people

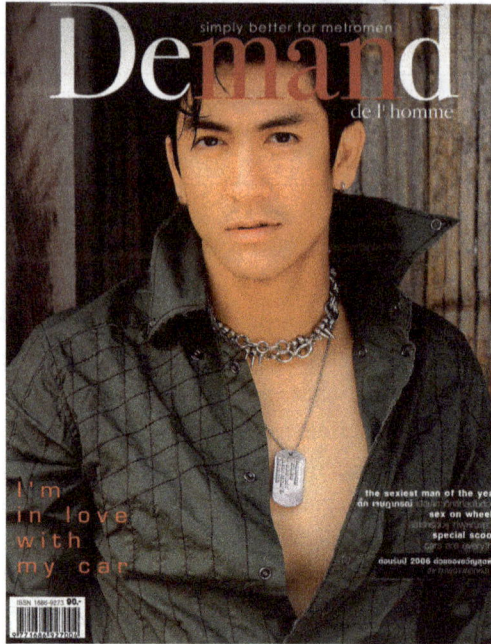

FIGURE 14.   Cover of the glossy men's fashion and lifestyle magazine *Demand de l'homme: Simply Better for Metromen* (2005), featuring actor Tik Jesdaporn Pholdee (b. 1977). Celebrities and actors became the faces of the Thai metrosexual look. Jesdaporn, widely known by his nickname Tik, was voted the sexiest man of 2005 in the Thailand edition of the Durex Global Sex Survey conducted in that year.

had the wherewithal to spend significant amounts on health care, beauty products, and services that had once been viewed as luxuries.

Fitness centers emerged in the context of this economic expansion and responded to the new trend of metrosexual men's emphasis on sports and health. This interest in health care, organic food, and male beauty redefined concepts of masculinity and changed perceptions of masculine body images. The rise of metrosexual lifestyles was reported in detail in Thailand in 2006 by *Positioning* magazine (*Positioning* 2006). The Thai metrosexual man was represented in images of male media and fashion celebrities as well as high-income urban men whose work and lifestyles centered on using new communication technologies such as mobile phones and laptop computers and for whom social status was marked by a consumerist, fashion-led way of life. The rise of the metrosexual was a commodified and mediatized phenomenon among urban, middle-class men and was closely related to the influence of commercial media on male fashion and ideals of masculine attractiveness.

FIGURE 15. Cover of the inaugural issue of *SOLID: Aspiring Fitness Magazine* (2012), a glossy full-color monthly devoted to homoerotic photos of men with highly developed physiques in brand-name swimwear and sportswear outfits. Targeting an upmarket readership, *SOLID* reflected the rapid rise of urban gym culture among middle-class Thai gay men. It included interviews with models on muscle development and the increased self-confidence that came with enhancing the masculine profile of one's body.

In the early 2000s, Thailand's new commercial physical culture was promoted in specialized publications that provided men with information about fitness activities and exercise techniques. The longest-running exercise magazine for men is the Thai edition of *GM*, which has been published since 1985. *Men's Health Thailand* has been published since 2006 and has become more popular among the younger generation. These two well-known exercise and health magazines are targeted to heterosexual men. Men who do not have enough money to pay for a personal trainer in a gym train by themselves by following the information provided in these magazines and watching television programs that provide guidance on how to work out. A Thai-language edition of the British gay magazine *Attitude* began publication under the banner *Attitude Thailand* in 2011 and included significant content on male physical culture. In 2012 the glossy full-color *SOLID: Aspiring Fitness Magazine* began publication. It was filled with images of Thai men with highly developed physiques in erotic poses. While not explicitly a gay magazine, the homoeroticism of its images was palpable, not unlike the homoerotic images in *Physique Pictorial* and similar Western physical culture magazines in the 1950s. Twelve issues of *SOLID* were published over the following two years. All these magazines were influential in the development of male gym and physical culture in Thailand.

As part of their consumer research, the advertising agency Ogilvy & Mather Thailand reported in 2005 that men who they defined as "metrosexual" earned more than forty thousand baht per month and were more interested in and paid more attention to health care, fashion, and beauty products than other Thai men.[5] This research estimated that at that time 10 percent of the male population of Bangkok, or approximately half a million men, could be regarded as living metrosexual lifestyles. Significantly, 20 percent of the informants in Ogilvy & Mather's survey reported that they made a point of exercising every day. In a 2010 online survey of attitudes toward metrosexual men, the mthai.com website reported that the singer and actor Dome Pakorn Lum (born 1979) was voted the most popular Thai metrosexual male superstar.[6] Participants in mthai.com's online survey judged Dome—who is of mixed Thai, German, and Singaporean heritage—the favorite metrosexual male personality of the year based on his good looks, fashionable dress sense, clean appearance, and healthy masculine body. In second place was the actor Aum Atichart Chumnanon (born 1979)—who is of Thai and British heritage. Third place went to the *hiso*-background actor Prem Budsarakamwong (born 1981). These male actor celebrities, several of whom were of mixed Asian and Caucasian heritage, symbolized the Thai metrosexual man in the early 2000s.

In 2011 the internet statistics service Truehits, provided by the Thai internet and mobile phone provider True, ranked mthai.com number three among the top ten most popular websites in Thailand.[7] In the early 2010s, mthai.com was one of the most popular online venues for content on health care, fashion, hairstyles, sex life, and fitness among both heterosexual and homosexual men. Discussions about sexual experiences and attitudes toward gay identity among webboard users on this website represented a cross-section of public attitudes toward Thai metrosexual men. The common association of the metrosexual style with gay men was reflected in the fact that when mthai.com identified Dome Pakorn Lum as the most popular metrosexual man of 2010, there was considerable online and offline gossip about his sexuality and lifestyle, although he has had a series of relationships with women. In the early 2000s, public perceptions and mainstream understandings of the Thai metrosexual man were encapsulated in the expression *phu-chai sam-ang*, "a man [interested in] cosmetics," which denoted elegant men who were careful about their physical appearance, a characteristic that intersected closely with urban, middle-class gay lifestyles and identity.

FIGURE 16.   The Eurasian or *luk-khreung* model Mike Lay, who is of mixed French, Vietnamese, and Thai heritage, on the cover of the inaugural issue of *Hey!* (2008). Lay reflected the fair-complexioned "white Asian" look that now dominates images of metrosexual masculine attractiveness among middle-class Thai gay men.

The Eurasian or *luk-khreung* model Mike Lay, who is of mixed French, Vietnamese, and Thai heritage, appeared on the cover of the inaugural issue of *Hey!* gay magazine in October 2008. Lay reflected the fair-complexioned "white Asian" look that now dominates images of metrosexual masculine attractiveness among middle-class Thai gay men.

Already established views about gay identity intersected with the characteristics of the metrosexual man, as both gay and metrosexual men came to identify in terms of body image and beauty. Metrosexual male superstars typically sported large muscles and good physiques developed by undertaking a bodybuilding regimen. It was rumored that the actor Aum Atichart trained at a fitness center in the Central Department Store shopping complex in Bangkok's Pinklao area, a gym where many gay men also came to exercise. In the early 2000s, metrosexuality, homosexuality, and fitness spaces were connected in the public imagination as body images based on health, beauty, and a more muscular physique became central to understandings of middle-class urban masculinity. It was in this setting that fitness centers and health clubs came to be widely regarded as spaces frequented by gay men.

In Western countries during the era of industrialization, dominant masculine discourses were based on the model of heterosexual relationships in which normative maleness was expressed by taking the insertive role in sex and exercising the power to dominate others. Normative patterns of gendering encouraged men to be active, powerful, and to exercise privilege in sexual interactions and family affairs. However, in neoliberal consumer cultures masculinity has been redefined by metrosexual lifestyles in which male body images have been produced to be consumed visually by both women and men. This metrosexual image was a new form of being a masculine man that was based on possessing a high level of taste literacy and resulted in a growing blurring of the lines that separate homo and hetero performances of masculinity (Clarkson 2005, 241).

In the early 2010s, there was much public discussion in Thailand about commercial fitness centers as gay spaces. Many people thought that while straight men exercised and played sports in public parks, working out in a fitness center was a gay activity. These attitudes were expressed in numerous webboard discussions of "gay men in fitness centers" among straight men and women on predominantly heterosexual Thai websites such as pantip.com. For example, in 2011 four male discussants who identified as straight posted on pantip.com and mthai.com.

> Thai men go to train and do bodybuilding at the sport clubs in public parks. But fitness centers are places for gay men who like to exercise.[8]

> My friend told me that ninety percent of the men in commercial fitness centers are gay. This is different from the straight men who always go out to play football and basketball. Straight men won't go to fitness centers.[9]

> Absolutely, more than fifty percent of the men who go to fitness centers are gay. Not many straight men go to those places. Most straight men go to exercise in public parks.[10]

> I've got a woman friend who's worked as a trainer at a well-known fitness center in Bangkok. She told me that almost all the men who went there are gay. Some male trainers and fitness center owners are also gay. I want to warn straight guys that you need to be careful of gay men when you go to a fitness center.[11]

While the fitness centers in public parks that emerged from the nation-building policies of the Phibunsongkhram era were predominantly marked as heterosexual spaces, the new air-conditioned spaces of commercial fitness centers became known as places patronized by large numbers of gay men. This common association of the different urban localities that are available for developing the male physique with men of different sexualities reflects the fact that expressions of modern heterosexual Thai masculinity are linked to the fitness spaces that emerged from mid-twentieth-century state policy while modern gay masculinities developed in the context of the capitalist marketplace. Modern Thai straight and gay masculinities have respectively emerged within different regimes of power, with state power having had a foundational role in defining patterns of modern heterosexual masculinity while the market and commercial media have been central influences in the molding of modern Thai gay masculinities. Even in the early twenty-first century, the Thai state bureaucracy continues to monitor and enforce the heteronormative gender norms that were introduced in earlier decades of the twentieth century. As Nattapol remarks, in Thailand "government institutions are places that straighten any display of queerness" (Nattapol 2022, 243). It is because of the entrenched heteronormativity of many organs of the Thai state that in the decades covered in our book, Thai gay men as well as homosexual women, trans women, and trans men, shunned involvement with the state and sought queer autonomy in the comparatively gay-friendly domains of commerce and the spaces of capitalism. Furthermore, the predominating influence of the market in modern Thai gay history and the socioeconomic stratification of Thai society is at the root of the evolution of the distinct middle-class and working-class forms of gay masculinity discussed in this chapter and in chapter 5.

Constructing the Middle-Class Thai Gay Body

In marked contrast to older stereotypes of the homosexual man as effete and effeminate, many heterosexual men and women in Bangkok now regard a man who has muscular arms and a more developed chest as more than likely being gay. The new image of the middle-class Thai gay man is of someone who engages in bodybuilding to develop a highly muscled physique. The men who train in fitness centers want to have a good physique and increase their muscle mass. They typically exercise their arms and chest as these parts of the body are important for affirming a sense of masculinity. Many middle-class Thai gay men now regard a big chest and strongly defined abdominal muscles as hallmarks of a sexually attractive male body. Having a good physique is a source of self-confidence and in the Thai gay community body image and appearance are very important in forming sexual relationships. In webboard discussions the major reason gay men gave for going to the gym to develop their physique was to be appreciated by others.

> Gays want to be accepted by society. They think that having big muscles is very attractive and other people will look at them admiringly. While straight men work out in fitness centers to be attractive to women, gay

men go there to find a man. It can be said that gay men are especially concerned about their health and body image.[12]

> Gay people like to see a smart, good-looking man, particularly a man with big muscles. So that's the reason that gays need to be in good shape, to be attractive to other gay men. However, it's very hard to identify who is actually gay, if they look masculine like a man.[13]

Men with highly developed arm and chest muscles are now colloquially called *kam pu*, "crab claws," a metaphor that compares their large biceps and upper arm muscles to a crab's large claws, which may look oversized compared to the rest of their body. This is a mildly derogatory expression that describes men whose large upper body looks out of proportion to their lower body and legs, an appearance that some regard as being unattractive. *Kam pu* is also a play on words, with the Thai word for "muscles," *klam*, often being pronounced *kam* in rapid colloquial speech. *Kam pu* describes the enhanced male upper body developed by intense physical workouts in combination with consuming muscle-building supplements such as whey protein and can refer to either gay or heterosexual men. Nevertheless, *kam pu* does tend to be used more often to refer to gay men.

Among Thai gay men who are not attracted to muscular physiques, gay musclemen are sometimes also called *mee* or "bears." In Thai gay culture *mee* or "bear" can refer either to a bodybuilder muscleman or to someone who is overweight, denoting a physique made large either by muscles or by fat. The physiques of the gay *kam pu* and *mee* are often similar and when Thai gays talk about a man with a big body or big muscles, they can use either term, such as "He is a *kam pu*" or "He looks like a *mee*." *Kam pu* is used by gay men who do not find large-bodied men sexually attractive, and at times *mee* can also be a mildly derogative term that implies being sexually unattractive. However, since the later 2010s, some large-bodied Thai men have identified with the term *mee* and "bear pride" events have been held in Bangkok pubs and bars. In contrast, *kam pu* has not become an identity label among Thai gay bodybuilders and remains a term of mild disparagement.

Not all Thai gay men regard the gym-enhanced physique of the middle-class gay *kam pu* as being sexually attractive. While well-built chests, shoulders, arms, and an abdomen sporting a six-pack are seen as attractive in contemporary middle-class Thai gay cultures, excessive body size marked either by muscle mass or fat are not generally seen as being sexy and there are significant differences in attitudes between classes. As detailed in chapter 5, younger working-class and lower-middle-class gay men in Bangkok regard a slim, lean physique as being more attractive than a body developed through fitness training. In January 2013, the postjung.com entertainment website reported a survey among Thai gay men of their preferred male body type, with four times more respondents preferring men with a slender physique to the larger *kam pu* body.[14] Surveys also found that many Thai women consider a man with larger than average muscles to be unattractive because it makes him look like a wrestler or a hoodlum. As one woman posted on the pantip.com discussion board as part of an online survey, "I don't like big musclemen. . . . I think bodybuilders are terrible. I like a clean-looking man who doesn't have overly big muscles."[15]

The new mainstream stereotype of the middle-class gay man as a *kam pu* bodybuilder also contrasts with gay men's diverse attitudes about the ideal masculine body, which, as detailed in the previous chapter, are marked by various types of masculine images. In the early 2000s, having big muscles was not the only idealized style of masculinity in Thai gay communities. Nevertheless, despite the change in understandings of what a Thai gay man looks like, heterosexual perceptions of gay body images continued to be marked by stereotypes that were often removed from actual gay experiences. The following examples from webboard discussions among straight men about gay men and fitness centers reflect the new stereotyping of gay men as having a *kam pu* physique.

> My friend was very surprised when he saw my big muscles. He thought that I look gay because I've been training in a fitness center. He told me that I must stop exercising in fitness centers. I got really angry when he said that.[16]

> In my opinion, I think that playing football is good exercise for men. But those men who train and build up really big muscles are attractive to gays. Unfortunately, [closeted] married men go to fitness centers to find other gays. I think fitness centers are gay places. Lots of gay men go there. I'm sure of that, so be really careful and watch out for *kam pu* guys.[17]

Men's fitness centers were not just places for exercise but also quickly became venues for sexual contact. Many men, irrespective of sexual orientation, experienced various kind of sexual intimacy in health clubs. In some Bangkok fitness centers, the men's bathrooms were implicitly designed as erotic spaces. There were no locks on the showers and the walls between shower stalls were often made of opaque glass, permitting the outlines of men's bodies to be seen. This type of design was especially common in the early years of the operation of commercial fitness clubs in Thailand. However, gay men's sexual activities in fitness centers were criticized in the media and after complaints caution posters were put on the walls of many centers detailing the rules of appropriate behavior and prohibiting sexual activity. Guards and cleaning staff began patrolling the bathrooms and if members broke the rules the police were sometimes called and the offending person's membership rescinded. The dress culture of gyms has also become conservative. A regime like that in some fitness centers in United States was introduced with men no longer being permitted to workout shirtless (Alvarez 2008).

In the early 2010s, many straight men detailed their negative experiences in fitness centers on the mthai.com webboard, especially while showering or relaxing in the sauna in venues where these facilities did not have locks on the doors. For example:

> I used to use the lockers at the fitness center to keep my clothes. But I don't use them now. I get ready in sportswear before going to the gym and so I don't need a locker now. When I've finished exercising, I go home in sweaty clothes. Because I've learned that the bathroom in fitness centers can be very dangerous for straight men. Lots of stupid things happen in the bathroom. The psychotic guys who intrude in the bathroom are really terrible.[18]

> I went to the fitness club at university and found that there were lots of gay guys there. Then, I moved to another fitness center, but there were still lots of gays. The guy who recommended that I go to a fitness center was gay. There are probably gay guys in every fitness center. I've been touched up by a gay guy. He poked his finger on my ass. I want to go to a fitness club that isn't overcrowded with gay guys.[19]

In the 2000s, the branches of California Fitness were especially popular among gay men in Bangkok. Before it closed in 2012, this fitness center was very popular because of its ambient dance music, bright lights, and colorfully decorated furniture.[20] Movie stars and celebrities were often profiled in the media as exercising at one or the other of this fitness company's branches, and it became known as a fitness center for Bangkok's wealthy *hiso* high-status crowd. However, as noted above, some straight men came to see California Fitness and other commercial health clubs as being crowded with too many gay men. Rumors circulated of gay men having oral sex in the bathrooms and the dry and wet saunas and, as a result, many straight men avoided these venues. Some straight men snarked that the branch of California Fitness on Silom Road near many downtown gay bars should have been renamed the California Gay Fitness Center.

The Thai Gay Middle-Class and Global Fitness Culture

The considerable expense of fitness center membership means that most of the gay men who work out in these venues are middle-class men and the forms of masculine body image that are cultivated in health clubs reflect middle-class perspectives and standards of homomasculinity. Furthermore, the connections between body image and urban lifestyles in Bangkok's class-based gay cultures are influenced by the economic, ethnic, and regional cultural forms of Thai society more broadly. Thai gay men negotiate their body images in relation to different styles of masculinity that come from a mix of Western, East Asian, and indigenous Thai influences. Although the consumerist urban lifestyles of Thai gay men share many features in common with international consumer culture, they nonetheless have their own ways of bodily and emotional expression. Jackson (2011a, 199) argues that Thailand's commercial queer scenes should be seen through the lens of local agency as indigenous phenomena, not as the outcome of either Western hegemony, exploitation by foreign capital, or the imposition of alien cultural forms.

Thailand's gay fitness culture emerged in the context of a global fitness industry that has shaped the commodification of health internationally. Arran Stibbe (2004) contends that in the West better-off, well-educated men typically embody a masculinist ideology and that the concern with health and fitness at the center of exercise culture reinforces male power and authority in late-capitalist societies. According to Stibbe, increasing muscle size is of paramount importance in middle-class fitness culture because it is a means by which higher-income men seek to confirm and affirm male power. Rosalind Gill, Karen Henwood, and Carl McLean (2005) argue that Western gym culture has become central to a late-modern identity project in which young gay and heterosexual men are equally anxious about their bodies and self-respect.

In the later decades of the twentieth century, gym culture became a focal social institution in American gay culture. In the United States gay gyms first became popular during the 1970s, when the politics of sexual identity encouraged many gay men to come out and create their own social spaces. At that time, the gay gym emerged as a social center for gay men to engage in a culturally influenced reengineering of the gay body image in masculine terms to challenge stereotypes of homosexual effeminacy and the queer sissy. American gay men believed that by building up their muscles they could make a claim to masculinity that placed them on a par with heterosexual men. Erick Alvarez (2008) maintains that American gay gyms provided spaces for homosexual men to reclaim the male physique, with forms of hypermasculinity becoming a new idealized body image in which muscularity came to be identified with the gay body.

Gay gym culture has also become highly influential in East Asian countries such as Singapore, Malaysia, Hong Kong, Taiwan, and, since the later 2010s, China. In all these countries predominantly gay men of Chinese-heritage have participated in the transnational gay consumer culture in which the muscular male body has been commodified as the idealized object of sexual attraction. Jack Kapac (1998) and Eng-Beng Lim (2005), among others, state that within Western gay communities Asian gay men have often been minoritized by a racialized gender hierarchy that feminizes Asian male bodies and locates them in a subordinate position relative to implicitly more masculine Caucasian men. This stereotype of Asian men's bodies as feminine has been challenged by a new style of the masculine Asian gay body developed through intensive gym work. East Asian gay men have not only sought to challenge heterosexist stereotypes of the effeminate homosexual within their own societies but have also resisted the minoritization of Asian gay men within an internationally dominant Western gay culture that has fetishized the Caucasian male body.

In contrast, however, the meaning of an attractive physique and the beautiful male body among Thai gay men is not the same as in either Western or East Asian gay communities. Significant numbers of Thai gay men do not prefer the strongly muscular male body of the gay hunk *kam pu* (crab claw) or *mee* (bear) who has large muscles on his chest, shoulders, and arms. While Thai fitness and gym culture reflects aspects of international gay consumer culture, there are local cultural varieties of meaning and multiple modalities of the sexually attractive masculine gay physique. As discussed in the next chapter, large numbers of Thai gay men seek to embody a slim, lithe mode of masculinity that contrasts with the middle-class *kam pu* or *mee*.

Thai Gay Fitness Culture and Aspirational Middle-Class Status

In the 1980s, the middle-class Thai gay man was regarded as someone with enough money to buy the sexual services of male sex workers. However, in the 1990s and early 2000s, as gay sexual relations shifted from purchasing sexual services from heterosexual men to seeking partnerings with other gay men, the need to be sexually attractive—often described as being "saleable" or "marketable" (*khai dai*) in Thai gayspeak—consequently increased. In Thailand's urban gay culture in the 2000s, a firm good-looking body was important for successful participation in the gay scene and large numbers of middle-class gay men became interested in presentation, appearance, and body image as the desire to be sexually attractive to other gay men came to dominate the forms of gay masculine expression. In this changed setting, access to gay sex nonetheless remained a wealth-determined privilege. In earlier decades, wealth had determined the privilege to buy sex, while in the early twenty-first-century wealth determined the ability to shape and sculpt the body in sexually attractive forms in the private spaces of members-only fitness centers. The gay men who enhanced their body image by working out in gyms were economically privileged and, indeed, in Thailand the developed musculature of the gay *kam pu* is as much a marker and statement of class identity in a hierarchical socioeconomic order as it is a claim for homosexual men to be recognized as masculine within a heteronormative culture.

The differences between middle-class and working-class Thai gay men can be understood in terms of the commodities and services they can afford to purchase and consume in their daily lives. Like expensive brand-name products, gym-enhanced versions of masculinity are reserved for high-income gay men. Luxury goods and services are not only associated with displaying wealth but in Thailand's class-structured social order are also viewed as indicating a man who "has good taste" (*mi rotsaniyom di*) and constitute forms of cultural capital that gay men from different classes strive to possess. For Thai gay men, possessing brand-name products and embodying a gym-enhanced *kam pu* physique are both associated with aspirations to enhance and exhibit social status. The distinctiveness of Thailand's gay gym culture emerges from its position within the country's class structure as an elite pursuit marked by claims to higher class status. The muscled body of the Thai *kam pu* does not just represent a wish for the masculinity of homosexual men to be recognized within a heteronormative order that devalues signs of femininity in males. This elite form of Thai gay masculinity simultaneously expresses a desire to be seen as urbane, cosmopolitan, and of a higher social standing than those gay men who embody other styles of masculinity that are marked as lower-class.

In the 2010s, the masculinity of the Thai gay middle class was increasingly constructed in relation to the global gym culture. However, images of the sexually attractive male body were interpreted through local sexual imaginations. On the one hand, the changing perceptions and ideology of masculinity among Thai gay men reflected how their urban lifestyle emerged in response to a consumerist logic in which the male body became a sexual commodity (Bronski, 1998) and cosmopolitan metrosexual lifestyles came to be signified by having a sexually attractive physique. On the other hand, however, the body transformations made possible by fitness culture were also linked to aspirational expressions of socioeconomic status. As Käng notes, among Thai gay men, "beauty practices . . . have a dual role of representing one's status during social interactions and increasing the level of class distinction necessary to demonstrate ongoing self-care and cultivation" (Käng 2021, 284). Nevertheless, the desire for a gym-enhanced body that marks both masculinity and middle-class status is far from universal among Thai gay men. In the next chapter we consider the alternative masculinity of working-class men in Bangkok for whom the masculine ideal is a slim physique, representing a refusal of the hegemonic status that the muscular male body has attained in sections of middle-class gay Thailand as well as in Western and East Asian gay cultures.

THE ALTERNATIVE MASCULINITY OF WORKING-CLASS COYOTE BOY DANCERS

This chapter details the alternative masculinity of coyote boy dancers who performed in gay bars and pubs in Bangkok in the early 2010s. Coyote boy troupes were composed of working-class men of diverse sexualities—heterosexual, bisexual, and gay—and their erotic dancing for predominantly younger gay audiences reflected the way in which these men negotiated their masculine gender roles and sexuality in different contextual situations. The highly popular coyote boy dance phenomenon was primarily a feature of Bangkok gay venues that catered to a local market of younger Thai gay men rather than the bars and pubs whose clienteles were international gay tourists and older Thai gay men. While called "coyote boys" in English, or simply *khoyoti* (i.e., "coyote") or sometimes *dek khoyoti* ("coyote kids") in Thai, these dancers were not children but young men in their early to mid-twenties. We explore the bodily practices by which coyote boy dancers performed their erotic shows and the forms of gendering they embodied in their stage personas as well as their offstage lives. This research does not consider customers' preferences or understandings of the masculine Thai male body but rather takes the perspective of the coyote boy performers.

The slim physiques of coyote boy dancers contrasted with the muscularity of middle-class gay men who worked out in gyms and took muscle-developing supplements. These performers represented a distinctive working-class masculinity that was regarded as an ideal of male sexual attractiveness among working-class and lower-middle class gay men in the early 2010s. Their performances reflected a stylization of urban working-class understandings of what it meant to act like a man, *kek man* or *ab man* in Thai gay parlance. They created shows that eroticized the masculine image of younger working-class men, and their dance styles and stage personas offer insights into what significant numbers of younger gay men in the early 2010s regarded as successful performances of *ab man* straight-acting masculinity. Indeed, coyote boys represented a commodification of the Thai gay masculine performative norm of *ab man* as the ideal of male sexual attractiveness.

The sexuality of coyote boy dancers was not fixed by either a heteronormative or homonormative sex/gender system as they had sexual relations with gay and bisexual men as well as with women. The most significant thing about coyote boy dancing was the performance of masculinity onstage. Each coyote boy had to present a masculine body image onstage, even if his private offstage behavior may not have conformed to normative notions of manliness. Indeed, many coyote boys acted effeminately and expressed feminine characteristics and behaviors in private within their groups. Thai coyote boys represented the development of an alternative masculinity in which both feminine and masculine characteristics were present and were not isolated into mutually exclusive gender binaries. They strategically deployed both masculinity and femininity to enhance their economic, social, and sexual opportunities and to forge friendships as well as romantic and intimate relationships.

Fieldwork for this chapter was undertaken from December 2011 to March 2012 and involved in-depth interviews with coyote boys who worked in a gay pub in the Lam Salee area of gay bars along Ramkhamhaeng Road in the east of Bangkok. The coyote boys interviewed were eighteen to twenty-five years old, were working class, and had migrated from rural areas of Thailand. Some had come to Bangkok to study as well as to find work, and most had made the move to the capital with other male friends with whom they shared rented rooms in the city. Also interviewed were go-go boy performers who worked in a gay bar in the Silom area, the owner of a gay pub in the Lam Salee area, and the manager of a gay bar on Surawong Road in Bangkok's downtown area of gay venues. This chapter is also based on observing coyote boy performances in gay bars and pubs and the interactions of the dancers with customers and friends. In addition, we draw on gay magazines and websites as sources on the histories of go-go and coyote dancing and the experiences of go-go boy and coyote boy performers in Bangkok gay bars and pubs.

The History of Male Erotic Dancing in Thai Gay Venues

Erotic dance performances have been a staple of Thai bars with commercial sex workers since the early 1970s. The first form of erotic dance to be performed in

Bangkok's gay bars and pubs was go-go dancing. Go-go dancing is a style of erotic dance that originated in the early 1960s in France and the United States, when female performers would get up on tables and dance the then-popular dance the twist to entertain patrons. The term "go-go" derives from both the French expression *à gogo*, meaning "a lot, galore," and the English phrase "Go, go, go!" used to encourage someone to engage in an energetic action. During the 1960s, go-go dancing became popular in nightclubs across the world and was a feature in gay clubs, where the performers were male dancers known as go-go boys. During the Vietnam War era in the late 1960s and early 1970s, go-go dancing by female performers was a common form of entertainment in the Bangkok and Pattaya bars and sex clubs that catered to American servicemen who came to Thailand on R&R ("rest and relaxation" breaks from active service). American serviceman also referred to *à go-go* dancing as "table dancing."

Male dancers called "go-go boys" in English and *dek off* or *dek bar* in Thai became common in Bangkok gay bars in the 1970s and have remained a staple of the entertainment provided in many gay bars in the country to this today. Go-go boy dancers are male sex workers who usually wear only underwear briefs with an identifying number attached and perform slow movement erotic dancing to pop music tunes on platforms and stages in venues. In many bars silver poles are also installed on the dance platform for pole dancing. Go-go boys dance erotically to display their bodies, advertising their availability to provide sexual services. Moving the body in time with the music in displays of dance skill and erotic action is known as *sai*, "to swing, sway or shake." Since their inception, gay bars with go-go boy dancers have catered to middle-class Thai customers as well as to Western and Asian tourists. As detailed in chapter 2, if a gay customer is interested in a particular go-go boy, he identifies the boy's number to the bar manager. The go-go boy goes to sit and drink with the customer before they go out together. The system of using numbers to identify go-go boys was borrowed from venues with female go-go dancers, with Thai gay commercial sex practices often copying patterns in pubs and bars servicing heterosexual clients. In a 1985 interview in *Mithuna Junior*, Suthat Chanket, the owner of Apollo Bar in the downtown gay precinct of Silom Soi 4, stated that in 1973 his venue had been the first gay bar in Bangkok to feature male go-go boy dancers (*Mithuna Junior* 1985a, 100).

Go-go boy dancing became increasingly common in Thai gay bars that provided sexual services, and the style of dancing also developed over time. In August 1985, Bar Beiry in Bangkok's downtown Surawong Road area held a go-go boy dancing contest to find the best male dancer in Thailand, and in the 1980s and 1990s this bar along with the nearby Twilight Bar became famous for go-go boy shows as well as male sex shows. From the 1990s, some go-go boy male danc-ers performed naked onstage and began to augment their dancing with candles, letting wax drip sensually onto their bodies, or using foam that highlighted the shape of their penis under their wet underwear. These kinds of erotic go-go boy shows attracted large numbers of gay customers as well as female tourists, with the 1990s becoming known as the golden era of Bangkok gay bars. Advertise-ments and articles in Thai gay magazines indicated that seventeen new gay go-go bars opened in Bangkok and its environs in 1990 alone. In the later 1980s and into the 1990s, there was often a rapid turnover of gay bars on the Bangkok com-mercial scene, with new bars regularly replacing older ones that were no longer successful and had shut down. The commercial success of a gay bar in this period depended on consistently providing good services and having a reliable stable of handsome men working as go-go dancers and sex workers. Inter Mustache's House, Super Lex, Bar Beiry, Twilight, Tulip, Violet, Tawan, and Adam were among the most successful go-go bars in Bangkok in the 1980s and 1990s, all of them staying in business for over a decade.

When this research was undertaken in 2011 and 2012, gay go-go bars were found in four major cities in Thailand. In Bangkok, the largest concentration of go-go boy bars was in Soi Pratuchai, located off Surawong Road. In 2011 eight go-go bars operated in this area. Another four go-go bars were in the Silom and Saphan Kwai areas. At that time, the most popular gay go-go bars in downtown Bangkok were Jupiter 2002, Dream Boy, X Boys, X Size, and Tawan. The Boyz Town zone in Pattayaland Soi 3 was the heart of gay pubs and go-go boy bars in Pattaya city. In 2012 nineteen go-go bars served gay clients in this city with the most popular being Boyz, Funny Boys, and Copa Showbar. The biggest and most well-known gay go-go bar in the southern resort island of Phuket was My Way, located in Patong Beach, while the longest-established gay bar in the northern city of Chiang Mai was Adam's Apple, where many go-go dancers entertained and provided sexual services for gay patrons.

Payment to a go-go boy for sexual services was in the form of tips that are mandatory but variable. Käng reports that in the early 2010s in Bangkok tips to male sex workers in gay bars were in the range of 1,000 to 1,500 baht for a short term and 1,500 to 2,000 baht for the night (Käng 2017, 199n29). In 2012 the price of a drink in a Bangkok gay bar was between 200 and 300 baht. The showtime for go-go boy dances was usually between 10 p.m. and midnight. Table 5.1 lists Thai gay bars in various cities that had go-go boy dancers in 2011.

In the early 2000s, go-go boy performances in Thai gay bars evolved beyond simply moving rhythmically in time to music to include more elaborate dance and entertainment routines, which highlighted the erotic appeal of the go-go

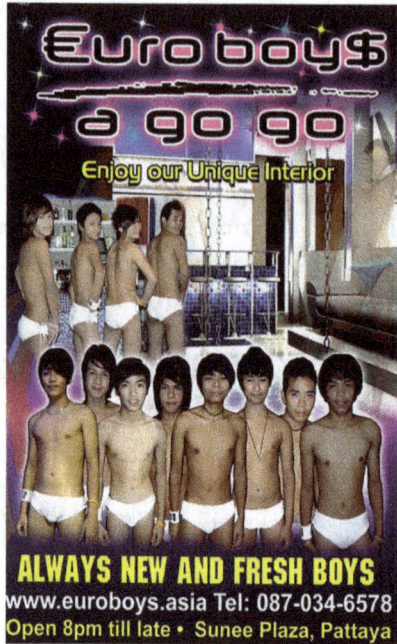

FIGURE 17.   Advertisement for the Euroboy$ gay bar in Pattaya with the venue's *dek bar* male sex workers wearing the house uniform of white swimwear briefs in which they perform erotic go-go-style dances. The slim physiques of the predominantly rural, working-class male sex workers in Thai gay bars contrasts with the highly developed musculature of many middle-class gay men. (Source: *Bangkok Desire* 2013).

boy's body and penis. In the early twenty-first century, different bars in Bangkok began to specialize in different styles of go-go boy shows:

- Uniform show: male dancers wore police or soldier uniforms or leather-man costumes and danced to Western pop music.
- Body paint show: the dancers wore bikini briefs and had their bodies painted in fluorescent backlight colors. The patterns were drawn from flowers, animals, or abstract designs and the dancers moved their bodies slowly to show off their painted body images.
- Penis show: the performers danced naked and walked around the bar to show their erection to customers.
- Fucking show: the performers engaged in anal sex in various positions and locations around the bar, such as hanging from the ceiling and lying on the floor.

TABLE 5.1 Thai gay venues with go-go boy dancers in 2011

LOCATION	BANGKOK	PATTAYA	PHUKET	CHIANG MAI
Number of go-go bars	14	19	6	2
Names of go-go bars	Be High	A Bomb	CU Tonight	Adam's Apple
	Boy Bangkok	Boyz Boyz Boyz	Mamasan	New My Way
	Classic 2nd Boys	Cartier	My Way	
	Dream Boy	Classic Boy Club	Passport	
	Fresh Beach Boyz	Copa Showbar	Superboy Bar	
	Golden Cock	Cupidol	Tangmo	
	Hot Male	Dream Boys		
	Jupiter 2002	Dinamite Boys		
	Ocean Boy	Four Seasons		
	Screw Boy Bar	Funny Boys		
	Solid Bar	G-U-Y Club		
	Tawan	Handy Boys		
	X Boys	Happy Place		
	X Size	Krazy Dragon		
		Lucky 777		
		Red Dragon		
		Super Star Showbar		
		Toy Boys		
		Wild West Boys		

Source: "Thailand Gay Guide City Directory" 2011.

- Candle show: the dancers held lit candles that they slowly moved around and over their bodies in time to the music.
- Bathing show: the performers bathed naked in a transparent glass bath.
- Golf show: the performers played golf by using their erect penis as a golf club to hit a golf ball into the hole.
- Foam show: naked dancers soaked their bodies with foam in time to the music.
- Masturbation show: the performers masturbated in front of customers, who dropped money into a glass jar on the stage. The first go-go boy to ejaculate took the money in the jar.

While widespread, these types of performances took place in a gray zone that skirted legality. Indeed, erotic male dancing in gay go-go bars was occasionally raided by the police, particularly in cases where it became known that teenagers under the age of eighteen were working as male sex workers and performing in a live sex show. Bar owners could be charged with promoting indecency and obscenity under sections 282 and 283 of the Thai criminal code (Kodmhai n.d.).

Payments for the performers varied according to the type of show, with go-go dancers who performed a fucking show getting more than for other types of performances. In 2012 performers in a fucking show earned from 350 to 600 baht per performance, while performers in the other shows were paid between 100 and 200 baht. The most important thing for performers in all these types of shows was that they have a big penis. In an interview, one male sex worker stated that gay go-go boy dancers were usually too shy to show their penis, while straight go-go boys were much less worried about performing naked and showing their erect penis to customers. Go-go boys used various techniques to help get an erection. Some took Viagra, while others watched porn clips or masturbated before going onstage. When they got an erection, they would keep it up with a rubber condom ring tied around their scrotum and the base of the penis.

Coyote Boy Dancers

In contrast to go-go dancing, which denotes erotic dancing on a specially constructed stage in a bar or pub, coyote dancing refers to erotic dance performances on bar tops or tabletops in venues. While go-go dancing in Thai gay bars has evolved into a set of stylized slow movements, coyote boy dancing is characterized by fast, jerky body movements. Informants interviewed in Bangkok's gay bars and pubs stated that they were not sure precisely when the coyote boy phenomenon first emerged in the Thai gay community. However, after the Hollywood movie *Coyote Ugly* (McNally 2000) was released, coyote girls who danced on bar tops and tabletops became popular in many heterosexual bars in Bangkok. *Coyote Ugly* was a romantic comedy based loosely on the experiences of female entertainers who worked at the Coyote Ugly Saloon, an actual venue that opened on New York's Lower East Side in 1993. As mentioned in the film, the name of the bar and the style of bar top dancing it became known for derives from a slang expression "coyote ugly." This refers to the feeling of waking up after a drunken one-night stand and discovering that one's arm is underneath someone who is so physically repulsive that one would gladly chew one's arm off without waking the person, just to be able to get away without being discovered. In the United States wild coyotes stuck in a trap are reputed to gnaw off their own limbs to escape.

Coyote boy dancing in Bangkok gay bars followed soon after this style of dancing was introduced in venues for heterosexual customers. One informant stated that he had started working as a coyote boy dancer in 2004. In the early 2000s, gay venue owners viewed the new style of coyote boy erotic dancing as a novelty to attract customers. One pub owner indicated that engaging coyote boys was an innovative business strategy in venues where customers wanted to watch male erotic performances. By the early 2010s, some Bangkok gay bars and pubs had their own coyote boy performers, while independent coyote boy troupes were also established. These troupes were hired to perform at several different pubs during the week and sometimes had more than one engagement a night. Coyote boy performances proved to be especially popular among younger Thai gay clients and were predominantly found in pubs where gay men socialized and cruised each other for sex rather than in gay bars with commercial sex workers. While some coyote boys did engage in sex work, they were not necessarily commercial sex workers. This contrasts with the go-go boy performers in bars, where all the dancers were commercial sex workers. In the early 2010s, the different styles of go-go boy and coyote boy male erotic performance catered to distinct gay niche markets.

Some venues included both go-go boy and coyote boy styles of erotic performance. In 2012 go-go bars such as Dream Boys in Bangkok's Surawong area had two coyote boy performances every night, with the shows respectively starting at 10:15 p.m. and at 11:30 p.m. At Dream Boys those working as coyote dancers were paid two hundred baht each night and were also sex workers who were available to provide sexual services for clients. At this venue, both coyote boy and go-go boy performers had identifying numbers pinned to their clothing. However, the status of coyote boys in gay bars was higher than that of go-go boys because they were regarded as having greater dance ability, which was viewed as being more artistic and requiring greater talent. Coyote boy dancers also tended to get more attention from customers than go-go boys. Their main customers were Thai college and university students and recent graduates in their twenties.

In 2012 the situation in pubs and discotheques was somewhat different. The coyote boys performing in these venues were not direct or formal sex workers but rather identified as erotic dancers and entertainers. Nevertheless, sexual contact between coyote boys and customers often took place on an informal basis. As Käng observes, the sex work of coyote boys was not as formalized as the go-go boy system in bars. "After coyote boy shows, the coyotes will generally frequent the tables of patrons who sent them tips, to show their appreciation. However, . . . coyotes are less committed to individual patrons [than go-go boys in bars, and] . . . move more freely throughout the bar space, looking for potential clients. Coyotes also do not expect to be offed [paid for sex] like go-go boys" (Käng 2015, 104). Coyote boys' primary occupational identification was as dancers rather than bar employees. Sex work was not as essential to their income and ongoing employment as it was for male dancers in gay go-go bars. Furthermore, the ratio between go-go boys and coyotes in venues was very different. As Käng notes of the situation in the early 2010s:

> In many go-go boy bars, there are as many or more go-go boys as there are patrons. Thus, the competition among go-go boys for patrons is very high. On the other hand, a dance club with several hundred patrons

may have a dozen coyotes. Coyotes thus do not feel compelled to seek a patron in as competitive a manner as go-gos. They thus have a much more casual manner in which they interact with patrons. Furthermore, as the dance bar does not control coyote boy interactions as a go-go bar would, they are able to more freely make connections and personal deals with patrons. For example, while visiting different tables, a coyote could exchange numbers with a potential patron and set up a date for another time to avoid off fees [paid to the venue owner], though some bars maintain a minimum number of off fines per month, typically one per month. While making private arrangements is possible in the setting of a go-go bar, it would first require that a patron use a staff intermediary to bring a go-go boy to him. Furthermore, while the go-go boy is working in a primarily foreign environment (mostly Asian and Western tourists), the coyote boy is working in a primarily Thai environment, where he interacts with patrons in Thai, and, though not communicating as equals, can interact more on his own terms. (Käng 2015, 105)

In 2012 coyote boy performances could be found in gay bars and pubs in both Bangkok and Pattaya.[1] In Bangkok two gay bars had regular coyote boy performances, Dream Boys and X Boys, both located on downtown Surawong Road, while eight gay pubs in several locations outside the downtown tourist precinct had nightly coyote boy performances, as listed in table 5.2.

As noted in chapter 2, in Thailand the term "gay pub" describes a nightlife entertainment venue that has dance music and serves alcohol and where gay men come to socialize, meet friends, and cruise other customers for sexual partners. In the West these types of venues would usually be called gay bars. Gay men

TABLE 5.2 Pubs and bars in Bangkok with coyote boy shows in 2012

BARS AND PUBS	LOCATION
Door Dum (pub)	Lam Salee (Ramkhamhaeng Road)
Dream Boys (go-go bar)	Surawong Road (Soi Pratuchai)
G.O.D. (pub)	Silom Road
ICK (pub)	Lam Salee (Ramkhamhaeng Road)
Isan First Love (pub)	Jatujak (Kamphaeng Phet Road)
Ratchada Soi 8 (pub)	Ratchada Road
Sa-Ke (pub)	Ratchadamnoen Road
See K Dance (pub)	Lam Salee (Ramkhamhaeng Road)
Sib Sean (pub)	Petchburi Road
X Boys (go-go bar)	Surawong Road (Soi Pratuchai)

Source: Compiled from data listed on the Camfrog website in 2011.

may cruise other customers for sex in Thailand's gay pubs, but they are not primarily venues for commercial sex. In contrast, in Thailand a gay bar is a venue whose main activity is commercial sex and whose employees are commercial sex workers. Another difference between Thai gay pubs and gay bars is that most customers in pubs are younger Thai gay men, particularly university and college students, while the customers in gay bars are older Thai men and foreign tourists. In the early 2010s, most of Bangkok's gay bars for foreign tourists were in the downtown Silom and Surawong areas while those for Thai customers were in the Saphan Khwai area in the city's mid-north. In contrast, gay pubs were in diverse localities around the city, closer to where younger gay men lived, notably Lumsalee in the east, Ratchada and Saphan Khwai in the city's mid-north as well as the Or.Tor.Kor. area near the Jatujak weekend market.[2]

However, the distinction between gay pubs and gay bars was not always clear-cut, as both types of venues welcomed gay men of all ages and backgrounds as well as straight men and women. One clear difference between these two types of venues was that while gay go-go bars often advertised as tourist attractions for both Western and Asian gay tourists to see sex shows, Bangkok's gay pubs generally did not advertise in tourist magazines but rather became known among younger Thai gay men through word of mouth or advertising on Thai social media platforms. During our research, few tourists were visible at the venues in the gay pubs and discos that had coyote boy performances. The patrons at the pubs where coyote boys performed were predominantly university and college students as well as lower-middle-class gay men with limited incomes. In contrast, the patrons at gay bars were mostly mature middle-class gay men with higher incomes. In the early 2010s, the different types of venues in Bangkok's commercial gay scene were structured on the expectation that younger gay men would socialize in pubs and find sex with each other, while older Thai gay men would visit bars and pay for sex.

Two types of coyote boy performers worked in gay pubs in the early 2010s. The first type was full-time employees who were paid monthly salaries of between 4,000 and 6,000 baht. The second type was part-time dancers who worked on weekends as a sideline and were paid about 350 baht per night by the pub owner. Coyote boys could also receive tips from appreciative customers, with some earning tips of up to 10,000 baht per night when this type of erotic dancing was first introduced to Bangkok's gay pubs and discotheques. In the early years of coyote boy performances, pubs might have had twenty-five to thirty coyote boys dancing on tabletops and bar tops. Some coyote boys formed their own troupes to deal directly with customers and perform at special events and private parties like birthdays and to celebrate festivals such as international New Year, Chinese New Year, the Thai New Year of Songkran in mid-April, and

FIGURE 18. A Bangkok coyote boy troupe showing the slim physique, fair skin complexion, gel-set hair style, boots, and jeans typifying the masculine style of younger, working-class gay men in Bangkok in the 2000s and early 2010s. (Source: *Axis* 2009).

the Loi Krathong festival at the end of the monsoon rainy season in November. These troupes worked in Bangkok as well as in other cities, according to the budget of the customer. For some special events, an individual coyote boy might earn up to 2,500 baht. Independent coyote boy troupes also moved between pubs that did not have their own full-time performers to do shows at several venues, which provided an additional source of income for skilled part-time coyote boys who worked on their own. As the coyote boy phenomenon developed, it became increasingly common for the dancers to become independent performers as they could earn more money that way. One bar owner said that customers liked to see new faces, and if a coyote boy moved to different venues, it would help a pub improve its business by getting a reputation for hosting different new performers (Ploy, September 20, 2012).

There were two types of coyote boy performances. The first was to perform shirtless in jeans or sportswear while the second was to dance wearing bikini briefs. In each type of show, coyote boys wore boots, which were central to the fashion style of the show. In most gay pubs, the first show of the evening was performed wearing jeans and lasted about fifteen or twenty minutes. The second

FIGURE 19. Xonix Coyote, a Bangkok coyote boy troupe performing their dance routine and wearing the boots, army-style underwear, and cut-back tank top uniform that symbolized working-class gay masculinity in the 2000s. (Source: *Max* 2009).

show took place after midnight and was performed wearing bikini briefs underwear. The bikini briefs show was the time for customers to tip the coyote boys by placing money in their underwear. This was also a time when members of the audience would give their favorite performer a bottle of soda water, which he poured over his torso so that his penis became visible under his wet underwear. This was known as "soda dancing" (*ten soda*) and was especially appreciated by customers. After the show, the coyote boys would come down off the tabletops to socialize with customers.

Coyote boys were recruited from among both gay and straight men who had a firm and slim but not overly muscular physique as well as a masculine presence. One coyote boy recruitment advertisement posted by the Door Dum Pub in Bangkok stated that the necessary qualifications were being between eighteen and thirty years old; being self-confident; having dancing ability, a good body, and good looks; being at least 170 centimeters tall and weighing no more than sixty kilograms. Most coyote boy dancers were twenty to twenty-five years old, with few remaining as performers beyond the age of thirty. Informants said that most coyote boys loved to dance and wanted to use this skill to earn a living. They were also attracted to becoming coyote boys by the excitement of gay nightlife and the opportunity to work in the ambience of a gay venue where they became the center of other men's attention.

A masculine presence was very important for coyote boy performances. As Käng states, the coyote dance style

> conveys a potent lower-class masculinity. The esthetics of coyotes are also similar to go-go boys. They both often style their hair based on Japanese manga characters, use make-up to whiten their faces and increase the contrast in their eyebrows, and maintain lean, fit bodies. Coyotes, however, will typically incorporate more masculine symbols in their costumes, such as arm or chest bands to highlight their muscles or wear camouflage patterns to reference masculinity in militarism, circuit parties, and Japanese pornography. (Käng 2015, 104)

The meaning of masculinity for a Thai coyote boy was not represented in terms of having a muscular body but rather by the performance of an image of manliness. For young coyote boys, this act of *kek man* or *ab man* manhood was more important than having a highly developed physique. In Thailand's diverse commercial gay scenes, the male body has been commodified for distinct markets, with this human commodity being produced in different masculine forms to conform to sexual tastes of different niche sectors. Appreciating the market—that is, the preferences of different gay audiences or consumers—is thus important for understanding the different types of masculine performance in the country's commercial gay spaces. While *dek bar* sex workers in bars designed their masculine performances to respond to the desires of tourists and older, middle-class Thai gay men, coyote boys who performed in pubs constructed their alternative masculine presentation for younger Thai gay audiences. Käng observes that it is notable that, "within local Thai gay bar spaces oriented towards Thai customers, class marks the type of sex worker available" (Käng 2015, 103).

Coyote Boys Onstage and Offstage

The stage in Thai gay bars and pubs is very important because it is the space at the center of the commodification of masculine bodies. The tabletop and bar top stages for coyote boys were spaces for the eroticization of their bodies as the object of the gaze of other young Thai men. Before coyote boys performed onstage, they got ready in four ways: choosing their clothing, preparing their dance steps, making up the male body, and highlighting the penis.

Fashion, Hair, and Makeup

Coyote boys needed to set their hair with gel to make them look "cool" (niap). They also applied a small amount of makeup, not overly powdered but enough to create a brighter face known as na deng. Some coyote boys wore earrings or ear studs as well as lenses to make their eyes look bigger. Some darkened their eyebrows with black coloring while others brightened their lips with a shade of pink lipstick, all of which helped brighten their face under the stage lights. Käng (2021) describes the procedures and cultural logic behind making the face look "brighter" (deng) as including Botox injections and "big eye" contact lenses (colored contacts with large irises) making the pupils appear larger. Käng observes that "the combined effect of these cosmetic procedures . . . is regarded as 'brightening' one's appearance, which means to look more alert and youthful, not to make one look Caucasian" (Käng 2021, 282). Some coyote boys sported a slim mustache as a sign of their virility. Each coyote boy in a troupe also wore a different distinguishing accessory, such as a hat, necktie, bow tie, handkerchief, belt, arm or shoulder belt, gloves, neck chain, or wings. Some had tattoos on their chest, arms, shoulders, stomach, or back. Many coyote boys believed that tattoos correlated with masculinity, and they got tattooed to enhance their sexual attractiveness. These accessories and fashions were seen as signs of both manliness and elegance. Some coyote boys had cosmetic surgery on their nose and lightened their skin color. Glutathione injections were common among coyote boys because this medical beauty aid helped them have whiter, brighter skin.[3] Having a fair complexion—"white skin" (phiw khao) in Thai—was viewed as a key attribute of a successful coyote boy's good image. Some worked out in fitness centers to build a firmer musculature.

A pub owner who was interviewed said that every coyote boy needed to whiten his face (na deng) and set his hair with gel. While using a small amount of makeup, both their appearance and costume needed to emphasize a masculine look (Ploy, January 7, 2012). The face and hair were especially important to the coyote boy look. One coyote boy who performed in a gay bar stated that

> it's a house rule of the bar that we need to set our hair. Each coyote boy will either set his hair himself or else get it done at a hair salon. Most have a standing hair style (phom tang). I make up my face with a little powder and draw my eyebrows with black color. My lips are shaded a bit pink. All coyote boys like to do this. For my own technique, I mix water with powder to lighten the whitening pigment. It helps to soften the powder so that it makes me have a natural-looking white skin. Also, I outline my eyelids with black color to highlight my eyes. If any coyote

boy doesn't make up his face or set his hair, Mama [bar manager] will complain and decrease his payment for that night. (Oil, December 10, 2011)

Dance Steps and Styles

The dancing styles of coyote boys were not formalized. Each coyote boy could independently create his own dance steps. However, most tried to control their dance routine in what Thai audiences regarded as a masculine way, by not swinging their body too much or in an excessively feminine way, just moving their arms and legs rhythmically. The basic pose was to stretch the legs and twist the body in time with the music, mostly Western dance tunes, while wearing a little smile and making eye contact with audience members. One coyote boy informant observed that

> each coyote boy has his own steps. There are different styles. My own step is seen as funny. The senior coyote boys suggested that dance step to me when I showed them my routine. I love hip-hop. I think it's an easy dance style. After I'd worked for some time, I found my own steps. This work is a kind of art that everyone who loves to dance can appreciate. The art of coyote dancing is to dance to entertain the customer. The successful coyote boys are the ones who can dance skillfully. I think I've still got a lot to learn about how to dance better. (Tar, January 6, 2012)

Coyote boys needed to dance in a way that pubgoers viewed as masculine, in which their dance steps were controlled with slow movements and not acting flamboyantly like a trans woman *kathoey*. One coyote boy related that he practiced in front of a mirror to check how to move like a man. He danced onstage like a sexy man, although he had feminine mannerisms in private after the show. He confirmed that many coyote boys who act like a man onstage are feminine or "girlie" (*sao*) when in the company of close friends (Sun, January 8, 2012).

Having a Firm, Slim Body

The masculinity of a coyote boy was expressed through having a slim body of medium muscularity and an average height of around 170 centimeters. The attractiveness of coyote boys lay in their embodying an eroticization of the look of a student or working-class man. Coyote boys ironically described their slim physiques as the look of the thin body of a drug user (*hun khi-ya*). This did not mean that they were in fact drug users but that they contrasted their slim body size to the much more developed muscularity of the middle-class *kam pu* bodybuilder described in chapter 4. While most coyote boys did some degree of physical training and exercise either at home or in a fitness center, they aimed for a comparatively smaller musculature of their chest, arms, and shoulders to maintain a slim build that was suited to the lithe body movements required by their work as erotic dancers. Only a few coyote boys displayed large muscles and six-packs (Tar and Man, January 6, 2012). One coyote boy related that "those coyote boys who go to the gym want to build their upper torsos, particularly the chest and shoulders. They want to develop a firm body (*hun firm*). You can develop a six-pack from dancing every day. The style of movement in coyote dancing that emphasizes using the upper body helps increase the muscles around the abdomen" (Oil, December 10, 2011). Nevertheless, many coyote boys did not maintain a regular exercise discipline. Their lifestyle often involved partying, going to nightclubs, drinking, and some also took ecstasy. They wanted to enjoy life and often did not invest time and energy in developing their bodies. They just cared about their masculine image when dancing onstage and regarded their body as a medium for acting like a man in their performances. Having developed muscles and a six-pack were less important than achieving a masculine look through fashion and hairstyle. One coyote boy stated that, "although coyote boys do exercise, they also like to take various drugs and drink alcohol. That makes their muscles a bit weak. They don't have the discipline to do regular physical exercise. Some do take whey protein supplements, the by-product of cheese production, to increase their muscularity rapidly when they train in a gym. However, when they stop working out, they'll accumulate fat around their muscles. They put on weight easily if they stop exercising" (Sun, January 10, 2012).

Maintaining a Visible Erection

Gay coyote boy dancing is an erotic performance in which the sexual attractiveness of the male body is emphasized. The outstanding indicator of a coyote boy's manhood was not developed musculature but rather a strong, erect penis. The sexual display of coyote boy dancing involved emphasizing the outlines of the penis under the jeans or briefs. Coyote boys used fluffing techniques called *pan K.*, an abbreviation of *pan khuay*, "to sculpt or mold the cock," to get and keep an erection. As with go-go boy dancers, some coyote boys took Viagra to help them maintain an erection, while others watched porn clips and videos to get aroused while masturbating in private areas of the pub before going onstage. The following statements from coyote boy informants reflect their experiences of maintaining an erection during their performances.

> Your cock should be hard when you're onstage. But some guys don't get an erection. Those coyote boys who've got a hard visible cock (*khuay khaeng*) will satisfy the customers. They'll be the ones who get tips, since

the customers want to see hard cocks. Weak, limp dicks (*khuay mai khaeng*) aren't appreciated. My friends watch porn clips in the pub's toilets before they perform, and they keep their cock erect (*khuay luk*) by using a cock ring. (Man, January 11, 2012)

I take Viagra before the show to keep a hard on. I also use a cock ring around my hard dick and balls (*krapok*). It keeps my dick hard while I'm dancing. For sure, behind the scenes I can see all my friends' cocks. Everyone is naked in the dressing room and some guys like playing funny games with their cocks when we're getting ready to perform. (Keng, January 12, 2012)

Coyote Boy Lifestyles: Aspiring to Live the Thai Gay Dream

Becoming a coyote boy was one way for working-class gay men with limited life options to be able to live the dream of a gay consumer lifestyle. The coyote boy profession was attractive for many younger gay men from less privileged backgrounds because it provided them with a regular income as well as the opportunity to participate in the urban gay lifestyle, find sexual partners, and establish romantic relationships without needing to engage in either commercial sex work as a bar boy or undertake strenuous manual labor—historically, the restricted range of occupations available to lesser-educated working-class men. Coyote boys' lifestyles reflected Bangkok's gay nightlife, and their everyday life was associated with consumer culture and sexual commodification. The life patterns of coyote boys were connected to five dimensions of sociality: emotional attachment, cosmetic surgery, gossip, a consumerist lifestyle, and nightlife.

Emotional Life

The working-class men we interviewed indicated that they had decided to become coyote boy dancers because it provided them with an opportunity for sexual contacts with men they found attractive. The easy availability of sex with other men was a key factor in influencing a decision to become a coyote boy. This contrasted with young men's decision to become a bar boy or go-go boy, for whom the key factor was financial. While in the earlier years of Bangkok's commercial gay scene go-go boys were typically young straight men, in the early twenty-first century growing numbers of working-class gay men also turned to this work as a means of affording an urban gay lifestyle.

As part of their work, coyote boys met people from many different backgrounds. It was common for them to be flirtatious and to have affairs as their occupation required them to aim to please the men who came into their lives. Some customers invited coyote boys to go out on dates and one bar owner related that handsome coyote boys were especially favored, with rich customers often trying to induce them to be their boyfriend (Ploy, January 7, 2012). Some coyote boys did go to live with a customer. However, as was also the case with relationships between customers and *dek bar* go-go boy dancers in gay bars, many of these relationships ended after a short time. The money that a coyote boy could derive from a customer-lover might not be enough to quench his desire for independence. Serial love affairs and broken relationships were common experiences in many coyote boys' lives.

In addition to having relationships with customers, coyote boys also fell in love with each other. Working together every day often led to emotional intimacy and some coyote boys lived together as lovers in their own apartments. Although some gay bars and pubs had a rule prohibiting relations between workers, it was nonetheless common that many bar boys and coyote boys formed deeper relationships beyond the controls exercised by pub owners and bar managers. Within their romantic and sexual circles, many coyote boys also found themselves working together with the former lovers of other coyote boys. One interviewee related that it was not surprising that coyote boys had many boyfriends because it was very easy to meet cute guys on the internet, on social media, and in discotheques (Sun, January 10, 2012). Coyote boys frequently changed boyfriends within their circles and networks, with relations among troupe members at times being marred by romantic competition and jealousy.

Cosmetic Surgery

The coyote boy community was highly competitive. Each dancer had to take special care of his image and appearance to make sure that he presented his body with the maximum sex appeal when dancing onstage. Coyote boys who got more tips from customers were regarded as successful dancers but also became the focus of envy by other coyote boys. To be favored by customers, each boy had to concentrate on his appearance, including the style of clothes, hair styling, makeup, accessories, dance steps, and body presentation. When onstage, each boy had to try to be outstanding in one way or another. In some cases, coyote boys undertook cosmetic surgery such as rhinoplasty nose realignment and skin-whitening procedures. Undergoing this type of surgery and taking time with beauty care required both economic and social capital. Coyote boys learned about these forms of enhancing their appearance from friends in gay bars and pubs.

The preferred rhinoplasty procedure was to make the broad nose typical of many Asian men slightly narrower and more prominent. Botox injections on the face to enhance a youthful appearance were also very popular. Botox is used to sculpt a less-rounded, more slender and angular face (*na riao*), which was considered to be more masculine and more attractive. In the early 2010s, a series of Botox injections cost between six thousand and twelve thousand baht, with the effectiveness of each procedure lasting from six to eight months. As noted earlier, white skin was also very popular and many coyote boys tried to lighten their skin color by injecting glutathione. While rhinoplasty cosmetic surgery and Botox injections were done in commercial clinics, coyote boys often self-administered the skin-whitening glutathione treatment by injecting it themselves. Both white skin and a slender face were important for the body image of coyote boys, with access to glutathione and Botox being widely viewed as essential aspects of improving one's appearance. Technologies of body modification were thus important elements of creating coyote boys' designer bodies that conformed to the norms of masculine attractiveness among young working-class gay men.

Gossip

Sex, love, and body image were all lively topics of gossip in coyote boy circles. Onstage, every coyote boy had to try to stand out to attract the attention of customers who could provide tips. However, anyone who tried too hard to be prominent or noticed onstage was said to "grab the scene" (*yaeng scene*), which often became a source of jealousy. Coyote boys also gossiped about their body images and appearance, especially when another coyote boy may have had cosmetic procedures to change his nose or face. The appearance of nose, lips, eyes, cheeks, and chin were common topics of gossip and teasing, and a performer who was the target of disparaging comments about his appearance may have sought to undergo cosmetic surgery. Rumors often circulated within coyote boy circles about who had good, and not so good, outcomes from cosmetic surgery. In the early 2010s, the starting price of cosmetic surgery for single procedures on the face was around eight thousand baht in Thai clinics.

The love lives and sexual exploits of other coyote boys were also hot topics of gossip and innuendo, with performers who were rumored to have lots of sexual partners being teased as well as being criticized as being easy lays. Better-looking boys who got more attention from a pub owner or a bar *mamasang* were also envied and given a hard time by other dancers. Another focus of gossip in troupes was coyote boys' contrasting images of public masculinity onstage and their private effeminacy offstage. While coyote boys made a living from performing masculinity onstage, they may not have been manlike when in the company of gay friends.

Consumerist Lifestyles

Coyote boys tried to express themselves by wearing trendy fashions and accessories. Having a fashionable image helped them attract the attention of customers. Brand-name shoes, watches, clothing, wallets, and mobile phones were important to enhance their image and signify social acceptance, status, and elegance. Those who possessed brand-name goods would be viewed as rich and considered to be successful dancers. To own a car would lead to even more acceptance. The monetary value of commodities was a much sought-after signifier that upgraded a coyote boy's status in the eyes of his peers. The prices of brand-name fashion items and consumer goods was an indicator of economic inequality among coyote boys and operated to establish social hierarchy within their groups. The more expensive a fashion item or accessory the better, and coyote boys typically showed off their new purchases to others in their troupe in displays of competitive consumerism. Unfortunately, in some cases expensive purchases were only temporary possessions that might need to be hocked at a pawn shop when a coyote boy needed cash.

Becoming a coyote boy was about achieving upward social mobility. It was a young working-class man's occupation that enabled him to participate in an aspirational urban lifestyle. Coyote boy dancing was a good choice for young gay men who loved to dance and wanted to explore the opportunities for an autonomous gay lifestyle offered by Bangkok's nightlife. Like go-go boys in gay bars, many coyote boys were from the provinces and the two groups often had similar class backgrounds. However, in the status-conscious Thai gay scene, being a coyote boy in a pub was viewed as a higher-status occupation than being a go-go boy male sex worker in a bar, as the coyote boy lifestyle offered considerably greater autonomy in forging an independent gay life. Coyote boys also typically made considerably more money than go-go boys, which enabled them to afford more expensive purchases and lead a more lavish lifestyle.

However, not every coyote boy had a chance to earn enough money to buy expensive brand-name items. Some were supported by customers in buying fashion items while others saved their own money for purchases. Some coyote boys stated that to impress their friends as well as customers they changed their mobile phone every two or three months to own the latest, most fashionable model. In their consumption-based displays of status, it was just as important for coyote boys to show off their latest-model phones to other coyote boys as to pub customers. In the late 2000s and early 2010s, Blackberry smartphones were the must-have brand of mobile phone among Bangkok gay men. Smartphones were a common item in displays of status in troupes because it was a product that most coyote boys could afford to buy with their own financial resources. The circulation of money was critical for coyote boys because their image among customers, sex partners, and fellow dancers depended on the thickness of their wallets and the number and quality of their material possessions. Without money or supporters, a coyote boy would be seen as a failure.

Nightlife

Nightlife was at the center of coyote boys' existence. They tended to sleep during the day, wake in the late afternoon or early evening, then go to work as performers until after midnight. Their free time for relaxing with friends in gay pubs and discotheques would be from 2 a.m. to 6 a.m., a lifestyle that often relied on cigarettes, alcohol, and drugs. After work, many socialized by going out drinking and dancing in after-hours gay venues such as G-Star discotheque located in Ratchada Soi 8 in Bangkok's mid-north. In the early 2010s, G-Star was a highly popular gathering place for younger gay men and coyote boys to enjoy the company of friends. Coyote boys were often described as being among Bangkok's "people of the night" (*khon klang-kheun*), with many using expensive party drugs such as ecstasy (*ya E*) or ice (crystal methamphetamine, *ya ice*) as stimulants to help them continue socializing into the early hours and to arouse their libido when dancing in discotheques. Some coyote boy interviewees said that ecstasy aroused their libido and heightened their sexual feelings, with this drug being especially popular among those who enjoyed the opportunities for anonymous sex with patrons in the restrooms and dark rooms that some Bangkok gay pubs installed in the early 2000s. Another reason for using ecstasy was that it was widely viewed as something that would whiten the skin.

However, in some cases, taking too much of these drugs could lead to a loss of self-control and depression as well as damage to the body, eyes, and brain. These drugs were expensive yet regarded as "toys" (*khorng-len*) by many coyote boys. The act of drug use was called "to play or do drugs" (*len ya*), or simply *hi*, from the English "to get high," and was often communal, with coyote boys pooling their money with friends to buy party drugs. In 2012 one dose of ecstasy cost between 2,700 and 3,000 baht in Bangkok.

The Gender and Sexuality of Coyote Boys

Thai coyote boys reflected nonnormative forms of gender and sexuality, as the performance of their male gender role was not fixed within the patterns of heteronormative masculinity. Most of the coyote boys interviewed identified as gay, but some at times also slept with women and they negotiated their masculine image in various situations. They did not always act strong and tough on the normative model of virile Thai masculine gendering and could also be effeminate when with gay friends, such as by using expressive gestures and the polite feminine speech particle *kha* in conversation. The gendering of coyote boys was an alternative, highly contextualized masculinity that was demonstrated publicly through the enactment of stylized performances of manhood and privately through more feminine modes of expression.

Our informants said that they had to *ab man* onstage but confessed that most acted effeminate or *taek sao* when offstage. These masculine *ab man* and feminine *taek sao* forms of gender expression were context-specific, with the former characterizing performances in public spaces and in sexual interactions and the latter being typical of private spaces of socializing among gay friends and acquaintances. While coyote boys were unlikely to be criticized as being *kathoey* or *tut*, "faggots," in the gossipy repartee that characterized the conversation style of their dance troupes and groups of friends, they might nevertheless have been ribbed as *sao taek* or girlie if signs of effeminacy slipped through the public performance of masculinity. This flexible gender enactment contrasts with heterosexual male gendering, which is formed within a singular masculine ideology that views the expression of any feminine characteristics as a threat to the normative male role and status characterized by toughness and virility.

In terms of sexual pleasure and eroticism, coyote boys expressed their homosexual desire for other men, whether male friends or gay customers. Nevertheless, coyote boys did not restrict their sexual pleasure to the binary opposition that sustains the normative gender system. Coyote boys could have sex with both men and women, and their sexual desire and expression were as flexible as their alternative male gendering. Indeed, some women attended coyote boy performances and sought them out as partners, while some coyote boys also had girlfriends whom they met at the pubs where they performed or at other venues. All coyote boys, whether they had male or female partners, socialized together and participated in the same complex gendering and physical self-enhancement practices described above. The community of coyote boys did not conform to either a strictly homosexual or heterosexual modality, just as the gender culture of this community blended masculinity and femininity in its onstage and offstage lifestyles.

Coyote Boys' Alternative Masculinity

The body and physique of the coyote boy was a site for negotiating both masculine and feminine images. Coyote boys engendered their bodies through fashion, makeup, hairstyling, working out, and dancing as well as body modifications through tattooing, Botox and glutathione injections, and cosmetic surgery. The bodies of coyote boys were eroticized canvases on which sexualized materials that represented homoerotically charged images of working-class masculinity were inscribed. The masculinity enacted by coyote boy erotic dancers differed from hegemonic heterosexual Thai masculinity in that it was not fully separated from feminine characteristics. The effeminacy of coyote boys was visible in their hairstyling and on their faces, where they used makeup around their eyes and over their eyebrows, eyelids, lips, and cheeks. However, in contrast to trans women *kathoey* and cross-dressing effeminate gay men, coyote boys dressed in male, rather than female, clothes.

The performances of Thai coyote boys as erotic dancers reflected the dominant patterns of Thai gay culture, which emerged within a field of homosexual consumerism where masculine images are valued sexually while feminine characteristics are common in the aesthetics, practices, and speech forms of everyday gay interaction. Coyote boy performances in Bangkok's gay bars and pubs were not just forms of entertainment. They expressed fundamental patterns that regulate the sexualization of the male body and the playful contextualization of masculine and feminine gender roles that characterizes Thailand's gay culture more broadly. The masculine image of the coyote boy was a blended construct that was formed from multiple sources—from trendy metrosexual fashions to sports styles that support a healthy life, as well as Korean styles that focus on fair skin, a clear bright face, and beauty. The Korean-style male beauty represented by Korean boy bands comprised of cute young men with fair skin, dark eyebrows, slim lips, and prominent noses had a significant influence on the aesthetic of Thai coyote boy masculinity.

As sites for the expression and consumption of eroticized images of masculinity, Bangkok gay bars and pubs in the early 2010s were spaces where both coyote boy dancers and gay customers performed *ab man* masculinity. In these venues all the gay men present, both customers and dancers, performed masculinity for each other to consume visually. Gay pubs had parallels with Bangkok's gay saunas, which are spaces of sexual exploration and expression where the Thai gay men who cruise each other also act in an *ab man* way to attract sexual partners. In Thai gender culture, masculine and feminine genderings are often as strongly marked in discourse and speech forms as in the visible domains of physical expression, body language, and fashion. In the public space of the gay pub, both customers and coyote boys used masculine speech forms such as the masculine sentence particle *khrap*, while offstage and in private both groups often playfully switched to using feminine sentence particles such as *kha, ja,* or *ha*.

As we argued in chapter 3, in contrast to the situation in Western gay cultures in the later decades of the twentieth century, masculine gender presentation in Thai gay cultures was not part of a gay liberation political agenda. This was also the case with Thai coyote boys. For coyote boys, sexual pleasure and sexual attractiveness were more important than ideas of sexual liberation or sexual citizenship. The masculine bodies of coyote boys were not fashioned in terms of a politics of identity but rather as a sexual commodity in response to the market and the individual search for sexual pleasure. And in this commodified gendering, coyote boys' masculine characteristics were not entirely separated from feminine mannerisms.

Cross-Cultural Reflections on Thai Coyote Boys and *Kam Pu*

Historically in the West, male homosexuality and effeminacy were often indelibly associated, sometimes even becoming synonymous. As Bethany Coston and Michael Kimmel observe, "Male homosexuality has long been associated with effeminacy (i.e. not being a real man) throughout the history of Western societies; the English language is fraught with examples equating men's sexual desire for other men with femininity: molly and nancy-boy in 18th-century England, buttercup, pansy, and she-man of early 20th-century America, and the present-day sissy, fairy, queen, and faggot" (Coston and Kimmel 2012, 183). George Chauncey (1985, 1994) points out that masculine-identified homosexual men living in early twentieth-century New York detested the "fairies" or effeminate men they nevertheless had sex with. Manly homosexual men looked down on "sissy" men and instead identified themselves as "queer." These different homosexual identities of fairy and queer emphasized the valorization of masculinity and the denigration of femininity. In Western gay cultures the embodiment of masculinity and femininity has at times become embroiled in vehement rhetoric and cultural politics. In earlier decades, some masculine-identified gay activists argued for a separation of more feminine gay men from masculine gay society. Jack Malebranche (2006, 48) argued that in the West homosexuality assigns the stigma of innate femininity to all men who engage in sex acts with other men. To resist this stereotypical attribution of effeminacy, he contended that males who love other males should live their lives away from effeminate gay culture, and he termed masculine loving between men "androphilia" (2006, 53). Malebranche's sex/gender politics involved setting up a boundary between masculinity and femininity in gay culture, so that love between men could be reimagined in terms of masculine ideals. He also argued that achieving political and legal rights required a separation of gay masculinity from the stigmatized effeminacy that dominated stereotypes within heterosexual culture. Tim Bergling (2001) observes that in this context many straight-acting gay men came to see effeminate gay men as slowing their progress toward achieving equal rights.

However, the cultural politics of excluding feminine men did not go unchallenged. Bergling (2001) argues that Western gay prejudice against feminine men and the valorization of masculine straight acting is rooted in a gender hierarchy that positions men above women and supports a misogynistic culture in which men look down on womanly behaviors in other men. Kittiwut Taywaditep (2001) similarly contends that the ideology of hegemonic masculinity is built on a value system in which men and masculinity are considered superior to women and femininity, while Peter Hennen (2008) maintains that negative attitudes toward unmanly gays, which he terms "the effeminacy effect," emerge from a discursive disciplining of male gender that positions it in opposition to the gender of women and effeminate homosexual men. Coston and Kimmel (2012) are of the view that gay men who conform to hegemonic norms secure their position in the gender hierarchy by adopting heterosexual masculine roles that subordinate both women and effeminate gay men. For Michael Messner (1997, 83) this separation of marginalized effeminate traits from a newly constituted hegemonic gay masculinity involves a politics of identity in which mainstream gay culture collaborated with patriarchy. In a similar vein, Michael Kimmel (1994, 2001) argues that contemporary gay manhood was born from a renunciation of the feminine that produced an at times rancorous separation between femme and macho gay men during the gay liberation era and spawned a politics of masculine gender conformity in many Western gay communities.

Thai Gay Effeminacy and Coyote Boy Masculinity as Gender Play

In contrast to the historical politicization of gender roles in some Western gay communities, early twenty-first-century Bangkok gay cultures presented a more complex picture of diverse influences and trends of gendering. On the one hand, the culture of middle-class Thai *kam pu* could be seen as reflecting Western and international gay cultures that devalue femininity and discriminate against "sissies." On the other hand, working-class coyote boy gendering was an example of considerable playfulness with gender.

In contrast to the polarized separation of masculinity and femininity in the culture of gay *kam pu* bodybuilders, the gender culture of coyote boys was a gender pastiche that drew on both masculine and feminine characteristics. The mixed gendering of working-class coyote boy performers was more playful than the masculine presentation of middle-class gay *kam pu*. This blending of genders, in which coyote boys played with both feminine and masculine traits and negotiated womanly and manly behaviors in various social situations, is a common form of gender nonconformity in some sections of Thailand's gay communities. Coyote boys respectively expressed masculine and feminine characteristics in different social situations, and in their working-class communities the male body served as a platform on which the boundaries of the masculine and feminine poles of the heteronormative gender binary were often blended.

Judith Butler's (1988, 1990, 1993) account of the performativity of gender provides a conceptual lens for appreciating working-class Thai gay men's playful acting with feminine and masculine genders. This theory of gender is based on a notion of speech acts in which masculinity and femininity are brought into being from the repetition of gendered actions. Butler argues that gender is an enforced cultural performance that is compelled by social sanctions and compulsory heterosexuality and does not express an inner core or pre-given identity (see also Jagger 2008, 20). For Butler (1990) the performances of drag queens represent the instability of the relationship between sex and gender and attest to the contingent nature of both masculine and feminine identities by exposing gender as a cultural code that relies on imitation and practiced repetition.

We can draw on Butler's account to understand the feminine acting practiced by many Thai gays, whose contextual effeminacy playfully imitates dominant gender norms. However, in contrast, the feminine acts of Thai gays do not represent a challenge to the regulatory regime of compulsory heterosexual genders. Rather, Thai gay effeminacy is a form of gender play in which feminine expression is used to create social networks among gay friends. At the same time, Thai gay men negotiate masculine forms of expression in sexual settings. In contrast to Butler's view of drag performances as a form of subversive gender politics that challenges heteronormative hierarchies, Thai gay men use varieties of feminine and masculine expression to respectively construct peer groups and form sexual relationships. Thai gay gender play does not have a political goal but rather is a form of contextualized sociality.

There are three key findings in understanding the alternative masculinity embodied by Thai coyote boy dancers. First, their performance of masculine images and characteristics is open-ended. While their onstage masculine performance is regulated within the straight-acting norms of *ab man*, coyote boys tactically engage these norms in different contexts. Their masculinity is a nonnormative gendering that blends both feminine and masculine traits. Furthermore, coyote boys' masculine identities are not necessarily linked to normative patterns of male sexuality. They live their sexual lives and find sexual pleasure with both men and women. In breaking from the heteronormative gender ideology that views sex as a supposedly natural and determinative foundation of gender, their male sexual physiology does not limit either their gender expression or their range of sexual experiences.

Second, Thai gay culture's commodified spaces of bars and pubs have formed sites where coyote boys' bodies are displayed to service the sexual desires and imaginations of gay customers. Customers regard coyote boys' masculine body expressions as sexual objects and coyote boys accordingly have learned to create images of masculinity that both attract and satisfy their gay customers. Onstage, *ab man* manhood enacted according to heteronormative patterns has attained economic value. However, offstage after the show, they often express feminine characteristics when in the company of other coyote boys and among gay friends. Their masculinity is not static but rather fluid and depends on the *kala-thesa* "time and place" social context.

And third, the masculinity of working-class Thai coyote boys represents an alternative male gendering that demonstrates continuities between straight-acting *ab man* and feminine-acting *taek sao* according to context and social setting. This alternating, dual expression emerged from processes of social learning that are found not only among coyote boys but also among Thai gay men in general. The sexualized commercial spaces of gay bars and pubs have provided opportunities for public recognition of and economic reward for coyote boys' learned *ab man* acting like a man, while private spaces offstage have provided sites for expressing equally learned *taek sao* effeminate behavior. Coyote boys thus constitute one instance of broader patterns found across Thai gay culture and by which homosexual men negotiate their nonnormative gender status in terms of both masculinity and femininity.

The multiple masculine and feminine performances of coyote boys in Bangkok's gay venues reflect class-based patterns of gendered socialization among working-class and lower-middle-class Thai gay men, the majority of whom have migrated to the metropolis from provincial towns and rural villages. Their masculinities are not restricted by the ideology of hypermasculinity embodied by middle-class bodybuilder gay men, who by contrast are constrained within a more rigidly disciplined gym-based form of manliness that dominates commercial media both within gay communities and among the wider public. The differing masculine images of these class segments of Thai gay men are regulated by distinct gendering discourses. Among working-class coyote boys, the masculine body is subject to looser controls that can incorporate feminine characteristics while, in contrast, middle-class gay men subject themselves to more constant forms of self-surveillance to avoid expressing feminine traits and behaviors.

Part III

THE INTERNET AND THE MASCULINIZATION OF GAY SEX

6

CONFIRMATIONS OF MASCULINITY IN THAI GAY VIDEO CHAT ROOMS

In this chapter we consider the masculine discourses and sexualized embodiments represented in Thai male same-sex video chat rooms in the Camfrog online platform. This research provides an understanding of same-sex desire in the masculine culture of mostly younger Thai men at a historical juncture in the early 2010s when online platforms began to supplant gay print magazines as the main media by which homosexually oriented Thai men consumed images of attractive male bodies. Camfrog was perhaps the most influential and widely accessed web-based chat platform for younger homosexually inclined Thai men in the late 2000s and early 2010s. In the years immediately before smartphone technology became widely available in Thailand, and gay dating applications like Grindr, Hornet, and Blued became influential platforms for facilitating gay hookups in the country, Camfrog was the most important platform for online sexual encounters and hookups for both homosexual and heterosexual men and women in the country. Ronnapoom Samakkeekarom and Pimpawan Boonmongkon (2011, 121) cite media research undertaken in 2006 that revealed Thailand ranked third in the world for use of Camfrog, following the United States and China. The importance of Camfrog in facilitating and informing the male same-sex cultures of this period is reflected in studies of how this online platform was important for sexual health promotion in Thailand (see, for example, Ronnapoom and Pimpawan 2011; Ronnapoom et al. 2008a, 2008b.[1] As networking for sexual hookups in Thailand relocated from real spaces of public parks, pubs, bars, and saunas to online domains, interventions for communicating sexual health messages among homosexually active men also needed to relocate to the virtual world.

Here, we consider the dominant forms of discourse that structured interactions in the male same-sex chat rooms on Camfrog. While the men who met and engaged in virtual sexual interactions on Camfrog remained largely silent on the question of their identity as gay or homosexual, male same-sex practices were nonetheless framed as strong confirmations of masculine gender identity. As an online video platform devoted almost wholly to sexual interaction, relations on Camfrog were formed within accentuated and intensified patterns of the *ab man* masculinity detailed in preceding chapters. The new medium of web-based video brought into even sharper relief the patterns of eroticized masculine performance that had been nurtured by gay print magazines in earlier decades.

"Men Who Have Sex with Men Are Real Men"

This chapter also reveals the importance of distinguishing between sexuality and sexual identity, on the one hand, and gender and gender identity, on the other. We argue that the sexual activities of male users of Camfrog did not constitute forms of sexual identity but rather were expressions and confirmations of masculine gender identity. The same-sex erotic practices enacted by male Camfrog users took place in a highly masculine expressive and discursive setting, which was underscored by a common idiom among users: "Men who have sex with men are real men" (*chai dai chai kheu yort chai*). Camfrog gay chat room users constructed and recognized alternative masculinities through an affirmation of their status as *bi*, which, while an abbreviation of the English term "bisexual," was used in Camfrog chats to denote masculine same-sex eroticism rather than an actual interest in both female and male partners. Male Camfrog users exhibited a wide range of characteristics that were differentiated in terms of finely nuanced masculinity that distinguished between greater and lesser degrees of ascribed manhood. The DJs who managed interactions between men in Camfrog's chat rooms referred to participants simply by the borrowed English term "user" (*yusoe*); and following this usage we also use "male user" or "user" to refer to the men who entered the male same-sex video chat rooms. The term "male user" is not a notion based on sexual identity but rather here connotes the masculine presentation of the men who logged on to Camfrog and who emphasized their virility.

We use the expression "Camfrog gay chat rooms" to refer to the online spaces of male same-sex eroticism on the Camfrog digital platform, even though, as discussed below, the word "gay" itself was largely absent from the discourses communicated in these virtual domains. An increasing association of "gay" with perceptions of effeminacy made this term problematic for many younger men in the early twenty-first century. While it was rare to find the word "gay" in the messaging and conversations between the men who accessed Camfrog's video chat rooms, many of these rooms did include "gay" in their names to indicate that they were private spaces for men who were looking for male-male sexual activity. The word "gay" was used in the names of these rooms to differentiate them from other rooms on Camfrog that had a heterosexual focus. While these online spaces were called "gay video chat rooms," the men who accessed them claimed diverse sexual identities and in no way did these chat sites cater exclusively to interactions among men who identified with the label "gay."

This chapter presents a contrast to the findings detailed in previous chapters on the impact of gay print media magazines in the 1980s and 1990s, which emphasized gay identity formation among middle-class men of working age. Rather than affirming homosexual identity, new online spaces such as Camfrog were accessed by younger men of high school and college age from a range of socioeconomic backgrounds, including both working class and middle class, and were marked by a deemphasis on gay identity. However, this chapter does confirm the findings detailed in the preceding chapters that a distinctive feature of modern Thai gay cultures is the greater importance of masculine gender identity relative to same-sex sexual identity. While differentiating between sexual identity and gender identity is important in much Western gay studies and queer theoretical analysis, as well as in studies of East Asian and Sinophone homosexual cultures, in Thailand's Southeast Asian cultures of same-sex eroticism the boundaries between gender and sexual identity are much less clearly drawn.

Most users of Camfrog chat rooms were younger men in their late teens and early twenties. In the early 2000s, these men were the first generation of Thai males for whom online platforms were central to their search for sexual interaction and identity formation. In these years, internet cafes that offered relatively cheap access to online media became common features of Thailand's cities and towns. These internet cafes were not limited to downtown locations and were found across urban spaces, including outer suburbs and older commercial precincts with cheaper rents. High school boys and college and university students were among the largest group of customers in these internet cafes, which often separated terminals with office partitions that provided a degree of privacy, enabling the more daring users to expose themselves and masturbate in front of the webcams. The cheaper internet cafes were also accessible to significant numbers of working-class men. Unlike the case of the earlier generation of print media gay magazines, whose price largely limited their circulation to middle-class men of working age, the proliferation of cheap online access in the early 2000s enabled men of almost all class backgrounds to interact in virtual domains.

In this period, increasing numbers of working-age men could also afford personal computers, enabling them to access online chat rooms in the privacy of their own homes. The proliferation of online access across almost all social strata in the country's urban centers meant that the virtual spaces of platforms such as Camfrog enabled both working-class and middle-class men, as well as younger and older men, to meet virtually in these domains. The growth of online access also enabled younger men who were still in high school or college to access sexual images and discourses that had been unavailable to males of earlier generations.

This chapter analyses the impact of digital media on Thailand's gay cultures in the period when online access was negotiated via computer terminals that required cable connections and were fixed in place. This work was conducted in the years immediately before the arrival of mobile internet connections accessed from smartphones and reflects a period when online technologies first provided access to discourses, images, and performances of same-sex eroticism beyond Thailand's middle class. This was a period that also marked the progressive decline and eventual demise of Thai gay magazines, with almost all gay media having migrated online by the middle years of the 2010s.

The gender culture of Thai Camfrog reflected the importance of notions of masculinity among emerging cohorts of homosexually active young men in the early 2010s. This study of Camfrog users shows that the culture of gay masculinity that emerged in print media in the later decades of the twentieth century was perpetuated among younger men in the early twenty-first century, and indeed was accentuated by the first generation of online media. In Camfrog the norms of masculinity that had been established in preceding decades through gay magazines became the standard of male sexual attractiveness among men whose first contact with Thai gay culture was often online rather than in real spaces of gay venues. Conformity to these norms of masculinity was a requirement for being seen as sexually attractive in these online communities. In particular, the online spaces of Camfrog often reflected the slim style of masculinity exemplified by coyote boys rather than the gym-enhanced bodies of middle-class *kam pu* gay musclemen. This indicates that Camfrog was primarily a space for lower-middle-class, working-class, and younger gay men rather than wealthier middle-class gay men.

Shaka McGlotten (2007) argues that video chat rooms provided possibilities for constructing and intensifying alternative intimate scenarios. Users could decide to engage in a range of erotic acts including, but not limited to, undressing, showing their face or their naked body, exposing their cock or ass, and filming themselves having sex with a partner. At the time our study was conducted in the early 2010s, McGlotten's account provided an accurate picture of Thai cyberspace as enabling the construction of intimate interactive scenarios in which sexual desire was free and largely unfettered. Käng (2015, 98) notes that several years later, in the mid-2010s, there was a series of media exposés of students selling sex to older Thai men on chat room platforms such as Camfrog. Both teenage boys and girls engaged in this practice, though the more common trope reported in the media was of girls using the money from online sex work to buy luxury consumer goods like designer handbags. This situation was often media fodder for conservative tirades that new media were leading to a decline in morals among Thailand's increasingly materialist youth.

In the following years, internet surveillance units of the Thai Ministry of Culture and the Thai police sought to regulate or even ban some same-sex online chat rooms. For example, in 2021, the Thai authorities intervened in the Only-Fans online site. However, at the time we were studying Camfrog in the early 2010s, Thai online chat rooms were free of state monitoring and regulation. This lack of regulation meant that male same-sex video chat rooms provided new virtual sites for enacting different modes of masculinity, where users could express sexual desires and seek pleasure and forms of intimacy with other men without being concerned about their sexuality or identity. Virtual spaces enabled men to reach out to other users whose masculine images attracted and interested them, and Camfrog provided opportunities for expressing alternative masculinities by enabling users to privately explore more diverse senses of gendered being.

This research was conducted as an exercise in virtual ethnography. Narupon began using Camfrog in late 2011, registering and creating an ID that enabled him to access male same-sex video chat rooms and chat with other users. This permitted the author to read the messages posted and observe the sexual activities between users and the DJ who coordinated them. Camfrog chat rooms combined audio, video, and text interactions, and the author could observe and interact with users via microphone, camera, and keyboard. Conversations with some users were recorded, as were conversations between users and DJs. These conversations were transcribed and analyzed to interpret the discourses of masculinity that they reflected.

Male Same-Sex Video Chat Rooms on Thai Camfrog

A video chat room is a software program used for communicating with others on the internet. The Camfrog video chat software program was launched in 2003 and was supported in many languages, including Thai. Camfrog permitted people worldwide to find partners in a wide range of chat rooms on internet-accessible personal computers, enabling users to chat in real time using both audio and video. After installing Camfrog on their computer, a user chose a username ID, or nickname or handle, and a password. After logging on, a user could select from a range of icons for diversely named chat sessions, called "rooms." When they clicked on the icon of a room that interested them, a user could see a directory of the IDs of the other registered users who were then currently logged on and accessing that room. To start a video chat, a user first sent an instant message (IM) to the person they wanted to communicate with. Clicking on a user's nickname ID would then start video chat with that person.

In the early 2010s, the Thai-language Camfrog platform included many male same-sex video chat rooms. Users distinguished between two types of same-sex chat rooms depending on the degree of sexual content permitted. The first type was called a "white room" (*horng si-khao*), which prohibited sexual activities and explicit video content. An example of a white room was one labeled the "Gay Best Friends" room. The second type of chat room was a sex room popularly called "a cock-showing room" (*horng cho* [show] *khuay*), which allowed users to use the camera on their device to expose their bodies and show sexual acts. At the time of this study, Camfrog chat rooms could only be named using the Roman alphabet. Nevertheless, the Camfrog sites for Thailand included many same-sex "cock-showing rooms" that often had explicit names, typically based on idiosyncratically spelled hybrid English-Thai terms and acronyms. The names of some of the "cock-showing rooms" on Thai Camfrog in 2011 were Gays Mans GKBT; Gay 4 Guy Mail; Gay 4 Guy Server; Gay 4 Men M9; Gay Uniform; Gay 17Up Club X; Gay 18Up Man; Gay 18Up Boy; Gay 7Eleven Live; Gay Bad BoyG; Gay Café Candy; Gay Cam City; Gay Hot Thai Bar; Gay K Boy (i.e., "gay cock [*khuay*] boy"); Gay M Boy 4; Gay Narok X Menz (i.e., "gay hell X men's"); Gay Xshow; and Men 4 Men N9. These "cock-showing" sex rooms were much more popular than the tamer "white rooms." Gay chat rooms were also created for different cities and localities across the country, such as Chiang Mai, Chonburi, Khorat, Phuket, Udonthani, and Phitsanulok. These regional chat rooms typically included the name of the city in the name of their icon.

Camfrog provided information on the number of users who logged on and accessed each chat room each day; this data enabled us to understand the relative popularity of different rooms. Among the various video chat rooms on the Thailand Camfrog site, the male same-sex rooms were among the most popular in the country. On each day of the research period, the top five video chat rooms always included at least two or three male same-sex rooms, reflecting the importance of Camfrog for Thailand's cultures of same-sex interested men in the early 2010s. Each night of the period of online research in 2011, popular male same-sex chat rooms such as Gay 4 Guy Server and Gay 4 Men M9 were accessed by at least twelve hundred users. Table 6.1 shows the highest number

TABLE 6.1   Top five Camfrog gay chat rooms in 2011

GAY CHAT ROOM	HIGHEST RECORD OF USER NUMBERS	DAY OF RECORD
Gay 4 Gay LCD	1,901	November 11, 2011
Gay Cam City	1,482	August 5, 2011
Gay 4 Guy Mail	1,321	October 8, 2011
Gay Bad Boy	721	March 18, 2011
Gaythai Esan Plaza	658	October 5, 2011

Source: Compiled from data listed on the Camfrog website in 2011.

TABLE 6.2   Monthly rental fees for chat rooms on Thai Camfrog in 2011

NUMBER OF USERS	ROOM RATE—BAHT PER MONTH
50	700
100	1,000
200	1,300
300	1,500

Source: Compiled from data listed on the Camfrog website in 2011.

of users in several male same-sex chat rooms on Thai Camfrog recorded during the research period.

These same-sex chat rooms were each operated by an owner who rented the online space for a fee paid to the Camfrog Thailand Company. Table 6.2 lists the room rates, which were based on the number of users who could log on and enter a room at any one time.

Only the owner of a Camfrog chat room needed to pay a fee to Camfrog Thailand. After registering their online username ID for Camfrog, users could access these rooms for free. The owner of a chat room had authority to determine permissible interactions and regulate everything that took place in each room. Each room also had a moderator, called a DJ, whose role in encouraging sexual activity among users is detailed below.

When they logged on and accessed a video chat room, users' ID names were listed in different colors in a user directory to identify the various categories of users online at any given time. The owner of a room, who exercised overall control of users' activities, was identified in red. The owner had the authority to eject or "kick out" (*te*) users who were reported by the DJ moderator as having breached the rules or etiquette of a room. For example, if someone criticized the DJ or used crude or impolite words with other users, that person would be refused access and kicked out of the room. When someone was kicked out of a chat room, an automatic message was shown that was visible to all users. Such a sample message was, "Camfrog server kicked out Monkykala for swearing.

Please don't flood." "Don't flood" (*ya thuam*) was a slang expression used by room administrators to mean not to disturb other people in the chat room or flood other users with excessive chat.

The ID icon of the room DJ or moderator of a room was identified in green. The DJ played an important role in talking with the users through the online microphone and playing recorded music and songs to set the mood of the room. The DJ had access to the webcam on each user's computer and so could see all users who were logged on at any given time, and all users could also hear the DJ's voice. Each user could also see and chat directly with the DJ by clicking on his ID and sending a message.

In addition to moderating activity in the room they were responsible for, DJs promoted the products and services of the room's commercial sponsors, with sponsors paying between 500 and 1,500 baht per month to have an advertisement placed in a chat room. The main products advertised were men's underwear, oil for enlarging the penis, Viagra, skincare and skin whitening products, weight loss pills, gay bars and discotheques, and gay movies and porn on VCDs and DVDs. Camfrog's gay chat rooms were commercial ventures, with an important role of the DJ being to encourage the maximum number of users to stay logged on to the room that he managed to generate income from advertisers. Each gay chat room had ten to twelve DJs, who logged on to entertain users at different times of the day, with all the rooms operating twenty-four hours a day. DJs usually worked for shifts of one to three hours. Table 6.3 lists the online ID names and work times of the DJs who moderated the Gay for Guy video chat room on December 6, 2011.

While the DJs and users were all identified with online names, the identities of the owners of the different chat rooms were not made public and could not be identified for this project.

TABLE 6.3   ID names and work times of DJs moderating the Gay for Guy Camfrog chat room on December 6, 2011

TIME	NAME OF DJ
00:00–02:00	Pae
02:00–05:00	Sherry
05:00–08:00	Dek Ram
08:00–11:00	Plaeng Thap
11:00–14:00	Gibsey
14:00–18:00	Khao Oat
18:00–20:30	Luckker BB
20:30–22:30	New
22:30–00:00	Han and Tee

The DJ used the color blue to identify users who he regarded to be attractive and handsome, with the men whose IDs were highlighted with this color being especially appreciated by other users. The DJ used the color gray to identify users who were masturbating, having sex, or exposing their penis. These men would then become the focus of attention for other users who would come to view their sexual activities. While watching other users engage in sexual activities was a primary interest, all users nevertheless still had to respect the rules laid down by the DJ. The color black was used to identify general users who accessed a gay video room to chat with the DJ, friends, or sexual partners. All users were able to post their messages on the main page of the room to invite others to chat with them via direct messaging.

Users were able to present themselves in five different statuses including online, private, hiding, away, and busy. Some users accessed a room but kept their computer camera turned off and so hid themselves from other users. In such cases, the DJ would ask them to turn on their camera and not pause the video. If anyone failed to follow the DJ's suggestions, they would be denied access to the room. Users could ask the DJ for their ID to be marked with a specific color when they logged on, but the allocation of a color was at the discretion of individual DJs. For example, users could ask to be identified in blue to mark them as attractive, but if a DJ did not regard them to be good-looking, he might criticize them publicly in front of the other users who were logged on.

Some of Camfrog's gay chat rooms were especially popular and it was often the case that more users attempted to log on to these rooms than the server could support. Access to a room would be stopped when it reached its capacity number of users. To accommodate this situation, each gay video chat room also had a "reserved room" for users who waited to be granted access to the main room. At times when the server had reached its capacity, the owner would post a reserved room message on the page to indicate that users should log on to the reserved room and wait there to be granted access to the main room. For example, the reserved room for the Gay For Guy main room was given the name Gay For Guy SMS. The most popular main gay rooms during the research period were Gay For Guy, Gay 18Up, Gay Cam, Gay Hot Thai, GayX, Guy GBKT, and Man 4 Men. These popular gay rooms permitted online sexual activities for users. There were also some automated messages from other rooms that invited users to move to chat in that room. If users became bored with the room they were logged into, they could easily change rooms to look for potentially more interesting activities. DJs could also send messages to users to let them know that there were other rooms that still had space to welcome them.

Most users accessed the rooms to chat and watch other users engage in sexual activities. When a user wanted to chat with another logged-on user, he would send an instant message, IM, directly to that person. While the names of chat rooms and user IDs were restricted to using roman script, users could chat with other users in Thai. If a user just wanted to see another user via his computer camera, he would click on the user's ID and his video would appear on-screen. This kind of observing other users without sending an IM was called *sorng*, "spotlighting," "focusing on," or "lurking." *Sorng* denotes following an internet post but not commenting or identifying yourself to the author of that post. Some users posted messages that invited others to join them privately. These users often wanted to exchange videos of their exposed bodies and masturbate together in a private communication known as *wet*, abbreviated from the English word "private." Users could change their status by clicking on a private mode icon symbolized by "P." Users understood that when they agreed to a private contact, they would be expected to expose their genitals and engage in cybersex. Some users were regulars in the same chat room and had friends in the room who would join them for a virtual party. The owner of a main room could also set up a party for members as a special event.

Some men from working-class backgrounds who identified as "real men" (*phu-chai thae*) also accessed Camfrog's chat rooms to seek out gay men looking to buy sex. These men used Camfrog to freelance as sex workers and would chat with users who might be interested in meeting them in real life and pay for sex. Some DJs intervened to prevent users from arranging to sell sex, but often these arrangements fell under the moderator's radar or else were tacitly allowed to take place. Anecdotal reports indicate that some women also used Camfrog's heterosexual chat rooms to sell sex to men. While gay video chat rooms served various purposes for men from diverse backgrounds and of different sexual orientations, masculine expression was very significant for all of them. Every man who accessed these rooms presented himself in a manly way in terms of both language use and bodily mannerisms.

Sexual Communication in Camfrog Gay Video Chat Rooms

It was common for the users of Camfrog gay chat rooms to use an ID name with sexual connotations. User IDs had to be written in roman script, and many men were creative in mixing romanized Thai and English terms to create a user ID that referred to sexual organs, sexual activity, and masculine attractiveness. Not all users chose IDs with sexually explicit meanings. However, those that did used expressions that reflected three dimensions of manliness—namely, general masculine characteristics, the male genitalia, and sexual acts.

Users chose names that often suggested they were a top, preferring the insertive *ruk* role. Many of the terms in usernames were borrowed or adapted from English, such as *man*, *bi man*, *boy*, and *king*. Popular Thai terms in IDs were *lor* ("handsome") and *ruk* ("top" or "insertive"). *Man* was a term used to confirm manliness and reject effeminacy. As noted in previous chapters, in Thai gay parlance *man* denotes having a masculine presentation rather than possessing a male physiology. Many users also specified that they worked in masculine occupations such as soldier, policeman, engineer, or personal trainer in a gym. Many users also created a name that included the letter "X," as in "X-rated," to denote sex and erotic expression. The following list provides examples of masculine usernames on Thai Camfrog. Nonstandard spellings of Thai words were often used in creating roman script usernames. Where relevant, the standard transcription of Thai terms in usernames is included in parentheses.

Username	Meaning
Army_Staff69	A man who works in the army and likes oral sex
Armythai999	Refers to a soldier in Thai army
Bigboyhotmale	A teenage boy who enjoys hot sex
Biman69	A masculine (*man*) bi-identified user who likes oral sex
Boy_2in1_Man	A masculine (*man*) teenage boy who is both insertive and receptive (i.e., two-in-one)
Dek_Mor_5_Man	A masculine (*man*) teenage boy (*dek*) who is in senior high school year 5 (*mor 5*)
Engineer_Biman	A masculine *bi*-identified user who is an engineer
Kingmans	A masculine (*man*) user who prefers the insertive sexual role
Man_dudee	A good-looking (*du di*) masculine user
Man4man	A masculine user who wants another masculine user
Manlove35	Thirty-five-year-old user seeking the love of a masculine (*man*) guy
Mantopmanz	A masculine user who plays the top role in sex with masculine guys
Man_X_Guy	A masculine user who loves sex
O_X_Man_Show	An exhibitionist masculine user who loves others to watch
Playboy_XK	A playboy who loves sex and cocks (K, i.e., *khuay*)
X_Armyboy_X	A teenage boy in the army who loves sex
X_Men_King5	A top who loves sex with masculine guys

The second type of username emphasized the male sex organ. The Thai terms used most often in this regard were *khuay* and *kador*, both of which were often shortened to the letter *K*, the first letter of the transcriptions of these two words. The crude slang term *kador* could also be signified by the less confrontational abbreviated roman script forms of "dor" or "door." In gay video chat rooms, including *khuay* in a username was very attractive because it would be understood that the user was ready to show his cock and wanted cybersex. Many users also cited their penis size. *Jet niw*, "seven inches," was a popular penis size that was taken as denoting a big penis. The list below provides examples of usernames that referred to the penis. Playful nonstandard spellings of Thai words were also often used in creating this variety of roman script username. Where relevant, the standard transcription of Thai terms in usernames is included in parentheses.

Username	Meaning
Bigdoor_7	A big seven-inch cock (*dor*, from *krador*)
Dekdekkbig	A teenage boy (*dek*) with a big cock (K)
Deklor_K_Yai	A handsome teenage boy (*dek lor*) with a big cock (*khuay yai*)
Door_dek_naluk	The cock (*dor*) of a cute teenage boy (*dek na-rak*)
Doordektai	The cock (*dor*) of a teenage boy (*dek*) from southern Thailand (*tai*)
Kadoordek	The cock (*kador*) of a teenage boy (*dek*)
K_boyman	The cock (K) of a masculine (*man*) teenage boy (*boy*)
K_gay_show_K	A gay user ready to show his cock (K)
KKK_BIG_KKK	An exceptionally big cock (K)
K7Biruk_man_man	An active (*ruk*) bi-identified user who is very masculine (*man man*) and has a seven-inch cock (K7)
K7K7_Krub	seven-inch cock (*krub* denotes the masculine sentence particle *khrap*)
K7man	A masculine (*man*) guy with a seven-inch cock
Kuaydek_M_Pai	The cock (*khuay*) of a teenage boy in the final years of high school (M_Pai = *mor plai*).
Munyaimakcodcod	A very big penis, literally "It's very big, my cock" (*man yai mak*; "cod" refers to the English term "big")
7X_formen	A seven-inch cock for men

The third type of username referred to sexual practices and intercourse. A popular Thai term was *yet*, "to fuck," and its variants. Because *yet* is regarded as exceptionally crude, it was often softened to the abbreviated form *ye* in gay slang. The English "yes" was also sometimes used in place of *yet* because many Thais pronounce a final "s" of English words as "t," with "yes" sometimes being pronounced as "yet." A less common term for anal sex was *at*, "to stuff/press in." Another popular term in usernames was *mok*, an abbreviated form of the English term "smoke," which has become a slang term for oral sex. A preference for mutual oral sex was denoted by "69," while masturbation was typically referred to with the Thai expressions *chak wao*, "to fly a kite," or simply *wao*. In Thai flying a kite is referred as *chak wao*, literally "to pull on (*chak*) a kite (*wao*) string." The act of repeatedly pulling on the string of a kite as it flies into the wind is compared to the movement of the hand when masturbating. Masturbating was also often called *tok*, abbreviated from the English "stroke [the penis]." The use of terms for sexual acts in a username indicated that a user was prepared to engage in explicit acts online. The following list provides a sample of usernames that indicated sexual activity. As in the previous lists, nonstandard and playful spellings of Thai words were often used in creating roman script IDs. Where relevant, the standard transcription of Thai terms used is included in parentheses.

Username	Meaning
Dek_Mok_Show	A teenage boy (*dek*) who shows oral sex (*mok*).
Dek_Yed_Dee	A teenage boy (*dek*) who fucks well (*yet di*)
Fuckkin69	Fucking and mutual oral sex (*kin* ["eat"] 69)
Gu_Yak_Don_Ye	I want to be fucked (*ku yak don yet*)
HI_HI_YED_GUN	Get high (i.e., chemsex) and fuck each other (*yet kan*)
K_Chon_K	Cock (K) rubs against (*chon*) cock
King_7_Yedkeng	An active (*king*) user with a seven-inch cock who is good at fucking (*yet keng*)
Manudman	A masculine user who fucks (*at*) another masculine guy
Munmun6969	Mutual oral sex (69) is great fun (*man man*)
Nam_Ja_Tack	I'll cum (*nam* [water or cum] *ja taek* [will break out])
69Yed_Free	Sucking (69) and fucking (*yet*) for free
3Yet	Three-way/threesome fucking (*yet*)
Wowkan	Wank each other (*wao kan*)
Wow_Wow_King	An active user into masturbation (*wao*)
X_yes_ok_69	Fucking (*yet*) and sucking (69) are both OK
Yak_Don_Yes	I want to be fucked (*yak don yet*)
Yedfreeyeddeedee	Free for great fucking (*yet di di*)
Yedmoo	Group fucking (*yet mu*)
Yed_Sod_Out_Door	Bareback fucking (*yet sot*) outdoors
Zeedwow	Masturbation (*wao*) is horny (*sit* = denoting an intense experience, an onomatopoeic word for the sucking sound of satisfaction made when first tasting exceptionally spicy food)

Messaging on Camfrog

When users logged on to a gay video chat room, they would hear a DJ's voice and music and see a user directory on the right-hand side of the computer screen. Many user messages were on the front page and users could write and post their own messages. These messages could include information about where a user lived, their original hometown, and their masculine features. Users typically indicated their sexual role as either top (*ruk*) or bottom (*rap*) and their sexual preferences. Lust and strong sexual craving, known as *ngian* or feeling horny, were often expressed. Some users sought a man for casual sex, while others wanted to find a regular lover. The most sought-after partners were insertive *ruk* and *bi*-identified men. For this reason, indicating a masculine image was especially important in attracting chat partners and messages including terms such as *man*, *bi*, *bi man*, *ruk*, and *bi ruk* were often used to indicate a user's masculine status. The English term "man" was also often duplicated as *man-man* to emphasize masculinity. Effeminate gay men labeled *sao* were not preferred on Camfrog. Being *man*, "masculine," and avoiding expressing femininity were very important to participating in Camfrog gay video chat rooms. The following are sample messages that reflected the masculine characteristics and desires of users. The messages were written in Thai and are here translated into English.

> I'm a basketball player, tall, with a good figure and fair skin (*phiw khao*), looking for a handsome *bi* guy who has a good body and is masculine (*man*).

> I'm looking for a male student studying in university. Nobody knows that I'm gay. Effeminate gays (*sao*) needn't bother coming to chat with me.

> I'm *bi* and have a big cock (*khuay yai*), looking for another *bi* who has a good body and a six-pack.

> I'm *bi* and nobody knows [that I'm gay]. I have a girlfriend. I'm looking for a *bi* who also has a girlfriend. I'd like to arrange secret hookups.

> I'm looking for a senior high school boy who is bottom and masculine (*pen rap pen man*). I'm *bi* and I'm waiting for you.

> I'd like to talk with handsome *bi* university students. Nobody knows [that I'm gay].

> I'm an active *bi* (*bi ruk*) looking for a cute, receptive *bi* (*bi rap*) who is sincere and masculine (*man*) to come and be my lover (*faen*).

I want group sex with really masculine (*man-man*) guys. I don't like effeminates (*sao*) because nobody knows that I like having sex with men.

I'm good-looking and tall with a good body. I'm looking for a masculine guy (*man-man*) like me. Let's meet and have sex (*mi sek kan*).

I'm an active *bi* (*bi ruk*) who wants to be fucked (*fai rap*).

I'm dark and handsome with a mustache. I'd like to chat with fair-complexioned masculine (*man*) guys.

I'm looking for a masculine *bi* (*man bi*) or top (*ruk*) who has a good physique and works out.

I'm a *bi* working guy who wants a younger guy (*norng chai*) to suck my cock.

I'm masculine (*man*) looking for a young guy (*norng chai*) studying in senior high school.

Many closeted men accessed Camfrog, with the expression "Nobody knows [that I'm gay]" (*mai mi khrai ru*) indicating that they had a masculine presentation and passed as straight in everyday life. "Nobody knows" worked as a confirmation of masculinity alongside terms such as *man* and *man-man* in Thai gay Camfrog chat rooms.

The Role of the DJ in Camfrog Gay Chat Rooms

Sexual activities by and among users in Camfrog gay video chat rooms were encouraged and choreographed by DJs. Without the DJ, many online sexual activities would not have taken place. DJs could observe the activities of all the users who were logged on to the chat room that they managed and spurred on, and at times cajoled, users to show their cocks, masturbate, and engage in sex shows. The communicative role of the DJ in Camfrog gay chat rooms can be understood in several regards. First, the DJ brought users' attention to logged-on users who he regarded as cute and handsome. Second, the DJ encouraged individual users to show their cock and masturbate, while urging couples who logged on together to have sex. Under the direction of the DJ, Camfrog gay chat rooms often took the form of online orgies with multiple users engaged in diverse forms of erotic and sexual activity.

DJs often used the term *na-rak*, "cute," to identify users whom they regarded as handsome and to have sexy bodies exposed to the camera. Men identified as *na-rak* were often senior high school students and those dressed in sports clothes and uniforms. Young men identified as *ti*—a Chinese dialect term for "younger brother" widely used in Thailand to denote young, fair-complexioned men of Chinese appearance—were especially often described as cute. This reflected a growing preference for fair-skinned or "white Asian" (see Käng 2015, 2017) partners among many gay men in Thailand since the 1990s.

A small moustache, tattoos, and earrings were often identified by DJs as making men especially attractive, a combination that reflected the masculine style of lower-middle-class youths identified as "*waen* boys," *dek waen*. *Waen* is an onomatopoeic word for the sound of a revving motorcycle, like "vroom," and *waen* boys refers to gangs of young men who ride their motorcycles at high speed noisily through city streets late at night. *Waen* boys have slim physiques and a masculine style similar to the coyote boys detailed in the previous chapter.

DJs would tell users about handsome men and invite them to click on these men's usernames using the term *sorng*. The DJ would announce the first two or three letters of a handsome user's ID, using this shortened name in a flirtatious, teasing way to indicate a cute man. DJs would also flirt with handsome users, saying that they would like to have sex with them and describing such users as *na-kin*, "tasty" or "worth eating." The Thai verb "to eat" (*kin*) is often used in slang expressions for sexual attractiveness. As noted earlier, Camfrog chat rooms were advertising venues for a range of products marketed toward gay men. By keeping users logged on to their chat room, DJs sought to ensure that information about advertisers' products and services reached as large a market as possible. DJs sought to keep the maximum number of users in the room they moderated by pointing out handsome guys and highlighting their username in blue, so other users could then click on that username and see the guy's webcam image. DJs tried to assess how many users were focusing or spotlighting on guys they identified as handsome by asking users to press a certain number or letter on their keyboard if they were watching the specified guy. This was an important method for DJs to determine whether they were keeping the attention of users. Below are samples of how different DJs brought users' attention to handsome guys who were logged on.

> You can meet up with really handsome and cute guys here. I'll tell you when I find them. Users, please stay with me in this room. Now, focus on TA. Take a look at (*sorng*) him. Then go and look at P and AN.

> I've found a guy. There are so many great, sexy (*seksi*) and perfect bodies in this room. Don't go anywhere now, stay in this room. If I find any cute guys, any handsome men, I'll tell you for sure.

Toto, you have to stay with me. Don't run away. I'll keep looking for cute guys in the room. You don't have to show your cock, but just stay in this room. You see, Sor has left the room, but Toto don't go away. If you want to leave the room, please tell me.

If anyone sees a cute guy, please tell me. Message me and let me know. All the blue-colored users are so cute, I guarantee.

Put a spotlight on (*sorng*) Bi [user's ID]. You can focus on (*sorng*) him right now. Wow! Can I be your boyfriend? You've got such white skin and a sexy body (*hun seksi*) too. Your nipples are really sexy. I'd like to suck your nipples and eat you. I'm looking at you. Whoever thinks Bi is very handsome, please key in the number 8. Quickly! Users, can you see Bi? How come you're so handsome, Bi? I really want to be your boyfriend. Will you let me be your boyfriend? Other users, you'll have to wait until I've finished having sex with Bi.

I've found another guy. Listen carefully now, Dave is really handsome and has a good masculine body. How come you're so handsome? When I see his body, my heart pounds really fast. Dave should get a blue color marker [on his username]. Can you stand up, Dave? Oh, . . . , I can see his black pubic hair. I really want to see his cock.

Mai is really popular. Let's take a look at (*sorng*) him now. Does anybody like Mai? Please key the number 1 for me if you do. Who's focusing on Mai right now? I want to know how many of you are looking at Mai now. Users who've just come into this room, please go focus on Mai.

Another aspect of DJs' communication was to urge users to show their penis and engage in sexual activities in front of their webcams. The act of encouraging sexual practices online was called *cheer*. In Thai the borrowed English term "cheer" has taken on the meaning of supporting or encouraging an individual or sports team, as in the expression "cheer squad." Being prepared to masturbate online was called *jat nak*, "getting heavy duty," and DJs encouraged such users "[to keep it up] a long time" (*yao pai loei*). When telling the audience about a user who was masturbating, the DJ would use an aroused tone of voice as if making love and he would raise two fingers to make a V-for-Victory sign when a user achieved orgasm. Users also showed the two-finger V-for-Victory sign when they came, which was called a "dam break" (*kheuan taek*). A DJ would also indicate which user had just cum by adding a flower symbol and a licking icon (*na-lia*, "worth licking") against that user's ID. In Thailand, flowers are often given to symbolize gratitude and appreciation. The following dialogues are samples of various DJs' online use of "cheer" to encourage users to engage in sexual activities in front of their webcams:

> ZeroZeroZero [username], grab your cock.[2] Can you do that for me? Users, go focus on ZeroZeroZero. He's so handsome and has a good physique too. ZeroZeroZero, do you have a boyfriend? Oh, . . . , can you all see ZeroZeroZero's cock? It's so hard. Please, give it to me. I'm waiting with my mouth open to suck your cock.
>
> Who'd like to see P.A.'s cock? Please type the number 1 for me on our room. Come on, key in the number 1 quickly now. If you don't key the number 1 P.A. won't show his cock. So, please type the number 1 for me. Hurry up, now! P.A., lots of users want to see your cock. P.A., can you hear me? I want to see it too. Oh! P.A. is wanking right now. Users, hurry up and focus on him! . . . Oh, PA is cumming. Oh, my god (*o mae jao*). His cum is spurting out like a fountain. Let's give him the flower and licking icon. Please, give him the flower to thank him. Ah, . . . his cum is spreading out all over his stomach. I really want to eat his cum.
>
> Let's spotlight on So [username], now. Can you take hold of your cock and wank (*chak wao*)? Please do it so we can look at you now.
>
> Users, look at Aen quickly! He's wearing black underwear. His cock is so big. Users, focus on him and wank together with him.
>
> Come and look at BIG [username]. I'll only tell you once. BIG, can you wank (*chak wao*) for us to see? Please! Your body is so sexy (*seksi*). I like you so much. I like guys with your physique. I really like to have sex with guys with masculine (*man-man*) bodies like yours. If users like BIG, please type the number 2. BIG, can you take your cock out of your pants? Oh, . . . he's pinching his nipple. I feel a spasm in my nipple. BIG's nipple is so nice. It should be sucked. I want to eat (*kin*) BIG. Oh, rub your cock on my face. Wank into my face.
>
> Wow, M.I. is wanking. Keep on wanking, please. Why are you so slow cumming (*set cha jang*)? Will it take you an hour to finish? Who likes M.I.? Please type the number 1. Oh, . . . he's really horny. He's cumming now. Give him a flower and a licking tongue icon right now. Show him some gratitude. Oh, his cum is so white.
>
> Bi-Big [username] has a hard cock. He's got a big cock. Oh my goodness (*o mae jao*), I can't stand it. He's using his foot to rub his cock. Oh, . . .

now he's fucking (*yet*) the pillow. Put the pillow underneath your body, please. Yes, fuck it. Oh, . . . yes, do it slowly. Anybody who likes Bi-Big, please type the letter B. Oh, . . . yeah, keep fucking the pillow. Yes! That's it. Fuck me, darling. I'm so horny. Oh, . . . yes, slowly please. Change your position a bit and show me your ass. I want to see your balls when you're fucking the pillow. Can you do that for me? Oh, . . . are you close to cumming? Show your two fingers when you cum. Yes, that's it. He's cum now. My voice made you cum for sure, right? I'd really like to know whether you'd prefer to fuck the pillow or my ass. Do you want to cum again? I'll suck your dick if you want to cum a second time.

A third aspect of the DJ's persuasive influence was to encourage male couples to engage in live sex shows online. DJs paid particular attention to users who logged on with a partner, encouraging couples to perform oral and anal sex in live sex shows that were called *nang sot* ("live show"). Below are sample dialogues of DJs' encouragement for couples to engage in sex online:

Both of you, let us see you suck your partner's nipple. Can you suck his cock, please? Whoever wants to see these two guys, please type the number 8 when you're watching them. Nam-ja-taek [username, "I'm cumming"], can suck his cock for us? Suck him until he cums, OK? You and your partner should go to bed and fuck. Users, quick, focus on these guys.

Let's focus on Nok-yung Thorng [username, "golden peacock"]. Oh, he's got a partner! Any users who want Nok-yung Thorng to suck his boy-friend's cock, please type the letter N. Nok-yung Thorng, you have to suck his cock. Understand? If you don't, I'll get angry with you. Please suck his cock. OK? They're touching each other's cocks. Users, focus on them, look. Oh, Nok-yung Thorng is wanking his boyfriend's cock.

Now 085 [username] will do a fucking show. Let's watch them. 085, you can switch to private mode so other people can't come in to watch your video. Your partner is really cute. Please, can you bring your partner into the camera too. Is your partner a bottom (*pen rap*)? Maybe your partner is shy and doesn't want to show his face. Can I see you fuck him? What's going on? I can't see what's happening. Oh, they're taking off their clothes. Yes, he's sucking his boyfriend's cock. Please move into the center of the camera. Now, they've started to suck each other's cocks. Yes, oh, fuck him really hard. The bottom guy (*fai mia*), lift your legs, please.[3] Let's watch 085. They're fucking each other.

Rethinking Gay Cybersex and Culture

Accounts of the forms of gay sex in cyberspace and virtual environments, and of cybersubjects as sexual subjects and identities, are often framed in terms of a tension between embodiment and disembodied possibilities—of cybersubjectivity as emerging at the intersection of the two worlds of the imagination and material bodies. Kate O'Riordan (2007, 17) suggests that the intersection of queer lives and cyberspace can be seen as the blending of two promissory discourses, which both unfold through utopian imaginaries made possible by the potentialities presented by technologically mediated futures. O'Riordan (17) points out that queer cultures and cybercultures both emerged in the same period as the ways of thinking about and reconfiguring the materiality of the present through reimaginings of the future.

Studies of cyberculture have also tended to assume that the cybersubject is free to perform an identity of choice online, and that queer people who enter virtual spaces will find opportunities to imagine diverse modes of sexual identity. This assumption draws from conceptions of correlations between embodied experience and authentic identity. D. J. Phillips and C. Cunningham (2007) observe that concepts of self and identity predominate in studies of how gayness is coded in cyberspaces, with a common theme being the tension between an authentic identity constructed within a material bodily physiology and an articulated identity found in virtual space. Both authentic embodied and articulated virtual identities are understood as being related by online media as sites of gender and sexual expression.

The notions of sexual self and identity discussed in accounts of virtual spaces have often drawn on Western paradigms of the construction of the subject, and queer studies scholars have been interested to consider how forms of sexual subjectivity are maintained and practiced in cyberspaces. Queer studies accounts of cyberspace have often seen online lives as demonstrating queer theoretical claims of the fluidity of both sexuality and gender and as providing confirmation of Butler's (1990, 1993) argument that gender and sexual identities are not stable or given but rather are constructed and materialized through performatively repeated ritualized actions.

Nonetheless, queer theoretical approaches to understanding cybersex and virtual sex among gay people have often centered on considerations of gay identity. For instance, Ragan Fox's (2007) *Gays in (Cyber-)Space* is a study of online performances of gay identities in which cyberspace is seen as offering an arena for gay men to witness and rehearse homosexual and homosocial possibilities. Fox argues that performative practices such as writing online blogs constituted affirmations and confirmations of gay cybersubjectivity. A main finding of Fox's study of gay-identified men's use of internet communications is that gay male subjectivity is multiple, not singular. Fox's account of fluid gay identities, however, is conceptualized around Western ideas of homosexuality and gay individuals who identify as sexual beings. As detailed below, this approach is problematic when applied to the study of same-sex online relations in cultures such as Thailand, where gender performance rather than sexuality-based identity is at the center of cybersexual relations.

To an extent, sexual practices in everyday life are mirrored in online sexual cultures. In a society where sexual desire and eroticization are framed primarily in terms of masculine and feminine social practices, sexual activities in cyberspace are not necessarily understood as modalities of sexuality or sexual identity but rather as forms of social conduct that establish the meaning of varieties or gradations of masculinity and femininity. Irmi Karl (2007) suggests that cyberspace is a domain where human sociality is reconstructed in novel ways that cannot be defined in terms of set identity categories such as gay or straight. Our research confirms that Thai men's engagement in gay video chat rooms in the early 2010s was not based on affirmations or explorations of sexual identity. Rather, online sexual activities and intimacies correlated with confirmations of masculine expression. A corollary of this understanding is that in some settings sexual relations, intimacy, and desire between men are not imagined through the lens of sexual identity. This finding from our study points to Thai same-sex chat rooms as being spaces of diverse masculinities and fluid genders, adding further detail to the account of multiple Thai masculinities presented in the preceding chapters.

Images and Discourses of Masculinity in Thai Gay Video Chat Rooms

It is not easy to classify the young male users of Camfrog same-sex chat rooms within clear-cut categories of either heterosexual, bisexual, or homosexual forms of sexuality. They typically presented themselves as Camfrog "users," often without reference to sexual identity labels. Many of those who accessed the same-sex chat rooms on Camfrog identified as "men" (phu-chai) and were eager to engage in explicit forms of sexual pleasure that emphasized masculine characteristics. Manhood, virility, and masculinity were the prime movers for accessing Camfrog's gay video chat rooms and the users in these rooms participated in sexual imaginaries in which pleasure was based on the exchange of erotically charged masculine images. Understanding the men's masculine gender presentation and performance is more relevant than seeking to classify them in terms of their sexuality.

In their research on users of Thai Camfrog gay chat rooms, Ronnapoom and Pimpawun (Ronnapoom et al. 2008a, 2008b; Ronnapoom and Pimpawun 2011) observed that in the early 2000s young Thai men who had sex with men (MSM) had limited opportunities for expressing their sexual desires and identities because they lived in settings dominated by a mainstream heteronormative ethos. The term "MSM" used in Ronnapoom and Pimpawun's studies of Thai male Camfrog users is derived from biomedical and epidemiological research of sexual acts and behaviors regarded as placing men at risk of HIV infection. This term is prevalent in the fields of sexual health and HIV/AIDS research and tends to emphasize physical acts of sexual intercourse, especially anal sex, between males without necessarily considering the social and cultural contexts of the men's sex lives. Gary Dowsett et al. (2006) contend that the biomedical category of MSM does not correspond to any identity category. Epidemiological populations of MSM are not united by any common cultural traits, with this category simply including sexual behaviors between biological males without taking into account different sexual preferences. In contrast, we contend that it is important to regard the male users of Camfrog's same-sex chat rooms as men who engaged in the imagining and practice of masculine-gendered sexual pleasure.

Ronnapoom and Pimpawun (Ronnapoom et al. 2008a, 2008b; Ronnapoom and Pimpawun 2011) describe preferences for insertive, *ruk*, and receptive, *rap*, male sex as respectively denoting forms of gender identity among Thai gay men. In contrast, in analyzing the interactions on Thai Camfrog, we did not find that the terms *ruk* or *rap* were used to refer to opposing masculine and feminine gender roles. As noted in chapter 1, the terms *ruk* and *rap* are borrowed from the terminology of Thai boxing, Muay Thai, in which "offensive" punches or strikes are called *tha ruk*, while "defensive" positions are called *tha rap*. In Muay Thai, *tha ruk* and *tha rap* are equally masculine, referring to strategies of male-male physical engagement and contestation rather than to a gender binary that positions one party as masculine and the other as feminine. In the early 2010s, the *ruk* and *rap* same-sex practices signaled and enacted in Camfrog did not indicate a masculine-versus-feminine gender binary among the male users but rather referred to sexual relations between males in which each partner embodied masculinity in a different degree. Camfrog same-sex chat rooms were characterized by gradations of masculinity along a same-gendered spectrum, with insertive *ruk* partners being understood as being more masculine than receptive *rap* men but in which sexually receptive men were nonetheless still considered masculine, not feminine.

Rather than identifying as homosexual, the users in Camfrog's video chat rooms represented themselves in terms of diverse modes of masculinity, notably as *ruk* (insertive), *rap* (receptive), *bi* (bisexual), *both* (versatile), and *man* (masculine). All these terms were collectively contrasted with *sao* (effeminate). The men who preferred the receptive *rap* role did not identify that position with feminine traits. Rather, they often emphasized their manliness by using the term *bi rap*. The use of the term *bi rap* reflected disidentification with the stereotypical images of the feminine *kathoey* and the effeminate *gay sao*, and identification with the ascribed masculinity of a bisexual man. This represents a discursive reconstruction of male-male sexual interactions as a pairing of two masculine partners and a resistance to heteronormative Thai discourses that define receptive anal sex as feminine, relocating receptive anal sex from the feminine to the masculine. The focus on gender identity rather than sexual identity in the discourses of Camfrog's male users finds parallels in Megan Sinnott's (2011) account of female users' self-reference terms on the Thai lesbian website Lesla. In the early 2000s, the most popular terms on this website were *les king* and *les queen*, which indicated complementary sexual roles between an active *les king* partner in relation to a receptive *les queen* rather than to a masculine-feminine *tom-dee* pairing of female same-sex partners.

In their studies of Thai gay Camfrog, Ronnapoom and Pimpawun emphasized sexual activities and power hierarchies among male users, arguing that room owners and DJs were the most powerful people in these interactions. Although the room owners and DJs regulated activities in different chat rooms, they could not command users to do many things. Users could choose to leave any room in which they felt uncomfortable, or bored, at any time. As seen in the transcripts of DJs' interactions with users, DJs continually tried to attract and keep the attention of users so that they did not log off or move to another potentially more interesting chat room. In contrast to Ronnapoom and Pimpawun, we contend that the power structure in Thai same-sex chat rooms was not hierarchical or top-down but rather horizontal and more evenly distributed by negotiation among users, owners, and DJs through online conversations and camera connections. Whether a given video chat room succeeded or failed in attracting users depended on users' willingness to participate, not on any regulation or censorship exercised by room owners or DJs.

Camfrog's Gay Video Chat Rooms as Sites of Fluid Masculinities

When reflecting on sexual practices between Thai men, we need to consider the cultural contexts in which male intimacy and sexual pleasure are regulated by social norms. In everyday life, young heteronormative Thai men may express forms of eroticism and emotion with a girlfriend, a female sex worker, or a trans woman *kathoey*. Among male friends, young men also often engage in sexual high jinks such as showing their cocks and masturbating. These locker-room-type practices are not necessarily seen as reflecting forms of homosexual desire but rather as demonstrations of masculine horseplay. Between young male friends, sexual joking and teasing are relatively common and typically elicit laughter and amusement. Furthermore, in macho youth cultures dominant masculinity is often constituted by minoritizing younger males. Men with smaller cocks may become the butt of jokes and criticism while less masculine male friends may be ridiculed and subject to teasing and forms of sexual harassment referred to as *plam*. *Plam* can denote rape but in male youth cultures also denotes forms of bullying and harassment when younger or more effeminate boys become sex objects in male horseplay. Hazing rituals (*phithi rap norng*) for military conscripts and for freshmen in predominantly male technical and engineering colleges may also include activities that would more generally be associated with sexual practices. Hazing rituals may include commanding new recruits and students to strip, and in extreme cases, freshman may be ordered to masturbate. These kinds of "risqué" or "indecent" (*thaleung*) practices serve to reinforce virile behavior and normative masculinity in all-male settings.

Hazing rituals are institutionalized in many Thai schools, colleges, and universities as well as the armed forces, where it is called SOTUS, an acronym of the English terms "Seniority, Order, Tradition, Unity, Spirit." Emily Brown (2020) describes SOTUS ritualized hazing of freshmen by seniors as instilling the importance of hierarchy into young Thai adults.[4] The homoerotic aspects of Thai SOTUS rituals were highlighted in the popular 2016 Boys Love (BL) genre television series *SOTUS: The Series* produced by GMMTV and in which an initially abusive relationship between a male senior and a freshman in an engineering college transmutes into an emotional relationship.[5]

The arrival of digital communication technologies provided private spaces where these types of masculine scripts and sexual horseplay based on the dominant Thai male gender culture could be enacted as forms of online sexual socializing among homosexually interested men as well as men who claimed a normative "real man" (*phu-chai*) status. Camfrog's gay chat rooms re-created a gender culture in which normative masculinity was constituted and affirmed through eroticized forms of interaction between men. This intersection of normative masculine gender culture with same-sex eroticism opened spaces for the participation of both homosexual and ostensibly heterosexual young men. While men who viewed themselves as normative "real men" affirmed their masculine gender status through interactions on Camfrog, homosexually attracted men achieved sexual pleasure from the audiovisual representations of same-sex acts.

Camfrog was a virtual space in which Thai men who claimed diverse sexual orientations could meet in the mutual construction and consumption of images of sexually desirable masculinity. The intense masculine culture of Camfrog's gay chat rooms highlighted significant features of the gender culture of the Thai gay communities that had emerged in previous decades when gay print media were the main source of images of sexually attractive male bodies. In the early 2010s, Camfrog formed a virtual domain of sexual imagination and experimentation by and for young men who could not necessarily find avenues of sexual expression or masculine gender confirmation in daily life.

The formation of Camfrog's gay chat rooms as spaces where both heterosexual and homosexual men met to affirm a shared masculine status was facilitated by the absence of the word "gay" from interactions. As already noted, most of the primarily young men who accessed Camfrog's gay video chat rooms did so without specifying a gay identity and, indeed, the discourses of Camfrog's gay chat rooms were characterized by an absence of homosexual identity categories. This absence of "gay" or "homosexual" identity categories among Camfrog's users created a domain in which ostensibly heterosexual men, who claimed a status as "real men" (*phu-chai thae*), often participated. The participation of these "real men" in the gay video chat rooms and the pleasure they enjoyed in exposing their bodies online for the appreciative gaze of other users was not taken as denoting an exclusive homosexual preference but rather as a variety of masculine sexual entertainment.

For Thai men familiar with the masculine culture of male sexual horseplay in which sexual acts are seen as entertaining, performing a sex show for a male audience in a video chat room in which a DJ praised their manhood could be understood as affirming masculine libido and virility. Indeed, Thai men who accessed the gay chat rooms sought to define their manhood in relation to other male users by comparing the quality of their masculinity. Exposing and exhibiting the penis in Camfrog's gay video chat rooms was often seen as essential to confirming a user's masculinity. DJs repeatedly praised those users who dared to show their penis as "men," *phu-chai*, while denigrating users who were reluctant to expose themselves as effeminate *sao*, as seen in the following comment from one DJ: "The user's name is Ban-ban, he and his partner are both effeminate (*sao*).[6] They don't dare show sex online."

A common view on Thai gay online chat platforms was that more masculine (*man*) users were more sexually daring and prepared to show their bodies and perform sex online, while more feminine men were more reserved in their online engagement and less prepared to take off their clothes and perform sex shows online.

The Discourse of *Bi* in the Constitution of Camfrog Masculinities

The men who accessed Camfrog's gay chat rooms participated in an intensely gendered milieu of eroticized masculinity. While various kinds of manly expression were found in Camfrog's gay video chat rooms, users nonetheless always indicated that they were a man who needed a man. While eschewing the word "gay," many users did identify as *bi*, a term that confirmed masculine status. In Camfrog's online chat the meaning of *bi* differed from the concept of bisexuality as the sexual orientation of a person who is attracted to both men and women. As used on Camfrog, *bi* did not so much indicate a sexual identity as a masculine gender status with the potentiality of eroticism and intimacy with other masculine-identified males. *Bi* emphasized that a male user was not effeminate and sought pleasure with other masculine males. As a masculine gender term, in the early twenty-first century, *bi* has become widely used among generations of younger homosexually oriented Thai men who want to express their sexual desire for men within a masculine frame. The use of *bi* in gay video chat rooms confirmed a user's manliness and was useful for attracting the attention of other users and finding sexual partners.

In the early twenty-first century, *bi* came to denote a privileged masculine gendering of male-male eroticism rather than bisexual preference per se. It became a popular term among younger generations of homosexually interested Thai men whose primary access to images and discourses of same-sex intimacy and eroticism was through online media. For these younger generations, *bi* connotes a more acceptable image of masculine homosexual gendering than gay. While linked with the privileged masculine status of the presumptively heterosexual "real man," *phu-chai* or *phu-chai thae*, *bi* nonetheless still implicitly connotes homosexuality. This ambiguity has enabled it to become prominent among younger men for whom online chat rooms have afforded safe spaces for sexual exploration.

While denoting a masculine gender identity, *bi* did not specify any preferred sexual role, whether top or bottom. For this reason, users with a preference for being either top or bottom often added an additional specifying term to their self-descriptors. A *bi* user who preferred the insertive role was described as *bi ruk*, an assignation that assumed a higher status in the gendered hierarchy of Camfrog same-sex relations. In contrast, a *bi* user who preferred the receptive role was called *bi rap*. *Bi ruk* users would seek out *bi rap* men to have private online sex shows in the gay video chat rooms. *Bi rap* users were still required to perform an adequate degree of normative masculinity and were not regarded as *sao*, effeminate or girlie. Users who identified as *bi ruk* also differentiated themselves from men labeled as "gay," and typically rejected approaches from more effeminate gay users.

The Effeminization of "Gay" in Early Twenty-First Century Thailand

In the early 2000s, "gay" came to imply a more feminine homosexual male and Camfrog users differentiated *bi* from gay, using *bi* to secure and confirm a masculine gender identity. The meaning of the term "gay" has undergone significant changes since it was first borrowed into Thai in the 1960s. Jackson (1999) observed that in the 1960s "gay" was widely used to refer to male prostitutes, especially those Thai men who sold sex to male foreigners. This sense of "gay" as a foreign influence that was often viewed as undermining Thai morality and traditions arrived at the same time that Western psychological ideas of homosexuality as an illness and perversion also took hold in Thai medical and educational circles. This compound of influences saw "gay" take on negative senses among sections of the Thai public as denoting a combination of sexual deviancy, mental illness, and abnormal behavior. However, during the 1980s, "gay" was reappropriated by Thai homosexual men and took on positive connotations of pride in same-sex preference, with many of the magazines discussed in previous chapters using "gay" to affirm a positive sense of male homosexual identity.

In the 1980s, "gay" took on positive meanings for urban homosexual men who were in the process of differentiating themselves from both heterosexual men (*phu-chai*) and trans women *kathoey*. "Gay" came to be a label for a different kind of man and reflected the acknowledgment and recognition of the different masculinities that were expressed in sexual relations among Thai men. In this sense, gay formed part of a continuum of masculine identities and descriptors, including *bi* and *man*. The men labeled by these three terms—gay, bi, and *man*—which were borrowed and adapted from English, were all seen as expressing manliness to a greater or lesser extent. Nevertheless, on the few occasions when it was used in Camfrog's same-sex video chat rooms, "gay" marked a status that was regarded to be less masculine than the men who were labeled as *bi*. "Gay" was also distinguished from presumably heteronormative males identified as *phu-chai*.

In Thai same-sex virtual spaces in the early 2010s, *phu-chai, bi ruk, bi rap*, and gay respectively marked different degrees of masculine status. *Phu-chai thae* (real men) were positioned at the top. *Bi ruk* and *bi rap* were respectively placed second and third, with males labeled as *gay ruk* (insertive gay) placed fourth, and *gay both* (sexually versatile gays) in fifth place in the online masculine gender hierarchy. Yet further down the scale of masculine privilege were men labeled as *gay rap*, with the lowest rank in Camfrog's scale of masculine privilege being ascribed to *gay sao* or effeminate gay men. *Gay sao* were seen as the least masculine, and hence the least sexually attractive, class of users. Indeed, effeminate *sao* or "girly" users were strongly out of favor in Camfrog's chat rooms. It was the progressive effeminization of the connotations of the term "gay" in the early twenty-first century that led to its effective absence from Camfrog online discourses.

In the early twenty-first century, the masculinization of male-male sex was not only a feature of Camfrog but Thai gay online interactions more broadly. In gathering information from Thai gay webboards—including gay.postjung. com, thaiboyslove.com, and msngaythai.com—and from gay dating applications such as Blued and Hornet we found that most Thai gay men on these sites also described themselves and those they were looking for in masculine terms. A key expression in the personal classified advertisements on these sites and apps was *mai sadaeng ork*—that is, to be straight acting or able to pass as heterosexual. Many also described themselves with the English-derived expression *bi man*. In gay dating apps most men stated that they were looking for masculine partners and described themselves as top (*ruk*) and *man*. Some samples of the types of brief messages from gay dating webboards that emphasize masculinity are summarized below:

> I'm a sportsman, good body. Looking for a receptive (*rap*) cute *bi man*.

> I'm a top (*ruk*) *bi man* looking for a handsome male student.

> Looking for a top gay (*gay ruk*). I'm a bottom gay (*gay rap*).

> I'm a *bi man*, but nobody knows (*mai mi khrai ru*) [I'm gay]. Looking for a boyfriend who acts like a *man*.

> I'm a Chinese-looking *man*, good body, play football, and work out. Looking for top (*ruk*) gay men.

> I'm a soldier bottom (*rap*). Looking for a *bi man*.

> I've got fair skin, *man*, insertive (*ruk*), work out. Looking for a guy with a nice body, bottom (*rap*).

The sample messages above indicate how masculine images predominate in gay dating contexts. In these settings effeminacy or feminine mannerisms, denoted by the terms *sao* or *taeo*, are strongly undesirable. In addition to emphasizing a preference for masculine-identified partners, messages posted on the msngay-thai.com webboard in 2012 also reflected prejudice against effeminate *gay sao* in sexual contexts, as seen in the following messages posted by a range of users:

> I'm a *man*, only looking for a masculine boyfriend. Don't be older or effeminate (*sao*).

> I'm looking for a lover. I'm tall. Don't be older, fat, or effeminate (*sao*).

> I'm looking for a handsome *man*. I won't welcome effeminate (*sao*) guys.

> I don't want to be lonely. Looking for a *man*. Don't be fat or effeminate (*sao*).

> I'm only looking for a handsome top (*ruk*) *bi man* only. I don't like effeminate gay bottoms (*sao rap*).

> I'm a top *bi man* looking for a masculine bottom (*man rap*). Don't be effeminate (*sao*).

> I'm a bottom *man* (*man rap*) looking for masculine boyfriend (*faen pen man*). I don't want an effeminate gay (*sao*).

No one on the dating sites we surveyed stated that they were effeminate (*sao*). Some said they were sexually receptive (*rap*) but nonetheless affirmed that they were masculine and did not express effeminacy. They described themselves as *gay man rap*—that is, a masculine gay man who prefers the receptive role. In attracting a masculine gay partner, Thai gay men take pains to ensure that first impressions on dates and hookups do not convey any sense of effeminacy, as they believe that effeminacy will destroy any chance of success in establishing a sexual relationship.

If a Thai gay man fails in his attempts to establish sexual intimacy because his desired partner perceives him as being too effeminate, or not being masculine enough, this is described as *ab mai nian*, an abbreviation of *ab man mai nian*, "to be unsuccessful at straight-acting." It is also called *sao taek*, for "girlie effeminacy to break out." Judging whether a gay man is effeminate is a central element of sexual socializing at gay events and in venues such as dance parties, pubs, and discotheques. In venues, Thai gay men may seek to identify those who are *sao*, "girlie," by looking at their dance moves, with *gay sao* being regarded as expressing effeminacy through their dance steps or *tha ten*. In extreme cases, *gay sao* may be ridiculed by other gay men as *tut*, *taeo*, or *kathoey*, with the use of these terms to express disparagement reflecting the extent to which effeminate gays may be discriminated against. This prejudice against *gay sao* has developed within a gay culture dominated by masculine images promoted by gay marketing and media. A number of *gay sao* nonetheless engage in gender-blending practices such as powdering their face in a feminine way but using masculine speech forms such as the sentence particle *khrap*. Such a multiple gender presentation of an effeminate *gay sao*, visually effeminate but discursively masculine, is disparaged by many masculine Thai gay men.

TABLE 6.4 Comparison of terms for sexual roles on Thai gay webboards and dating apps

IDENTITY	SEXUAL ROLE	THAI TERM
Bi	Insertive (top)	Bi ruk
	Receptive (bottom)	Bi rap
	Versatile (both top and bottom)	Bi both or dai thang ruk lae rap
Gay	Insertive (top)	Gay ruk
	Receptive (bottom)	Gay rap
	Versatile (both top and bottom)	Gay both or dai thang ruk lae rap

Identity Labels, Complex Gendering, and Diverse Sexual Roles

Large numbers of men who joined chat rooms on gay dating webboards and dating apps described themselves as *bi* or *bi man*, with the majority identifying themselves as *bi ruk*. A smaller number identified as preferring the receptive role and described themselves as *bi rap*. As detailed in table 6.4, these varieties of *bi*-identified men expressed diverse sexual desires, reflecting how in the early twenty-first century male same-sex relations in Thailand took place in settings of complex sexual identities. Some men using gay dating webboards described themselves as *bi both*—that is, a *bi* man who is sexually versatile and interested in both insertive and receptive anal sex. The prevalence of sexual versatility in contemporary Thai gay communities is reflected in the existence of a variety of expressions such as *dai thang ruk lae rap*, "can be both top and bottom"; *both*, "both (top and bottom)"; and *dai mot*, "can do everything." In online dating sites, a man describing himself as *bi both* would be perceived as being more masculine than a man who used the label *gay both*. Just as *gay sao* occupies a complex zone at the intersection of feminine and masculine gender norms, the prevalence of the term *bi* in discourses in Thai virtual spaces reflects the complex experiences of masculine-identified homosexual men as they negotiate their sexual identity in different spaces.

The complex blending of degrees of masculine gender presentation and preferred sexual role is also represented by a range of compound gender-sex expressions that describe a hierarchy of identity categories on gay webboards and dating apps. The first term in these compound expressions is either *bi* or gay, depending on how masculine a man sees himself or wishes others to see him. Men who identify as *bi* typically add the gender term *man* to denote their masculinity (i.e., *bi man*) while gay-identified men may be referred to either as masculine *man* (i.e., *gay man*) or feminine *sao* (i.e., *gay sao*). Because *bi*-identified men are by

TABLE 6.5 Identity terms for gender presentation and sexual role on gay dating apps

GENDER PRESENTATION AND SEXUAL ROLE	THAI TERM
More masculine sexually insertive	Bi man ruk
More masculine sexually versatile	Bi man both, dai mot
More masculine sexually receptive	Bi man rap
Masculine sexually insertive	Gay man ruk
Masculine sexually versatile	Gay man both, dai mot
Masculine sexually receptive	Gay man rap
Effeminate sexually insertive	Gay sao ruk, sao siap
Effeminate sexually versatile	Gay sao both, sai mot
Effeminate sexually receptive	Gay sao rap

definition masculine, the compound *bi sao* is not found since it represents a contradiction in the schema of early twenty-first-century Thai gender and identity categories. Finally, a third term is added for preferred sexual position: *ruk* for insertive; *rap* for receptive; and *both* or *dai mot* for sexual versatility. The fine nuancing of these terminologies indicates the importance of both gender presentation and sexual role in the culture of men who have sex with men.

Table 6.5 lists the complex of identity labels used on Thai gay dating sites and smartphone apps, arranged in a gender hierarchy from the most masculine at the top to the least masculine at the bottom. Given the importance of masculine presentation in sexual contexts, Thai men do not use the term *sao* to identify themselves when communicating on webboards or social media, even if they may be effeminate. Terms that contain the word *sao* are ascribed identities, used by men to label those they regard as being effeminate, rather than being a category that a person seeking a sexual partner online would claim for themselves.

Sao Siap: Effeminate Gay Men Who Like to Top

Thai gays now separate the gender norms enacted in public from sexual positions adopted in private encounters. While masculine gay men can alternate their sexual activity from the usually expected role of being a top to also be a bottom, feminine gays who are expected to be a bottom may also take the insertive role in anal intercourse. Some effeminate *gay sao* can play the insertive role (*ruk*), and are often called *sao siap*, "penetrating girls," a term originally used among *kathoey* to describe preoperative transsexuals who take the active role in sex with male partners. Few Thai gays identify as *sao siap*. Rather, this term is used by other gay men to describe an effeminate gay man who is known to take the insertive role. Some Thai gay men are of the opinion that *sao siap* have become a novel phenomenon in the country's gay community because masculine gay men are comparatively rare. In this context, some effeminate gays have solved the problem of a lack of tops by taking the insertive role, which makes it easier to find sex with other gay men. While *sao siap* may be used to describe an effeminate gay man who is sexually insertive, this term is not used as an identity label in sexual settings.

The following quotes from conversations among gay men who posted on the gay webboard thaiboyslove.com when discussing sexual experiences with *gay sao* exemplify the complex intersection of gender presentation and sexual role in Thailand's gay communities in the early 2010s.

> If my partner is more feminine (*sao*) than me, I will top (*ruk*). Of course, when I find a masculine gay man, I will be the bottom (*rap*). It depends on different gay characteristics. (Tom, May 6, 2012)

> I've slept with a *gay sao*. He was very good as a top (*fai ruk*). I liked it a lot. (Oh Army, June 28, 2011)

> An effeminate gay top (*gay sao ruk*) needs to have sex with a masculine bottom (*gay man rap*). If he finds out that his receptive partner is feminine (*sao*), his sexual libido will disappear, and his cock will go soft. (Hi Tor-Mai, April 10, 2012)

> When I have sex with my boyfriend, I'll show my manliness (*khwam-pen-chai*) and take the top role. But when I stay with my close friends, I'll express feminine characteristics. It's a lot of fun to act like a woman. (Jan, November 26, 2011)

> I'm not romantically serious with effeminate gay tops (*gay sao ruk*), but I can have sex with them. If they have a good body and a big cock, I'll be happy. (Kob, November 24, 2011)

Even though masculine presentation is important in cruising for sex and looking for partners on online sites, in the private setting of sex, pleasure may override the gender that a man enacts in public. In Thai gay cultures there is not only a division between public contexts of masculine straight-acting to avoid being stigmatized as a feminine *kathoey* and private expressions of effeminacy when socializing among gay friends. There is now also an increasingly common division between *ab man* performances of masculinity when seeking a sexual partner in a gay venue or online and a possible effeminate expression when having sex. Public roles and sexual cruising are subject to the norms of masculine gender performance, while in sexual practice these gender roles may be forgotten when the desire for sexual pleasure becomes paramount. Contemporary Thai gay culture is constituted at the intersection of public forms of masculine and feminine gendering, and private sexual preferences characterized by the exploration of sexual pleasure. This further indicates the contextualization of Thai gender and sexual culture, and Thai gay men's ability to move between public and private contexts in which different normative expectations operate. The fine nuancing of Thai gay terminology—which combines terms for sexual identity, gender presentation, and preferred sexual role—reflects the widespread awareness and acknowledgment of the complexity and situational specificity of Thai gay gender/sex culture. This confirms Jackson's (2004b, 2013) observations that the Thai field of *phet*, the term by which the multiple phenomena detailed in this research are understood, needs to be considered as an imbricated gender/sex domain, rather than as constituting distinct fields of gender or sexuality.

Online Platforms and the Demise of Thai Gay Print Media

The differentiation of multiple gradations of masculinity as gendered modalities of same-sex expression has been intensified within the online media of Thai gay cyberspace. Digital media have facilitated a further differentiation of a scale of masculinities in Thai gay culture and have institutionalized to an even more heightened degree the hierarchical privileging of heteronormatively modeled forms of manhood in contrast to stigmatized effeminate genderings.

Masculine self-imaging was central to all the visual and discursive dimensions of Camfrog's gay chat rooms. Many users repeated the expression "A man who has sex with a man is a real man" (*chai dai chai kheu yort chai*). The literal sense of this expression is "a man who gets a man [sexually] is the peak of manhood." This often-used idiom, where the colloquial use of the verb "to get" (*dai*) may denote any variety of sex, whether top or bottom, reassured users that they could find diverse varieties of sexual pleasure with other men at the same time as affirming their masculine status. This expression was used to signify that gay video chat rooms are spaces where Thai men could attest to their masculinity through erotic exposure of their bodies to the gaze of other men. In Thailand's early twenty-first-century gay cultures, this sentence reflected a situation in which digital media accentuated the patterns of a homoerotic culture in which the possibility of male-to-male sexual relations was predicated on enacting scripted forms of masculinity. The expression "Men who have sex with men are real men" signaled a culturally constructed form of male same-sex eroticism that was not defined in terms of homosexual identity but rather by understandings that positioned men who have sex with other men as embodying a heightened degree of masculinity.

In virtual spaces such as Thai gay Camfrog, male users could express their desire for gender affirmation from other men without stigma. They could perform sexual acts that did not necessarily lead to them being labeled with any particular sexual identity but which operated as a means to enact their masculine gender status in relation to a finely differentiated hierarchy of manhood. Users clearly found pleasure in having their manhood affirmed through masculinized sex shows of masturbation and oral and anal sex. This attests to the importance of the notion of *bi* for younger Thai men who explored the intersections of their gendered identity and sexual desires through online platforms. In Thai virtual spaces, *bi* constituted an alternative masculinity in which manhood was a prerequisite for realizing sexual desire and achieving affirmations of homoerotic expression and intimacy.

Camfrog highlighted the masculine culture that had been nurtured by Thailand's gay print media in the latter decades of the twentieth century and came to dominate many sections of the country's gay communities in the early twenty-first century. While the gender culture of Camfrog perpetuated norms of masculinity that had been cultivated by print media, digital media such as this web platform soon sounded the death knell of Thai gay magazines. Print media could not compete with the ubiquitous and instantaneous access to communication and images enabled by the internet. While some print publications continued during the early era of online access when the internet was mediated by desktop computers, the arrival of smartphones with dating and other apps led to the ultimate demise of all gay commercial print publishing in Thailand. Thailand's last commercial gay print magazine, the Thai version of the English gay publication *Attitude*, ceased publication in 2018. The arrival of smartphones and dating apps from the middle of the 2010s also saw a rapid decline of desktop-based digital platforms such as Camfrog, which is now a relic of an already superseded era of online communication. The popularity of Camfrog in the late 2000s and early 2010s marked a moment of media transition in Thailand, when print publications and online sites coexisted, and when digital media drew on the gender and sexual cultural foundations that had been laid down by gay print media. Camfrog marked a historical moment when "readers" of print media transitioned to become online "users," when the print-based communication technology of gay magazines increasingly struggled to find a niche in an expanding market that accentuated immediacy and instantaneous interactivity. Our history of the roles of commercial media in the making of Thai gay masculinities ends at this moment of media transition.

CAPITALISM, CLASS, AND THAILAND'S MULTIPLE GAY MASCULINITIES

In exploring how Thai gay cultures relate to male body images and practices, we have engaged the contradictions by which male same-sex desire has been expressed through the lifestyles of capitalist consumer culture in a highly class-stratified social order. For almost five decades, Thai gay behaviors and practices have been influenced by the lifestyles found in bars, pubs, saunas, and disco-theques, and which have been represented in commercial gay media and encountered in visual erotica and pornography. These spaces of consumption have been significant in constructing forms of gay identity and community in which middle-class gay men have assumed privileged positions in both their social and sexual relations with working-class men.

Mithuna Junior, Thailand's first commercially successful gay magazine, reflected the mainstream of Bangkok's changing commercial gay culture from the early 1980s to the mid-1990s. In this period, the magazine developed close relations with Bangkok's gay bars to produce materials for middle-class gay men, such as erotic photo albums of male models and sexually explicit short stories, which provided platforms for new forms of social and sexual relations as well as classifications of sexual and gender identity. The homoeroticism of gay identities and lifestyles represented in *Mithuna Junior* and the other gay magazines that were soon published in Thailand was imbricated with sexual commodities whose advertisements were pervaded by masculine body images. Thailand's commercial gay print media and entertainment venues together played a major role in supporting the development of a sense of gay identity among middle-class homosexual men. At the same time, commercial gay magazines also reinforced modern homosexual norms that organized masculinity and sexual commodities in Bangkok's gay communities, and subsequently across the country.

A primary indicator of the new norms of gay masculinity was manifested in forms of commodification that encouraged middle-class homosexual men to identify as gay in the context of consuming sexualized representations of male bodies and by participating in commercial sex. A second component of Thai gay culture in this period was the reconstruction of male-male sexual relations from a masculine-feminine pairing to a relation of two masculine partners. The performance of masculinity by which gay people represented themselves as men whose presentation and behavior did not reveal their gay identity in the public sphere was called *mai sadaeng ork*, "not expressing [gayness]." The forms of straight-acting masculine presentation denoted by this idiom were not just strategies for avoiding being labeled and stigmatized as homosexual. In the following decades, this homonormative presentation of masculinity, now called *kek man* or *ab man*, "acting the man," came to be the standard of gay male sexual attractiveness. Heteronormative styles of masculine presentation that enabled a middle-class gay man to pass as straight, *mai sadaeng ork*, were integrated within a Thai gay culture where "acting the man," *kek man* or *ab man*, became a prerequisite for finding sexual and romantic partners. Thailand's masculine gay lifestyles also emerged as a system of homosexual categorization that marginalized gay men who were seen as embodying stigmatized feminine characteristics. More effeminate gay men were often labeled with half-humorous–half-derogatory expressions based on the term *sao*, "young woman," such as *ork sao*, "to express girliness," or *taek sao*, "for girliness to break out (through the performance of masculinity)."

Between Consumer Autonomy and Homonormative Subordination

In our chapters we have traced the pivotal role of commercial gay media in the construction of these contemporary norms of Thai gay masculinity and we have shown how the growth and increasing visibility of Thailand's modern gay communities and cultures has been associated with the dominance of consumer society and the expansion of gay commercial spaces. Jackson (2011a) has argued that queer studies is marked by a tension between accounts that view the capitalist consumerism of global gay cultures negatively as a form domination and those which interpret market cultures in a positive light as offering opportunities for queer autonomy from the heteronormative state and family. This tension in queer studies plays out in a theoretical field of post-Marxist analysis informed by critiques of Eurocentrism that contend that gay consumerism within globalization is not necessarily defined by processes of homogenization catalyzed by Western models of gay culture. While some accounts equate the cultural processes of gay consumerism with socioeconomic exploitation in which gay men are treated as passive sexual consumers, others point out that the gay market nonetheless provides avenues for gay autonomy and a greater sense of human rights than was possible in precapitalist societies or within heteronormative state bureaucracies. These contrasting approaches respectively see capitalist culture in terms of opposing effects and consequences for gay men, either as an oppressive force of queer subordination or as a vehicle for creating queer empowerment and opportunity. Our research points to both perspectives, reflecting the ambiguous relationship between Thai gay cultures and the commercial spaces and media that enabled them to come into being.

In studying the relations between gay identity politics and consumer lifestyles in the West, Tim Edwards (1994) delineates how a heterosexual ethos dominates the patterns of gender and sexuality within capitalist ideology, which, he argues, discriminates against and oppresses homosexual people. Edwards contends that within this capitalist logic concepts of masculinity and expressions of male gendering are strictly controlled under heteronormative institutions, with male homosexuality continuing to be classified as a sign of weakness and sexual deviance. In many Western societies this oppression of male homosexuality was the sex-political setting that incited modern gay movements which seek to create a positive homosexual identity. Gay identity politics developed through new senses of minority group membership and discourses of citizenship that emerged as social forms within a heteronormative consumer society. In this setting, the leading model of gay identity politics has been the strategy of coming out, which serves as the individual basis of sexual identity. Edwards notes: "Coming-out was now seen to work on three levels . . . : first, telling oneself that one is attracted to the same sex and is homosexual or gay in identity; second, telling others who are of the same identity in a safe, usually homosexually exclusive space; and third, and here there is the difference, telling the wider and usually straight society of family, friends and workplace" (Edwards 1994, 26). This coming out model of identity politics responded to a capitalist culture in which gay selfhood came to be defined in terms of consumer lifestyles. Indeed, many gay businesses grew on the back of this model of gay identity and the expansion of gay commodification. However, our study of Thai gay cultures highlights that the relationship between Thai gay men and their commercial spaces is also framed by the socioeconomic inequalities that structure the country's gay communities. While middle-class gay men may find personal success and fulfilment in Thailand's gay marketplaces, lower-income gay men may be excluded from the consumer lifestyles and hence the autonomy of a market-based homosexual identity.

Commodifying Male Bodies in an Apolitical Setting

In contrast to the situation in many Western countries, the Thai gay culture that emerged from the 1980s with the growth of gay print media and commercial venues was almost solely expressed through the logic of consumerism rather than through the medium of sexual politics or struggles for rights. From the early 1980s to the mid-2010s, the sense of collective gay identity for middle-class Thai gay men was not mobilized as a political tool to advance rights but rather was constituted to create safe spaces in everyday life. For many Thai gay men, confirming a gay identity was an aspirational strategy to achieve the status and advantages afforded by middle-class gay consumer lifestyles. Such as it existed in Thailand, gay identity politics was personalized, reduced to the level of the individual where it was exploited by consumer logics in which gay self-definition came to be subjected to the dictates of the market and the exchange of sexual commodities. Until the 2010s, the Thai project of gay identity formation did not find expression in a gay political movement for equal rights. Rather, it was translated as an expression of consumer rights in which gay men sought a place in modern Thai life by assimilating to the mainstream heteronormative social institutions of Thai capitalism.

In Western gay cultures, masculine body images have been constituted both within gay political movements—which sought to promote positive images of being homosexual as a strategic response to homophobia—as well as within consumer lifestyles that promoted masculinity as a homoerotic commodity. However, across the four decades of our research, Thai gay masculinity was not enacted within the politics of a movement for sexual liberation. Rather, it was situated in a network of market-centered relations of global and local appropriations. Until the early twenty-first century, Thai gay men were relatively politically disinterested when compared with the historical situation in Western gay communities. While homosexuality was minoritized within Thailand's heteronormative culture, it was not illegal or classed as a sin within the dominant religion of Theravada Buddhism. In not having been subjected to the religious and legal sanctions experienced by homosexual men in Western societies, Thai gay men did not have to mount as concerted a struggle to establish a place within their society, and as such capitalism rather than political activism has been the historically dominant influence on the formation of Thai gay identity and culture.

Because the autonomy of Thai gay men has been materialized by gay consumer lifestyles and homoerotic commodities, many in Thailand view capitalism more as a force for queer emancipation rather than subjection, and as a medium of local cultural differentiation rather than Westernizing homogenization. Nevertheless, while gay commercial media and spaces provide opportunities for forms of an autonomous gay life, Thai gay men cannot escape the unequal power relations that privilege higher-income men. When the performance of masculinity is primarily oriented toward becoming an indicator of gay consumer autonomy, this gendered form of sexual identity institutes new modes of discrimination. Market-based gay autonomy not only has the positive effect of enabling middle-class gay agency; it also reinforces forms of homonormativity in which different gay men are assigned unequal statuses based on relative degrees of masculine image and body appearance. This culture of masculine homonormativity is tightly bound with gay consumer lifestyles and regulates the standards of masculinity and sexual autonomy that serve as the norm for higher-income urban gay men.

The insertive *bi man ruk* found in online gay spaces exemplifies the privileged norm of Thai gay masculinity, being a more highly privileged status than either the sexually receptive *bi man rap* or effeminate gay men, *gay sao*. Since the early 2000s, this standard of gay masculinity has been promoted in both gay venues and cyberspaces. The masculine body and characteristics of the insertive *bi man ruk* has become the "must-have" sexual commodity and the popular image that many Thai gays have aspired to embody. This homonormative ideal, which is represented in both everyday Thai gay practices and in gay commercial scenes, is embedded within a structure of unequal social and sexual relations.

The commodified and mediatized settings of modern Thai gay life may appear superficially like gay cultures in the West and economically developed East Asian societies. However, such apparent similarity may obscure Thailand's deeply hierarchical class-structured social order as well as the distinctive meanings of localized concepts of homosexual being and identity that are articulated in Thai discourses. The full range of meanings of Thai gay masculinity can only be understood by distinguishing the different classes of gay men, whose daily lifestyles are often radically different. The socioeconomic dimensions of Thai gay social structures mean that Thai gay communities are not characterized by any common pattern of masculine gendering. Rather, there are diverse modes of expressing masculinity by which gay men from different classes perform, practice, and seek to define their gender for social advantage and personal benefit. The masculinities of Thai gay men not only afford an escape from homophobic sanctions but are also ordered by relations of economic and discursive power by which homosexual men both include and exclude each other. Thai gay masculine practices are not only means of social protection in a heteronormative social order; they are also critical for gay men's sexual subjectivity and social image in which socioeconomic status determines many activities. This understanding is the primary criterion by which we have sought to specify the kinds of masculinity that are created and negotiated by different groups of Thai gay men and how their respective masculine expressions are connected to the cultural politics of gender and sexuality in the country's gay scenes.

Thailand's Gay Class Divide and Alternative Masculinities

Appreciating how the two main socioeconomic fields of Thai gay masculinity—middle class and working class—are related forces us to rethink notions of hegemonic and alternative masculinity. R. W. Connell and James W. Messerschmidt's (2005) notion of hegemonic masculinity reflects historical and cultural settings in which the ideology of socially acceptable masculine sexual and gender roles is defined in relation to a male body that is expected to be strong, powerful, and invulnerable and which derives its meaning from a heteronormative patriarchal order that classifies manhood in relation to male sexual physiology and biology. In Connell and Messerschmidt's account, the ideological patterns of dominant forms of masculinity are regulated by social expectations that a man should fulfill the responsibilities of being a husband, father, and head of a family, and this cultural order maintains and stabilizes a binary gender system that privileges those men who uphold heterosexual norms.

However, this hegemonic masculinity is a social and cultural construct that does not correspond to the actual lives of all men. Although the norms of manhood are produced within a capitalist industrial logic in which men are required to live by wage labor, the cultural expectation that a man should be strong and powerful does not always relate directly to the lives of working-class men in societies such as Thailand. In Thailand's class hierarchy many men need to engage in compromises with the norms of hegemonic masculinity to create their own forms of being a man, which serve as alternative practices of embodying manhood. In Thailand to be a man is not merely to be inscribed within the dominant gender order. Thai forms of manhood are also further embedded within a class hierarchy that privileges middle-class men while minoritizing those from working-class backgrounds.

In Thai gay experiences of masculinity, conforming to patterns of normative masculinity is a response to complex relations between social images of masculine ideals, the sexual pleasure experienced by male bodies, and the economic and cultural hierarchies that privilege some men over others. These compounded relations between masculine ideals, desire, and class position lead to multiple layers and contradictions in the enactment of masculinity. Masculine expressions and representations are conducted within class-based social relations as discrepant forms of both hegemonic and alternative masculinity. Middle-class Thai gay men aim to conform to ideas of masculinity advertised by gay consumer culture, training their bodies in gyms and fitness centers to develop a masculine look that responds to ideas of the healthy metrosexual man. Lower-income, working-class men who work as go-go boy dancers, as well as the straight men who work as nude models in gay magazines, also participate in the dominant cultural order of masculinity. However, the masculine practices of male erotic dancers and nude models are not based on middle-class ideas of the healthy metrosexual male body. Rather, these men seek to embody notions of what is considered sexually attractive for middle-class gay clients, who pay to appreciate their bodies. The sense of masculinity of these working-class men, both straight and gay, centers on becoming an object of sexual consumption for middle-class gay clients. The gendering practices of working-class men operate to produce their bodies in desirable masculine forms fit to be marketed in Thailand's gay economy. In contrast, middle-class Thai gay men seek to embody norms of masculinity to affirm and confirm their subjectivity in terms of the two dimensions of gay identity and middle-class status. In Thailand's hierarchical social order, the sexual identities of middle-class gay men are privileged because they are constituted as masculine gay subjects, while the sexual identities of working-class gay men are minoritized because they form their masculinity to become objects of middle-class gay desire. Heterosexual men can also participate in this field of class-stratified masculine genderings where their masculine gender identity is affirmed by their ability to be appreciated as sexually attractive men.

Across the four decades of our research starting in the 1980s, the dynamics of the masculinities within Thai gay communities have represented how both gay and straight men have respectively recognized themselves within a variety of masculine body images in diverse contextualized *kala-thesa* time and place settings. The commodified masculinities of working-class gay and straight men are created under the influence of notions of hegemonic masculinity—that the ideal male body is defined by strength and toughness—and also in relation to the homoerotic desires of middle-class men. However, masculine practices are interspersed with somewhat feminine characteristics and ways of acting. In the case of coyote boy dancers, the male body is adjusted and modified in relation to both feminine and masculine characteristics. While coyote boy dancers may sport a masculine moustache, they also apply feminine makeup. This kind of oscillating masculinity is formed within the discursive power relations by which both gay and straight working-class men regulate themselves within Thailand's gay consumer culture, with both groups actively making and remaking their bodies as sexual objects.[1]

Thai gay men from different social and economic backgrounds have developed their own understandings of masculinity in a range of domains and spaces.

The print media space of gay magazines provided a platform for communication and sexual contact in which middle-class gay readers satisfied their sexual imagination by consuming photographs of male nudes. And for male models—who in the 1980s and 1990s were typically bar boys and other working-class men—these gay magazines were an economic space that afforded the opportunity to find economic support from high-income gay clients. The dancing stages in gay bars and pubs likewise formed sexualized spaces designed to satisfy the expectations of gay customers while also being economic spaces that were sites where go-go boy and coyote boy dancers generated their incomes. The spaces of commercial, members-only gyms served as locales for middle-class gay men to fulfill their sense of embodying a healthy, high-status masculinity. And the cyberspace of gay Camfrog chat rooms responded to the desires of gay and *bi*-identified men to find sex partners and reveal their bodies and sexual activities before live video cameras. And all these manifold spaces of diverse masculine practices across Thailand's modern gay cultures simultaneously reinforced while also challenging the normative patterns of male gender and sexuality in the country's heteronormative culture.

Class and Ethnicity

The class hierarchy of Thai gay masculinities is rendered even more complex by the fact that Thai gay cultures are also marked by an ethnicization of forms of masculinity. The ethnic diversity of Thailand, within which different regional and ethnic communities are characterized by different shades of skin coloring, has produced forms of ethnicized desire. The differential skin coloring and ethnic look of Thai men, as having either a fairer-complexioned (*khao*) Chinese-looking or a darker-skinned (*khem*) appearance, means that within each given socioeconomic class one may also find various ideals of masculine attractiveness. And these ethnicized differences within Thai gay cultures can be commodified to respond to multiple markets. While working-class men with a more Chinese "white Asian" look (Käng 2015) may produce their bodies for Asian gay customers, darker-skinned Thai-looking men may find work in venues catering to Western gay men. A working-class Thai man's "natural" appearance—whether as fair- or dark-complexioned—may influence which ethnocultural form of masculine attractiveness he strives to embody.

It nevertheless also needs to be acknowledged that not all lower-income working-class gay men are entirely excluded from homosexual consumerism or commercial gay spaces. Some poorer gay men and male sex workers may participate in aspects of the autonomy promised by consumerist gay lifestyles by engaging in sex work. Indeed, we have seen how many lower-income gay men—particularly go-go boy and coyote boy dancers—participate in gay consumer lifestyles in specific ways. They can obtain benefits from gay clients—whether money, material goods, or fashion accessories—that enable them to live and identify as gay consumers. Some coyote boys use their incomes to buy brand-name smartphones and fashion products and enjoy their spare time living a gay social life in pubs and discotheques. Their experiences of the autonomy of gay consumer cultures are enabled by the economic opportunities and support that comes from high-income gay clients, and their sense of gay identity is negotiated through their social and sexual relations with wealthier gay men.

In the 2010s and 2020s, economic status is no longer the sole factor that defines who can be afford a modern gay lifestyle. Digital media have meant that participating in aspects of a gay consumer lifestyle have become increasingly possible whatever a Thai man's social background, education level, or economic status. Virtual gay social networks in online spaces have enabled men from all backgrounds to satisfy their sexual desires and express their identity. In the early 2010s, some men sought sexual partners in gay video chat rooms and negotiated their sexual and gender identities within nuanced definitions of *bi man* (versatile masculine), *bi ruk* (versatile insertive partner), or *bi rap* (versatile receptive partner) aiming to convince their sexual partners of their masculine sexual attractiveness.

Thai Gay Gender Contextuality: Between Masculinity and Effeminacy

Connell's (1995) formative study of forms of masculinity in multicultural Western societies was given a plural title, *Masculinities*. Her notion of "multiple masculinities" denotes the genderings characteristic of racial, ethnic, and sexual minorities within a multicultural society, which may exhibit alternative norms of masculinity in contradistinction to the hegemonic forms that are characteristic of the dominant groups. However, in this model any given man is imagined as embodying just one of these hegemonic (heterosexual Caucasian) or marginal (gay or ethnic) masculinities. This is not the same type of gender multiplicity detailed in our book, where the same person may enact different, and equally normative, forms of being a gay man in different time and place *kala-thesa* settings. For Thai gay men the interrelationship between masculine and feminine practices and expression is realized through a continuity between acts of *ab man*, "to be masculine," and *taek sao*, "to be effeminate." Thai gay men respectively appropriate and re-create both masculine and feminine characteristics in association with their social and sexual activities. This does not constitute a source of sexual tension but rather takes place as social play that enables and facilitates the creation of multiple modalities of both masculinity and femininity.

Ab man masculine acting is expressed in response to social images that enhance Thai gay men's chances of being respected as a man in their social world and also as being sexually attractive to other gay men. Western gay straight acting is a masculine performance that emerged as an existential survival strategy from the need to pass in an often violently homophobic society (see Eguchi 2009). In contrast, Thai gay *ab man* acting is a masculine performance constituted from the need to present masculine images by which gay men can maintain good relations with friends and family as well as with gay lovers and partners. Furthermore, in contrast to Western gay straight acting, Thai gay *ab man* is an appropriation that is realized through a coordination of both masculinity and effeminacy. The unmasculine feminine characteristics known as *taek sao* are not entirely excluded from Thai gay men's gender dynamics. Thai gay men are highly context sensitive and adapt their gender performances to the setting of social activities and the circumstances of sexual intimacy. The duality and fluidity of Thai gay men's masculinity (*khwam-pen-chai*) and effeminacy (*khwam-sao*) effect a gender dynamic of constant adaptation. There is no necessary contradiction between a Thai gay man acting *ab man* in one setting while acting *taek sao* in another. In Thai culture skill in acting appropriately for the *kala-thesa* time and place circumstances necessitates adapting one's presentation, demeanor, and linguistic expression to each setting. In Thai gender and sexual cultures founded on a multiplicity of settings, it is incumbent on every man, and every woman, to develop skill in modulating their gender expression rather than maintaining a singular, hegemonic masculine or feminine presentation.

The experiences of Thai coyote boy and go-go boy dancers exemplify the masculine/feminine duality of Thai gay gendering, constituting a fluid and dynamic form of masculinity in which gay men draw on various sexual and gendered practices of both manhood and effeminacy. Thai gay men's masculinity cannot be interpreted as only constituting a resistance to or rebellion against effeminate expression. Rather, the forms of Thai gay manhood are expressed along a continuum that also includes acts that can be regarded as more or less feminine. For Thai gay men, the characteristics of masculinity are not established by means of an exclusionary binary that opposes masculinity to femininity as noncommunicating polarities. Through complex relations masculine traits are interconnected with feminine mannerisms. The gender differences found in Thai gay communities, which are represented and expressed by both masculine and effeminate body images and acting, are not constructed through a single categorization of heteronormative gender roles. Rather, they are actively adopted, repeated, and re-created from multiple sources of masculine and feminine expression.

The Blurred Boundary of Homosexual and Heterosexual Masculinities

In the middle decades of the twentieth century, the modernizing Thai nation-state required its citizens to conform to the dictates of its heteronormative gender ideology, under which men were directed to behave according to the ideal gender role known as the *luk phu-chai* or "real man." However, this idea of being a "real Thai man" has been negotiated in diverse ways by men from different social classes and economic statuses. Coyote boy and go-go boy dancers may engage in both heterosexual and homosexual sexual intercourse and participate in both insertive and receptive anal intercourse without anxiety about losing their sense of masculinity. Their sense of their sexuality is not attached to a fixed notion of masculinity and their sexual desire and pleasure is modulated according to different situations.

While Thai gay men may move between masculine *ab man* and feminine *taek sao* gendered performances, it is nonetheless the case that in sexual settings masculine presentations are valorized. This primacy of masculine gendering in men's sexuality also contributes to a blurring of the divide between homosexual and heterosexual interactions in some settings. The male models pictured in gay magazines redefined their masculine body image both in terms of homoerotic expression and heterosexual relations. Their maleness was not confined to the category of heterosexuality but rather was often associated with context-specific social practices and forms of sexual contact. In Thai gay Camfrog chat rooms, many men did not identify their sexuality but rather referred to a masculine imaginary in which the male who is labeled as *bi man ruk*, masculine and taking the insertive role in sex, is favored and admired. In this virtual space a confirmation of a man's sexual identity is not necessary if his gender identity is affirmed in the context of revealing his body to the sexual gaze of other men.

In these settings of affirming masculine gender identity the essentialist binary opposition of heterosexual versus homosexual masculinity is blurred. The masculinities of gay and straight men are not necessarily separated out in terms of different sexualities. Since the early 2000s, it is also no longer the case that straight men in Thailand necessarily present more masculine images or that gay men are viewed as being weaker. With the emergence of middle-class gay gym culture, some gay-identified men have developed increasingly muscular bodies to conform to images of the strong and healthy metrosexual man. This physical culture

of exercise has destabilized the boundary of gay and straight middle-class masculinities. It is necessary to exercise care in specifying what constitutes homosexual
or heterosexual masculinity as the embodiment of masculine characteristics and
maleness has been resituated within a dynamic complex of social interactions.

Gay Thailand After Print Media

Our book has dealt with the period from the early 1980s to the 2010s when commercial print publications were the dominant medium through which discourses
and visual representations of gay gendering and identity were communicated in
Thailand. Print publications have now been superseded by online media, and
Thai gay masculinities have continued to evolve in the post-print era of online
digital communications.

The hypermasculinity of gym-enhanced, middle-class *kam pu* male bodies has been perpetuated as Bangkok has become a regional center for regular
gay circuit parties, such as G-Circuit (see Narupon 2024). Established in 2007,
G-Circuit dance parties have become staples of Thailand's annual gay calendar, drawing thousands of gay tourists from across East and Southeast Asia and
from all parts of Thailand. The style of the participants in these expensive dance
events, with tickets selling for upwards of three thousand baht, is the gym-buffed
"white Asian" look (Käng 2015) with slimmer, darker-skinned men being in the
minority. The hypermasculinity of the international gym-cultured gay *kam pu*
has also been paralleled by alternative East Asian influences on Thai gay gender
and sexuality. The "soft masculinity" characteristic of Korean boy bands and the
popular Boys Love manga and TV series, called Y (from *yaoi*) in Thailand (see
Phuwin and Natthanon 2021; Baudinette 2024), has also influenced contemporary styles. And older forms of working-class slim masculinity continue to exist.
In summary, there has been a further multiplication of styles of masculinity in
the era of online media, with diversification and contextualization continuing to
characterize Thai gay cultures of masculinity in the 2020s.

The Rise of Thai LGBTQI+ Politics

One of the most significant changes in Thailand over the past couple of decades
has been the rise of community-based queer activism and the increasing relevance of LGBTQI+ rights issues in national politics. While Thailand's queer
communities emerged as some of the largest and most visible in Southeast Asia
in the second half of the twentieth century, at that time the country's political
leaders largely regarded LGBTQI+ people and their issues to be unimportant and

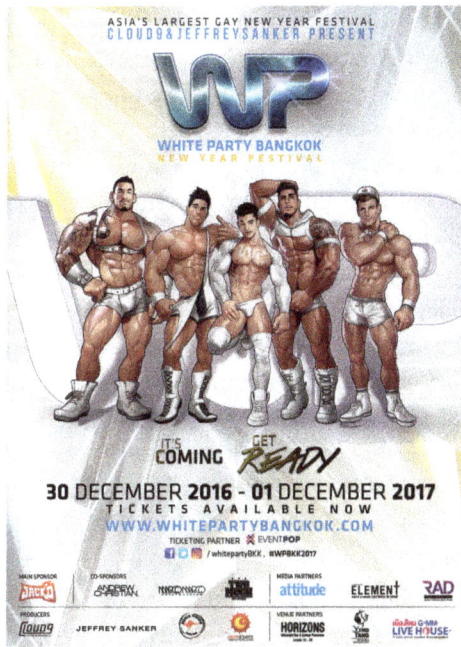

FIGURE 20. Poster advertising the 2017 gay New Year White Party in Bangkok. Bangkok is an international center for regular, themed gay circuit parties drawing in thousands of middle-class participants from across East and Southeast Asia. The muscular physiques of the cartoon images in the advertisement reflect the muscleman body style that increasingly typifies middle-class gay masculinities in Thailand and across many parts of East Asia.

not relevant to national political concerns. Exceptions were sections within the national health bureaucracy, which in the 1990s collaborated with new gay community organizations in combating the HIV/AIDS epidemic, and the Tourism Authority of Thailand, which regularly used the country's queer communities as advertising drawcards to promote international gay tourism. However, it is no longer the case that Thailand's gay communities and cultures of masculinity exist in an apolitical field dominated solely by the market and commercial media. LGBTQI+ issues have increasingly moved to center stage in Thailand's national politics. In 2021 and 2022 Thai queer groups for the first time joined with prodemocracy activists in public demonstrations against the military-led government. Nattapol describes queer participation in one of the prodemocracy street rallies held in August 2021: "LGBT rights activists [were] easily discernible among the pro-democracy protesters. They sported the rainbow-colored pride flags, dressed as drag queens, danced in the parade, and sometimes turned the street into a catwalk for a satirical fashion show aimed at the Thai monarchy. Their demands were inspired by the global gay rights movement, such as legalization of same-sex marriage and sex workers and educating about gender and sexuality diversity or *khwam-lak-lai-thang-phet*" (Nattapol 2022, 1–2).

In the late 1990s and early 2000s, occasional pride parades were held in Bangkok and other cities with large numbers of gay venues such as Pattaya and Phuket. However, these early parades, made up of floats organized by gay bars, were sporadic and were frequently sponsored by commercial gay venues. The participants in these early parades were often men and trans women working at gay bars, which reflected the dominance of commercial venues in Thai gay life throughout the twentieth century. Pride parades resumed in Bangkok in 2022 after the end of COVID-19 lockdowns and now had a markedly different character from the earlier events. In the place of bar workers, members of large numbers of community organizations representing gay men, lesbians, trans women, and trans men participated. Commercial involvement was also prominent, but instead of floats sponsored by gay bars the parades in 2022, 2023, and 2024 included rainbow-colored vehicles displaying the logos of mainstream businesses targeting queer markets, including airlines, car brands, and international fashion labels. And for the first time, political leaders also walked in the parades to show support for the country's queer communities. In 2022 the mayor of Bangkok, Chadchart Sittipunt, who in the 2010s had been deputy minister of transport in the national government led by Thailand's first female prime minister, Yingluck Shinawatra, attended the parade. In the 2023 and 2024 pride parades in Bangkok, prominent members of both the Move Forward and Pheu Thai parties, which together won the largest number of elected MPs in the 2023 national elections, also participated.

Pheu Thai, the main party in the coalition government that emerged after the May 2023 general election, appointed an LGBTQI+ policy officer during the lead-up to the vote, and several major parties actively courted the pink vote by including the legalization of gay marriage in their policy platforms. The Move Forward Party, which won the most seats in the 2023 election, has four openly queer members in the current Thai parliament. And in 2024, after over a decade of lobbying by a coalition of diverse community groups, Thailand's parliament passed a marriage equality bill, with Thailand becoming the first Southeast Asian country to legislate for gay marriage.

Multiple Thai Gay Masculinities in the Digital Era

Thai gay men made the transition from consuming print media to becoming users of online media platforms extremely rapidly. In 2014 the online marketing and services company Zocial Inc. surveyed gay Facebook users around the world to determine the number of gay people using this social media platform in different countries (Marketingoops! 2014). According to the report of the survey, in 2014 India had the highest number of gay Facebook users, totaling about three million men, followed by the United States and Egypt. With 340,000 gay Facebook users, Thailand ranked tenth in the world.

The 2010s were a period of rapid change for social media in Thailand as increasing numbers of gay dating apps jostled for dominance in the Thai gay market. In 2015 the popular Thai website and online discussion board pantip.com detailed the most popular gay dating apps in the country, reporting that Grindr was the most widely used app followed by Jack'd and Hornet (Pantip 2015). Other gay dating apps used in Thailand at that time were Guyspy, Boyahoy, Planetromeo, Gaypark, Scruff, Surge, Disco, and Tinder. In 2016 the Chinese gay dating app Blued launched a live function called HeeSay, by which users could broadcast various daily activities live. This new function led to Blued becoming extremely popular across Asia and, in 2016, 180,000 Thai gay men registered to use it. Blued also opened an office in Bangkok to develop Thai-language functionality to more directly target the Thai gay market (Techsauce 2016). In a 2018 study of Thai gay men between twenty and thirty-five years old who used more than one dating app, Blued, Hornet, Jack'd, GuySpy, and Grindr were found to be the most popular (Worayut 2018). Another study conducted a couple of years later in 2020 found that the most popular gay dating apps among Thai men at that time were Hornet, Tinder, and Blued, with self-identified bisexual men preferring to use Twitter and Facebook (Peerasek et al. 2020). In 2021 Benjarong Tirapalika (2021) found that Twitter (since renamed X) was widely used by gay men to facilitate hookups for group sex.

While the online technologies of gay dating apps enable instantaneous erotic communication in virtual space, establishing physical and emotional relationships still takes place in physical spaces. Face-to-face meetings with someone contacted on a dating app are now called *nat yim*, "meeting to smile (and be polite)." A *nat yim* is a date to check whether a person they contacted matches their online profile. A situation where a person's actual appearance does not match their profile is described as *mai trong pok*, "not the same as the image on the cover (of a book, etc.)." A hookup for sex with someone met on a gay dating app is now called *nat yet*, "meeting to fuck."

The short messages that gay users posted on Twitter in the early 2020s were similar to the self-descriptions of gay men published in the personal classifieds columns of gay magazines in the 1980s and 1990s. Twitter users defined their sexual preferences as either insertive (*ruk*), receptive (*rap*), or versatile (*both*), using terms that had become established on gay chat boards such as Camfrog in the early 2000s. And just as Camfrog users had identified themselves with sexually explicit IDs, the roman-script hashtags that Thai gay men used on Twit-ter accounts two decades later also used direct and often crude expressions. The use of idiosyncratic and often nonstandard roman transcriptions of Thai sexual terms evaded online censorship that was more oriented toward detecting English obscenities. Examples included #sex moo (i.e., *sek mu*, "group sex"), #taek nok (i.e., *taek nork*, "cumming outside [the body]"), #yed dek (i.e., *yet dek*, "boy fuck-ing"), #sod roo (i.e., *sot ru*, "bareback fucking"), #sod (i.e., *sot*, "barebacking").

The openness of many sexualities on Thai Twitter sheds light on how online communication has allowed groups of people who were previously marginalized in the dominant masculine gay culture to claim space. Larger-bodied gay men, effeminate gays, men interested in BDSM, and older gay men, among others cre-ated their own Thai Twitter groups and established networks outside the norms of gay masculine attractiveness that had been promoted by gay media. The newer generation of online communication platforms has allowed the normative forms of gay masculinity that dominated images in gay media in the late twentieth and early twenty-first centuries to be challenged (Benjarong 2021).

The OnlyFans platform was launched in 2016 and has become very popu-lar among celebrities looking to create content and earn money by collecting payments from online followers. Gay erotic content creators became common in Thailand starting in 2020, with male models from gay magazines and male dancers from gay bars creating porn distributed via OnlyFans. Like the hashtag groups of Twitter/X, Thai gay groups on OnlyFans reflect a wide variety of physi-cal appearances including slim, dark-skinned, short, tattooed, feminine, body-builder, older, and younger.

In the 2020s, social media have facilitated the emergence of increasingly diverse online sociocultural spaces where multiple expressions of gender are vis-ible, reflecting the fact that a larger range of different types of masculinity are now competing and challenging the representational norms that were established in the era of gay print media (Benjarong 2021). While online platforms such as OnlyFans have been criticized by Thai moral conservatives as bad influences on Thai youth, these media have enabled a new generation of Thai gay men to explore diverse expressions of sex and masculinity that are consistent with their own tastes and lifestyles. While emerging from a commercial foundation, digital media are nonetheless capable of creating dynamic social networks that engender increased self-respect by highlighting diversity.

The multiple dynamic patterns described in this book reveal that masculin-ity needs to be seen as a set of possible social and cultural practices that are not confined within any given category of gender or sexuality. Masculinity is not uni-fied within a single, fixed, or universal notion of manhood but rather is complex in a wide range of cultural settings (Cornwall and Lindisfarne 1994). Notions of masculinity are fluid and situational and need to be viewed through the lens of the multiple ways that human beings may understand what it means to be a "man" in any particular setting. Masculinities are defined, and redefined, in social interaction, being situated within contested practices and cultural discourses in everyday life. As Matt Mutchler (2000, 15) contends, gay men are sexual actors who adapt and innovate sexual scripts in light of shifting social and sexual environments and complex, dynamic cultural norms. Our case studies of the history of modern Thai gay masculinities reveal that the discourses and representations of masculinity available to gay men in molding their sexual identity and gendered subjecthood do not emerge solely as matters of personal choice. Rather, they develop from practices of signification in which commercial mass media have assumed a dominant role in the increasingly diverse worlds of gendered existence that globalizing capitalism has brought into being.

GENERATIONS OF THAI GAY MAGAZINES

Listed in alphabetical order with number of issues according to decade of publication.

Thai Gay Magazines from the 1980s

Commercial Magazines (nine titles)

Gay Prasopkan ("gay experiences"), 11 issues
Horng Ha Liam ("the pentagonal room"), 128 issues
Midway, 88 issues
Mithuna Junior, 96 issues
Morakot ("emerald"), 129 issues
Neon, 157 issues
Violet—Entertainment of Purple Friend, 29 issues
Violet Home, 7 issues
Yort Nai Baep Domon ("top Domon male models"), 15 issues

Thai Gay Magazines from the 1990s

Commercial Magazines (sixty-one titles)

Big Boy Lap Chaphor ("big boy top secret"), 2 issues

Big Boy Prasopkan lae San-banthoeng Chai Si-muang ("big boy experiences and entertainment of lavender men"), 14 issues

Body Magazine, 18 issues

Buddy, 1 issue

Canon, 2 issues

Chap, 8 issues

Child New Wave Magazine, 4 issues

Classique, 2 issues

Club 69, 2 issues

Dreamman, 5 issues

Dude, 7 issues

Flesh, 5 issues

Flesh Junior, 3 issues

GR, 27 issues

Grace Album, 23 issues

Grace Junior, 3 issues

Grace Magazine, 7 issues

Grace Male, 21 issues

Guy Magazine, 12 issues

H Magazine, 13 issues

Heat Collection, 4 issues

Heat Men, 131 issues

Heat Special Secret, 16 issues

Hero 1994, 2 issues

Him-01, 1 issue

Him Club Magazine, 3 issues

Hot Guys, 15 issues

Icon, 2 issues

Kamp, 3 issues

Lap Chaphor Chao Si-muang ("top secrets of lavender people"), 124 issues

Leo, 7 issues

Leon, 1 issue

Male, 49 issues

Male Album, 8 issues

Male Mini, 31 issues

Male Mini Special/Secret, 8 issues

Male Special, 7 issues

Male Sut-supda ("male weekend"), 19 issues

Man Studio, 10 issues

Na Ya ("Oh yeah!"), 4 issues

Neon Special, 20 issues

Neon Weekend, 8 issues

New Half, 4 issues

New Wave, 5 issues

Next Men, 2 issues

Prasopkan Khrang Raek Khorng Rao Chao Si-muang ("first experiences of us lavender people"), 5 issues

Queer, 2 issues

Uncensored by Male, 6 issues

Weekend Men, 92 issues

Weekend News, 4 issues

Young, 5 issues

Community Magazines (three titles)

Anjaree-san ("the Anjaree magazine"), 27 issues

Julasan Kunlagay ("good gay magazine") (F.A.C.T. Sheet), 42 issues

Pink Ink (in English), 5 issues

Thai Gay Magazines from the 2000s

Commercial Magazines (forty-six titles)

Back Door, 2 issues

Born: Up to the Top Models, 5 issues

Boy Models Extra, 10 issues

Boy Models Magazine, 27 issues

Boyburi ("boy town"), 1 issue

Boyzone, 1 issue

Cellman, 2 issues

Chai Chakan ("he-man"), 5 issues

Chai Chakan Special, 2 issues

Cock, 6 issues

D-Day, 21 issues

D-Diary, 4 issues

D Guy, 12 issues

Dark, 4 issues

Deep, 7 issues

Deer, 7 issues

Demand, 19 issues

DiK (a play on both "dick" and *K* for khuay; i.e., "cock"), 4 issues

Door, 43 issues

Door Dek ("door kid"), 7 issues

Emaid, 1 issue

Erotic Man, 5 issues

Exit, 2 issues

Exotica, 6 issues

G Zone, 32 issues

Glamour, 4 issues

Gray, 2 issues

Head Shot—New Gendar [sic] *Models Magazine*, 10 issues

Hey!, 43 issues

Hot-Man, 4 issues

I Am Guy, 10 issues

K Mag (i.e., "*khuay* [cock] magazine"), 23 issues

KFM (an acronym for "*Khuay* [cocks] for Men"), 2 issues

Khon Nork ("the outsider"), 8 issues

Lotud (a play on "lotus" and *tut* [ass]), 1 issue

Maxi—Magazine for Purple Friend, 3 issues

MM—Man to Men Magazine, 15 issues

Moke (from "smoke"; i.e., "to have oral sex"), 2 issues

My Way, 3 issues

Real—For Real Metro Men, 13 issues

Stage—Stage and Reality, 64 issues

Step by Stage, 31 issues

Thai Guys, 44 issues

V-Z Men, 4 issues

X Story, 12 issues

Z-Men, 16 issues

Community Magazines (two titles)

More Than Man, 24 issues

Sai-fon Ton Rung ("rain showers at the end of the rainbow"), 12 issues

Free Bar Magazines (seven titles)

Axis Magazine, 14 issues
Bangkok Gay Max, 17 issues
Bangkok Variety, 92 issues
Gay Guide Bangkok, 116 issues
Max Guide Line, 85 issues
Max Magazine, 140 issues
PLU Guide Thailand, 4 issues

Thai Gay Magazines from the 2010s

Commercial Magazines (twenty-seven titles)

Attitude Thailand, 66 issues
Firm, 23 issues
Firm Special, 4 issues
G Story, 3 issues
Glow—For Metro Men, 32 issues
Grease F&E, 11 issues
Hero, 2 issues
Jan Raem ("waning moon"), 11 issues
Ka-Door ("cock"), 1 issue
Khorng Khorng Khao ("his cock"), 1 issue
Lang Suan ("behind the orchard"), 1 issue
Mean, 6 issues
Mecs, 3 issues
Menthol—The New Way of Us, 2 issues

Nai Num ("young guy"), 4 issues
Nam Phrik Num ("young guy's chili sauce"), 5 issues
Need+, 29 issues
Norngmon ("young guy"), 4 issues
Omkoi ("suck cock"), 1 issue
Reuang Khorng Rao ("our stories"), 13 issues
Sexemen, 2 issues
Shake, 5 issues
Show K ("show cocks"), 1 issue
SOLID, 12 issues
Tom-Act (lesbian magazine), 60 issues
Uncut—Album Nude Magazine, 2 issues
Up!, 3 issues

Free Bar Magazines (eight titles)

Desire, 46 issues
GB Guide, 77 issues
GM Guide, 59 issues
Guta Magazine, 7 issues
Out in Thailand Magazine (in English), 60 issues
Spice!, 54 issues
Sticky Rice, 12 issues
Thai Puan ("Thai friend"), 76 issues

Glossary of Thai Terms

ab bao To feign innocence to appear attractive and cute while in fact being worldly and sexually experienced.

ab mai nian or *ab man mai nian* To fail or be unsuccessful in pretending to be straight acting or masculine, as when a gay man's performance of masculinity is undermined by an effeminate gesture or use of words.

ab man For a gay man to act in a masculine way, straight acting. See also *kek man*.

achip gay "The gay profession," an expression formerly used in the Thai press and media reflecting perceptions of gay men as male prostitutes and sex workers.

aep jit "A sneaky mind/persona," coined in the 1980s by the former academic and gay media personality Seri Wongmontha to translate "to be closeted" into Thai.

ai "That ... (guy)," a title used before men's or boys' names or in combination with other terms either to form derogatory third-person expressions to refer to heterosexual men and masculine gay men or, conversely, to show friendship or relationship in reference to men or boys. Compare with *ee*.

ai ha "That damn guy," "Damn you!," derogatory. *Ha* refers to a spirit believed to be responsible for the plague and is a term that occurs in a number of exclamations.

ai hia "That damn guy," "Damn you!," derogatory. *Hia* is a type of large monitor lizard, and the name of this reptile is one of the strongest derogatory expressions in Thai.

ai sat "That damn guy," "Damn you!," derogatory. *Sat* means "animal" in Thai.

antha or *luk antha* Technical term for the testes.

arom ying "Female emotions," an expression reflecting the view that gay men have feminine emotions and that femininity is embodied in the gay male.

awaiyawa "Organ," an abbreviation of *awaiyawa phet*, "sex organ."

awut "Weapon," a metaphor for the penis.

bandor A Buddhist term for nonnormative gendering, widely equated with the Thai term *kathoey* for trans woman.

bi Abbreviation from the English "bisexual," in gay usage may refer to masculine presentation rather than bisexual identity.

bi both From the English "bi(sexual) both," a masculine man who engages in both insertive (*ruk*) and receptive (*rap*) sex with another man. See also *dai thang mot, dai thang ruk lae rap*.

bi man From the English "bi(sexual) man," a masculine homosexual man.

bi rap A masculine man who prefers the receptive (*rap*) role in sex with another man.

bi-ruk A masculine man who prefers the insertive (*ruk*) role in sex with another man.

biang-ben thang-phet A technical term meaning "to be sexually deviant."

bo na or *bo paeng* To brush powder on the face.

both From the English "both (top and bottom)," a man who is sexually versatile and can be either top (*ruk*) or bottom (*rap*).

chai chakan A strong, brave man in the prime of life.

chai-chatri A brave man, a real man, one who is regarded as embodying the ideals of Thai masculinity.

chai dai chai kheu yort chai "A man who gets a man [sexually] is the peak of manhood."

chak wao To masturbate, wank; literally, "to fly a kite," denoting pulling (*chak*) on the string of a kite (*wao*) with a hand motion similar to masturbating.

chao dorkmai "Flower people," a metaphorical expression used in the 1970s and 1980s to refer to gay men in general.

chatri A male fighter or warrior.

chi niw Pointing the index finger to the front, regarded as a feminine form of body language as in female fashion shows.

chor laeo "Having been snipped or chopped," an idiom denoting postoperative male-to-female *kathoey* or trans women.

dai thang mot "Can [do] everything," to be sexually versatile, to be either top or bottom.

dai thang ruk lae rap "Can be both top (*ruk*) and bottom (*rap*)," to be sexually versatile. See also *both* and *dai mot*.

datjarit To act in an affected way, especially to be effeminate.

dek bar A male sex worker employed by a gay bar.

dek khai or *dek khai tua* A male sex worker.

dek nang drink A male sex worker employed by a gay bar; literally, "a young guy who sits and drinks (in a bar with a customer)."

dek off A male sex worker employed by a gay bar and able to be engaged to be taken off the premises for sex.

deng, also *na deng* To have a powdered or whitened face.

dian "I," an informal version of the feminine first-person pronoun *dichan*, sometimes used by *kathoey*.

dichan "I," a formal feminine first-person pronoun, sometimes used by *kathoey*.

dork-thorng "You slut!," a bitchy slang expression used by and for women, *kathoey*, and gay men. See also *ee-raet, raet*.

du mai ork "Unable to tell [whether or not a man is gay]," an expression used in reference to straight-acting gay men, a gay man who conforms to heteronormative patterns of masculinity.

dut khuay "To suck cock."

ee "That . . . (woman/girl/*kathoey*/gay man)," an informal feminine title used before the names of women, girls, *kathoey*, or gay men. Also used in combination with other terms to form derogatory third-person expressions to refer to heterosexual women, *kathoey*, and effeminate gay men or, conversely, to show close friendship or relationship among *kathoey* and gay men. Compare with *ai*.

Ee! An exclamation of fear or affected surprise, used by *kathoey*.

Ee-dork or *ee-dork-thorng* "Slut," "You slut!" See also *ee-raet, raet*.

Ee-pluak "That damn woman/*kathoey*/effeminate gay man," "You damn woman/*kathoey*/effeminate gay man"; literally, "Damn termite."

Ee-raet A bitchy, slang term, "You slut!" See also *dork-thorng, ee-dork, raet*.

Ee-ran A bitchy, slang term, "You slut!" See also *dork-thorng, ee-dork, raet*.

Ee-sat "That damn woman/*kathoey*/effeminate gay man," "You damn woman/*kathoey*/effeminate gay man"; literally, "Damn (female) animal."

fai rap The "receptive party" in sex, a bottom.

fai ruk The "insertive party" in sex, a top.

fang muk To insert small round objects such as pearls (*muk*) or glass beads beneath the skin of the penis as a sign of virility and masculine sexual prowess.

gay both A gay man who is sexually versatile, able to be both top (*ruk*) and bottom (*rap*) in sex with another man.

gay king A gay man who plays the insertive role in sex with another man, a top.

gay man both A masculine gay man who is sexually versatile, able to be both top (*ruk*) and bottom (*rap*) in sex with another man.

gay man rap A masculine gay man who is a bottom (*rap*).

gay man ruk A masculine gay man who is a top (*ruk*).

gay queen A gay man who is a bottom (*rap*).

gay rap A gay man who is a bottom (*rap*).

gay ruk A gay man who is a top (*ruk*).

gay sao An effeminate gay man, "a girlie gay man."

gay sao both An effeminate gay man who can be "both" top and bottom.

gay sao rap An effeminate gay man who is a bottom (*rap*).

gay sao ruk An effeminate gay man who is a top (*ruk*).

ha An informal sentence particle used by some men.

ham Northeastern Thailand term for the penis and testes.

hee khan "[You've got] an itchy cunt!," a derogatory expression used of a woman or *kathoey* who is regarded as showing too much interest in sex. Used by *kathoey* to mean that they feel horny.

hoei "Hey!," an exclamation and expletive used by masculine speakers.

hun firm To have a "firm body." Coyote boy slang for the firm but not overly muscular physique.

hun khi-ya Denotes the skinny body of a drug user, "to have the physique of a druggie." Coyote boy slang for having a sexually attractive slim body.

jampi A colloquial term for the penis; the shape of the boy's penis is often compared to a champaka (*jampi*) flower.

jao kha "Yes," a very formal expression used by women and *kathoey*.

jao lok "Lord of the world," slang term for the penis.

jik kat To blame in a bitchy, biting (*kat*) way; used by *kathoey*.

jik wik To put on a wig, used by *kathoey*.

ju Slang term for the penis, often in a cute sense, also *kraju* and *ai ju*.

K. Slang for the penis, the letter "K" is the first letter of the spelling of *khuay*, "cock," in roman script.

kadae To show off, used by *kathoey*.

kador See *krador*.

kam pu "Crab claw," a slang expression that denotes the large biceps and muscled upper torso of a male bodybuilder; a humorous, mildly derogatory expression denoting a man whose physique is regarded as overbuilt.

kari Prostitute, whore.

kathoey Trans woman.

kathoey khwai "A water buffalo *kathoey*," a derogatory expression for a *kathoey* with a large body and muscles and whose physique does not match the ideals of feminine beauty.

kathoey mai plaeng phet "Nontranssexual *kathoey*," a trans woman who has not had gender-reassignment surgery.

kathoey mi ngu "A *kathoey* with a snake," a slang expression for a preoperative trans woman, a *kathoey* who still has a penis or "snake" (*ngu*).

kathoey plaeng phet "Changed-sex *kathoey*" or "transsexual *kathoey*," a trans woman who has had gender-reassignment surgery.

kek To pretend, be pretentious, or put on airs; a slang term borrowed from the Chao Zhou or Tae Jiw Chinese dialect.

kek man To be "straight acting," a mildly derogatory idiom which implies that a gay man acts butch but is in fact girlie (*sao*) or effeminate; common in the 1980s and 1990s but largely replaced by *ab man* in the early 2000s.

kep akan "To maintain [a masculine] position or stance," for a gay man to refrain from extravagant bodily gestures that might reveal his gender nonconformity and thus lead to suspicion that he might be homosexual. See also *ab bao*, *kek man*, *khip luk*, and *mai sadaeng ork*.

kep meu "To keep [one's] hands [still]," for a gay man to refrain from extravagant use of his hands when speaking and so perform normative, restrained masculinity. Compare *kep akan*.

kha A polite feminine sentence particle used by women and *kathoey*.

khai "Eggs," colloquial term for the testes.

khai ham A collective term for the penis and testicles.

khip luk "To keep [a masculine] look," from English "keep look"; for a gay man to refrain from extravagant bodily gestures that might reveal his gender nonconformity and arouse suspicion that he might be homosexual. See also *ab bao*, *kek man*, *kep akan*, and *mai sadaeng ork*.

khong-kraphan Magical invulnerability ritual.

khong-kraphan chatri Masculine ritual to confer a man with magical invulnerability.

khorng "Thing," a common slang term for the penis.

khorng lap "Secret thing," common slang term for the penis.

khrap A polite masculine sentence particle used by men.

khrapphom A very formal masculine sentence particle used by men.

khreuang "Machine," a common slang term for the penis.

khuay The most common slang term for the penis, "cock" or "dick." Also an exclamation used by men, "Damn!"

khuay khaeng "To have a hard cock," to have an erection.

khuay luk To keep up an erection, such as by using a cock ring.

khuay mai khaeng A flaccid penis, to fail to get or maintain an erection.

khwam lak-lai thang-phet A formal term for sex/gender diversity.

khwam-pen-chai "Being a man," "being male," a formal expression for masculinity.

khwam-pen-ying "Being a woman," "being female," a formal expression for femininity.

khwam-sao "Girliness" or "girlishness," an informal cute or sweet expression; compare *khwam-pen-ying*.

khwam-witthan Sexual perversion.

king See *gay king*.

krador An impolite slang term for the penis used by men, also *kador*.

krajiao A slang term for the penis, also *jiaw* and *ai jiaw*.

kraphom A very formal first-person pronoun used by men.

krapok The testes, the scrotum.

ku An informal and at times crude first-person pronoun, mostly used by men but increasingly also used by women.

kunla gay "A good gay man," a term coined by gay activist Natee Teerarojjanapongs in the 1990s to denote a gay man who conforms to social norms and so is accepted within mainstream society.

len fitnet From "fitness," to work out in a gym to get fit.

len klam To work out in a gym to develop muscles.

lia khuay To lick or suck cock (crude).

lia nom To lick or suck the nipples.

luk phu-chai To be a real man, a man who embodies Thai ideals of muscular masculinity, to be "man's man." See also *chai-chatri*.

maeng A crude exclamation, an abbreviation of *yet mae meung*, "fuck your mother."

mai sadaeng ork "Not showing or expressing (one's homosexuality or gayness)," to be straight acting or passing as straight. Contrast with *sadaeng-ork*, "showing" or "expressing" femininity or effeminacy.

makheua phao "Grilled eggplant," slang expression for a flaccid penis or erectile dysfunction, with a wrinkled penis being compared to soft, grilled eggplant.

mamasang From "Mama San," the "madam" or "captain" of a gay bar who arranges sexual services between male sex workers and clients, a role often played by an older *kathoey* or effeminate gay man, hence the use of the female term.

man From "man," to act in a normatively masculine way.

mangkorn "Dragon," a slang term for the penis.

mee "Bear"; in Thai gay culture *mee* can denote either a fat gay man or a big-muscled bodybuilder. See *kam pu.*

na deng To have a powdered or whitened face.

na ya Colloquial feminine particles used by *kathoey.*

nai A title used before the names of men, similar to "Mr."

nak-klam "Muscle man," a bodybuilder.

nam taek To ejaculate, to cum; for semen (*nam asuji*) to break out (*taek*).

nang A title used before married women's names, similar to "Mrs." Also used among gay men as a third-person pronoun, "she/her," to refer to other gay men.

nang-sao A title used before unmarried women's names, similar to "Miss."

napungsaka "Hermaphrodite," a technical term used in Buddhist contexts.

nok khao Colloquial expression for having an erection.

norng chai "Little brother," a slang expression for the penis.

om khuay "To suck cock," to give a blow job.

ongkhachat Formal term for the penis.

pan K. An abbreviation of *pan khuay.* See below.

pan khuay "To mold the dick," to fluff the cock to get an erection.

pha laeo "Having been operated on" or more colloquially *chor laeo*, "having been snipped or chopped"; to have had gender-reassignment surgery.

phekha A very formal and polite feminine particle usually only used when speaking with royalty that can be used facetiously and playfully by *kathoey* to affect an upper-class status.

phet Sex, gender, or sexuality.

phit-phet To be sexually or gender deviant.

phit-pokkati To be abnormal.

phit-thammachat To be unnatural.

phuang sawan "A heavenly bunch," slang expression for the penis.

phu-chai A man; to embody the ideals of Thai masculinity; used to denote a heterosexual man in contrast to gay.

phu-chai thae A real man.

phu-ying A woman.

phu-ying kham-phet A formal term for a trans woman.

phu-ying praphet sorng "A second type of woman," a somewhat formal expression for a *kathoey* or trans women popularized by some trans-identified people in the 1980s and 1990s as a more acceptable polite expression. See also *sao praphet sorng.*

phu-ying thiam "An artificial woman," a trans woman.

queen See *gay queen.*

raet A bitchy slang term used by *kathoey* and gay men to mean "You slut!" See also *ee-raet, dork-thorng.*

rak-ruam-phet A biomedical term for homosexuality.

rap "To receive," to be the receptive partner in anal sex, to be a bottom.

ruk "To attack, invade, go on the offensive," to be the insertive partner in anal sex, to be a top.

sao A young woman.

sao praphet sorng "A second type of young woman," a polite way to refer to a *kathoey*. See also *phu-ying praphet sorng*.

sao siap Originally a *kathoey*-speak expression denoting a preoperative *kathoey* (*kathoey mi ngu*) who plays the sexually insertive role with a male partner. This expression has been borrowed by Thai gay men to mean an effeminate gay man who can play the insertive (*ruk*) role.

sao taek To act effeminately, for a gay man's inner "girl" (*sao*) to "break out" (*taek*) and undermine his performance of *ab man* straight-acting masculinity. See also *taeo taek*.

sombat "Treasure," a metaphor for the penis.

sorng To "spotlight," "focus on," or "stalk"; internet slang, to observe another person's online posts without letting them know one is watching.

taek sao See *sao taek*, *taeo taek*.

taeo A slang term for a *kathoey* or an effeminate gay man.

taeo taek To act effeminately, for a gay man's inner "faggot" (*taeo*) to "break out" (*taek*) and undermine his performance of *ab man* straight-acting masculinity. See also *sao taek*.

taep To hide any visible sign of the penis beneath the underwear. Perhaps derived from the English words "tab" or "tape," as cross-dressing drag performers often use tape to hold the penis close against the body so it is not visible when wearing tight-fitting clothes.

Tai tai! An exclamation or scream of surprise or fear, used by *kathoeys*.

tut A derogatory slang term for a *kathoey* or gay man.

wet Abbreviated from the English word "private"; when internet users exchange videos of their genitals and masturbate together in a private communication.

wiparit To be perverted.

yaeng scene "To steal the scene," Coyote boy slang for a performer who tries to outdo his peers onstage.

yet To fuck.

yusoe An internet "user."

Notes

INTRODUCTION

1. For accounts of research on sexual and gender diversity in Thailand published in both Thai and English, see Pimpawun and Jackson 2012; Narupon and Jackson 2013; and Narupon and Jackson 2017.

2. We adapt the heading of this section from the title of a roundtable, "Queer Asia as Method" (2021), held at King's College, London.

3. In Thailand the borrowed word "gay" has not been used to describe women and has not been used as an identity label by Thai homosexual women. From its first use in the country in the 1960s, "gay" has been used to refer either to cisgendered males or trans women (*kathoey*) (see Jackson 1997a, 2000). Modern Thai female same-sex identities have been labeled with distinctive terms such as *tom* (from "tomboy") for a butch lesbian and *dee* (from "la*dy*") for a femme lesbian (see Sinnott 2004, 2011).

1. THAI GAY LANGUAGE OF MASCULINITY AND EFFEMINACY

1. For extended analyses of Thai notions of *kala-thesa* as contextual sensitivity, see Jackson 2004a, 2020.

2. This is expressed in idioms such as *gay thuk khon mi khwam-sao yu nai tua* (Narupon 2010a; Pavadee 2016).

3. In the transcription system used here *ab* in the idioms *ab bao* and *ab man* would normally be written as *aep*. However, to avoid confusion with the term *aep*, which means "to be sneaky" or "act stealthily," we write it as *ab*. This also reflects the fact that some Thai scholars trace the origin of *ab* to an abbreviation of the English word "<u>ab</u>normal."

4. Descendants of migrants from China's southern maritime provinces make up about 10 percent of Thailand's population.

5. There are also differences in the performance and languaging of masculinity among gay men, straight men, and masculine-identified *tom boy* lesbians. Furthermore, there are also differences in the enactment of femininity among gay men, women, and trans women *kathoey*. In other words, there are distinctive cultures of masculine gendering among heterosexual men, gay men, and *tom*, as well as characteristic cultures and styles of femininity among heterosexual women, gay men, and *kathoey*.

6. For accounts of Thai discourses of *phet* see Cook and Jackson 1999; Jackson 2001, 2004b.

7. In North America this type of gay venue is usually called a "steam bath" or "steam." In Thailand the term "sauna" is used, borrowing from British, European, and Australian gay usage.

2. THAI GAY MAGAZINES, GAY BARS, AND BAR BOYS

1. For studies of patron-client relationships as a dominant pattern in social relationships in Thailand, see Akin 2005 and Amara and Preecha 2000.

2. For further discussion of debates about whether modern Thai gay culture developed from local processes or by copying Western patterns of homosexual lifestyle and culture, see Jackson 1999 and 2009.

3. "Public parks: Gay sexual marketplaces in the city" (*suan satharana—talat kamarom gay klang krung*) (*Mithuna Junior* 1986b, 41–48).

4. For an account of the rise of saunas as a major focus of Bangkok gay men's social lives, see Dacanay 2011.

5. See Jackson 2016.

6. In colloquial Thai, the borrowed English word "cheer" means to support, promote, or encourage.

7. The term *mamasan* to describe a woman in charge of a bar or brothel was coined by American soldiers serving in occupation forces in Japan after World War II. In the following decades, *mamasan* came to be widely used in Southeast Asia, including Thailand, to describe both a woman in charge of the female sex workers in a heterosexual bar as well as a *kathoey* or gay man who is in charge of the male sex workers in a gay bar.

8. The word for "dick" used here was *jiao*. Joon was called *Joon jiao yai*.

9. In addition to denoting the astrological sign of Gemini, *Mithuna* is also the Thai name for the month of June.

10. The owner of Domon brand, Boonsak Wattanaharuethai, was married with three children and does not seem to have been gay. Nevertheless, he initiated the handsome man contests that subsequently became common features of Thai gay venues when he sponsored Domon Man male model contests.

11. R. W. Connell (1992) has put forward a very similar idea in her account of "the very straight gay."

3. THE STRAIGHT MALE NUDE AND THAI GAY MASCULINITIES

1. Käng (2021) observes that the *prang kao yot* (nine stupa pinnacles) tattoo is now seen by some as *choei* or outdated. However, a magical tattoo that remains popular is a "modern" *ha thaeo* (five lines) tattoo on the back of the shoulder blade. The five small tightly composed lines of ancient Cambodian text represent a Buddhist incantation that functions as a protective talisman. This type of tattoo was popularized by the Hollywood actor Angelina Jolie after she adopted a Cambodian son, Maddox. She received the *ha thaeo* design tattoo from Ajan Noo Kanphai, one of the most famous practitioners of *sak-yan* magical tattoos in Thailand today.

4. FITNESS CULTURE, MASCULINITY, AND THAILAND'S GAY MIDDLE CLASS

1. While the name of the sauna is spelled Chakran in roman script, it is pronounced *chakan* in Thai.

2. Since the early 2010s, the formerly dark and leafy Lumphini and Jatujak public parks have had lighting installed, undergrowth has been cleared, and security guards and police conduct regular patrols, meaning that formerly private zones have been opened to the public gaze. The main gay outdoor cruising venues in Bangkok have now moved to other locations, such as the dark parklands under and around the many elevated highway interchanges that criss-cross the modern city.

3. *Business Brief* 2009.

4. *Phujatkan 360 rai-sapda* 2011.

5. MGR Online 2011.

6. Mthai.com was established in 2002 to convey information on the variety of entertainment for urban men and women (Mthai, In Focus, n.d.).

7. Truehits 2011.

8. Straight male (Pantip n.d., 30039518).

9. Straight male (Mthai n.d., 137021).

10. Straight male (Mthai n.d., 137021).

11. Straight male (Pantip n.d., 30323517).

12. Gay man (Pantip n.d., 30323517).

13. Gay man (Pantip n.d., 30323517).

14. Postjung n.d.

15. Woman (Pantip n.d., 32503265).

16. Straight male (Pantip n.d., 30039518).

17. Straight male (Mthai n.d., 137021).

18. Krit (Mthai n.d., 137021).

19. Casanova (Mthai n.d., 137021).

20. California Fitness closed in 2012 because of financial mismanagement (Suwipha 2013) and was declared insolvent by Bangkok Bank. The Thai subsidiary of the company that was first established in Hong Kong had a loan and outstanding unpaid interest totaling 75.87 million baht (Sanook n.d.).

5. THE ALTERNATIVE MASCULINITY OF WORKING-CLASS COYOTE BOY DANCERS

1. We were not able to obtain information on whether coyote boy performances were also found in gay venues in other locales with concentrations of gay bars such as Phuket, Chiang Mai, or Koh Samui Island.

2. Or.Tor.Kor. is the popular name of a market for agricultural products, being the Thai acronym for the Agricultural Marketing Authority (*Ongkan Talat pheua Kaset*) that administers the market.

3. Glutathione is an amino acid that acts as a melanin inhibitor, which lightens the skin by preventing the formation of dark pigmentation. The skin can be whitened through regular monthly injections of glutathione, often in combination with vitamin C to improve the results. Glutathione is also the active ingredient in skin-lightening beverages, soaps, and pill supplements that are readily available in Thailand. Käng notes that in the early 2010s, an injection of one ampoule of glutathione a month cost 1,000 baht at cosmetic surgery and dermatology clinics or 300 baht in beauty salons and during home visits from paraprofessionals (Käng 2021, 283).

6. CONFIRMATIONS OF MASCULINITY IN THAI GAY VIDEO CHAT ROOMS

1. For further studies of Thai use of Camfrog, see Ronnapoom et al. 2008a, 2008b; Pimpawan et al. 2008; Sarayut 2008; Nayti et al. 2011; Thaksin 2015.

2. In Thai the username was *Sun-sun-sun*.

3. Here, the DJ uses *fai mia*, "the partner who is the wife," to refer to the sexually receptive partner.

4. Brown (2020) contends that the goal of the SOTUS system in Thailand is to create unity within an age-peer group through activities, games, and punishments and to inspire loyalty and respect of younger students (*norng*) for their seniors (*phi*), which serves to reinforce traditional ideas about hierarchy within Thai society. Brown has observed an increasing spread and severity of the SOTUS system, including its wider extension to senior high schools, as well as the growth of protests against the system and the forms of gendered harassment that it stands for.

5. For more information on Thai BL television series, see Baudinette 2019.

6. *Ban-ban* means just an ordinary guy, with the appearance of a country guy from a rural village (*mu-ban*).

CONCLUSION

1. For comparative studies of the commodification of male bodies in Western societies see Pendergast 2000 and McGrath 2006.

References

Note: Following Thai custom and scholarly practice, Thai authors are listed alphabetically for both their Thai- and English-language publications. In Thailand the Buddhist Era (BE) calendar, beginning from the reputed birth of the Lord Buddha in 543 BCE, is used for the dates of publications. Here, the Common Era (CE) date of Thai-language publications is provided with the corresponding Buddhist Era date in parentheses, e.g., 2000 (BE 2543). The titles of Thai-language publications are provided with translations following in parentheses.

Adams, Mary Louise. 1997. *The Trouble with Normal.* Toronto: University of Toronto Press.
Agathangelou, Anna M., M. Daniel Bassichis, and Tamara L. Spira. 2008. "Intimate Investment: Homonormativity, Global Lockdown, and the Seduction of Empire." *Radical History Review* 100:120–43.
Akin Rabhibhatana. 2005. *Patron-Client System and Development.* Bangkok: Faculty of Economics, Thammasat University.
Aldous, Susan, and Pornchai Sereemongkonpol. 2008. *Ladyboys: The Secret World of Thailand's Third Gender.* Dunboyne, Ireland: Maverick House.
Altman, Dennis. (1971) 1993. *Homosexual: Oppression and Liberation.* New York: New York University Press.
——. 1996a. "On Global Queering." *Australian Humanities Review*, online edition. Accessed August 14, 2021. http://australianhumanitiesreview.org/1996/07/01/on-global-queering/.
——. 1996b. "Rupture or Continuity? The Internationalization of Gay Identities." *Social Text* 48 (Autumn): 77–94.
——. 1997. "GlobalGaze/Global Gays." *GLQ: A Journal of Gay and Lesbian Studies* 3 (4): 417–36.
Alvarez, Erick. 2008. *Muscle Boys: Gay Gym Culture.* New York: Routledge.
Amara Pongsapitch and Preecha Kuwinpan, eds. 2000. *Patron-Client System.* Bangkok: Chulalongkorn University Press.
Anderson, Benedict. 1983. *Imagined Communities: Reflections on the Origin and Spread of Nationalism.* London: Verso Books.
Au, Alex. 2011. "Speaking of Bangkok: Thailand in the History of Gay Singapore." In *Queer Bangkok: 21st Century Markets, Media, and Rights*, edited by Peter A. Jackson, 181–92. Hong Kong: Hong Kong University Press.
Axis. 2009. Issue 1.
Bangkok Desire. 2013. Issue 29.
Baudinette, Thomas. 2019. "*Lovesick, The Series*: Adapting Japanese 'Boys Love' to Thailand and the Creation of a New Genre of Queer Media." *South East Asia Research* 27 (2): 115–32.
——. 2024. *Boys Love Media in Thailand: Celebrity, Fans, and Transnational Asian Popular Culture.* London: Bloomsbury Academic.
Benjarong Tirapalika. 2021 (BE 2564). "Kan-poet-phoey Tua-ton Phan Kan-seu-san Pheua Sang Khwam-samphan Baep Klai-chit Khorng Klum Chai Rak Chai Nai

Pheun-thi Twitter" [Self-disclosure through online communication: Intimate interactions of men who use the internet to find relationships with other men on Twitter]. PhD diss., Naresuan University.

Bergling, Tim. 2001. *Sissyphobia: Gay Men and Effeminate Behavior*. New York: Harrington Park Press.

Berry, Chris. 1998. "Chris Berry Responds to Dennis Altman." *Australian Humanities Review*, online edition. Accessed August 14, 2021. http://australianhumanitiesreview.org/2008/05/01/chris-berry-responds-to-dennis-altman/.

Bishop, Ryan, and Lillian S. Robinson. 1998. *Night Market: Sexual Cultures and the Thai Economic Miracle*. New York: Routledge.

Boellstorff, Tom. 2005. *The Gay Archipelago: Sexuality and Nation in Indonesia*. Princeton, NJ: Princeton University Press.

——. 2007. *A Coincidence of Desires: Anthropology, Queer Studies, Indonesia*. Durham, NC: Duke University Press.

Borhan, Pierre. 2007. *Man to Man: A History of Gay Photography*. New York: Vendome Press.

British Library. n.d. Thai Rainbow Archive collection. https://eap.bl.uk/project/EAP128.

Bronski, Michael. 1998. *The Pleasure Principle: Sex, Backlash, and the Struggle for Gay Freedom*. New York: St. Martin's Press.

Brown, Donald E., James W. Edwards, and Ruth P. Moore. 1988. *The Penis Inserts of Southeast Asia: An Annotated Bibliography with an Overview and Comparative Perspectives*. Berkeley: University of California Center for South and Southeast Asian Studies.

Brown, Emily. 2020. "Hazing and Hierarchy in Thailand: SOTUS and Societal Change." Accessed December 23, 2022. https://seasia.yale.edu/hazing-and-hierarchy-thailand-sotus-and-societal-change.

Business Brief. 2009. Issue 2629.

Butler, Judith. 1988. "Performative Acts and Gender Constitution: An Essay in Phenomenology and Feminist Theory." *Theatre Journal* 40 (4): 519–31.

——. 1990. *Gender Trouble: Feminism and the Subversion of Identity*. New York: Routledge.

——. 1993. *Bodies That Matter: On the Discursive Limits of Sex*. New York: Routledge.

Cagle, R. L. 2000. "Beefcake." *Afterimage* 27 (6): 16.

Carter, David. 2011. *Stonewall: The Riots That Sparked the Gay Revolution*. New York: Griffin.

Chakrabarty, Dipesh. 2000. *Provincializing Europe: Postcolonial Thought and Historical Difference*. Princeton, NJ: Princeton University Press.

Chalermpong Kongcharoen. 2010 (BE 2553). *Rabop Setthakit Thai Korn Wikritkan Kan-ngoen Phor. Sor. 2540* [The Thai economic system before the 1997 financial crisis]. Bangkok: Thailand Research Fund.

Chalongphob Sussangkarn. 1993. "Labour Markets." In *The Thai Economy in Transition*, edited by Peter G. Warr, 355–400. Cambridge: Cambridge University Press.

Chauncey, George. 1985. "Christian Brotherhood or Sexual Perversion? Homosexual Identities and the Construction of Sexual Boundaries in the World War I Era." *Journal of Social History* 19 (2): 189–211.

——. 1994. *Gay New York: Gender, Urban Culture, and the Making of a Gay Male World, 1890–1940*. New York: Basic Books.

Chen, Kuan-Hsing. 2010. *Asia as Method: Towards Deimperialization*. Durham, NC: Duke University Press.

Clarkson, Jay. 2005. "Contesting Masculinity's Makeover: Queer Eye, Consumer Masculinity, and 'Straight-Acting' Gays." *Journal of Communication Inquiry* 29 (3): 235–55.

Connell, R. W. 1992. "A Very Straight Gay: Masculinity, Homosexual Experience, and the Dynamics of Gender." *American Sociological Review* 57 (6): 735–51.

——. 1995. *Masculinities*. Berkeley: University of California Press.

——. 2002. *Gender*. Cambridge: Polity Press.

Connell, R. W., and James W. Messerschmidt. 2005. "Hegemonic Masculinity: Rethinking the Concept." *Gender & Society* 19 (6): 829–53.

Cook, Matt. 2003. *London and the Culture of Homosexuality, 1885–1914*. Cambridge UK: Cambridge University Press.

Cook, Nerida M., and Peter A. Jackson, eds. 1999. *Genders & Sexualities in Modern Thailand*. Bangkok: Silkworm Books.

Cornwall, Andrea, and Nancy Lindisfarne, eds. 1994. *Dislocating Masculinity: Comparative Ethnographies*. London: Routledge.

Coston, Bethany M., and Michael Kimmel. 2012. "Seeing Privilege Where It Isn't: Marginalized Masculinities and the Intersectionality of Privilege." *Journal of Social Issues* 68 (1): 97–111.

Dacanay, Nikos. 2011. "Encounters in the Sauna: Exploring Gay Identity and Power Structures in Gay Places in Bangkok." In *Queer Bangkok: 21st Century Markets, Media, and Rights*, edited by Peter A. Jackson, 99–117. Hong Kong: Hong Kong University Press.

Deininger, Klaus, and Lyn Squire. 1997. "Economic Growth and Income Inequality: Reexamining the Links." *Finance and Development* 34 (1): 38–41.

Demand de l'homme: Simply Better for Metromen. 2005. Issue 6.

Department of Business Development. 2019. *Fitness Business*. Accessed January 27, 2023. Retrieved from https://www.dbd.go.th/download/document_file/Statisic/2562/T26/T26_201905.pdf.

Door. 2002. Issue 32.

Door. 2005. Issue 5.

Dowsett, Gary, Jeffrey Grierson, and Stephen McNally. 2006. *A Review of Knowledge About the Sexual Networks and Behaviours of Men Who Have Sex with Men in Asia*. Melbourne: Australian Research Centre in Sex, Health and Society.

Duggan, Lisa. 2003. *The Twilight of Equality? Neoliberalism, Cultural Politics, and the Attack on Democracy*. Boston, MA: Beacon Press.

Dyer, Richard. 2002. *The Culture of Queers*. London: Routledge.

Edwards, Tim. 1994. *Erotics & Politics: Gay Male Sexuality, Masculinity and Feminism*. New York: Routledge.

Eguchi, Shinsuke. 2009. "Negotiating Hegemonic Masculinity: The Rhetorical Strategy of 'Straight-Acting' Among Gay Men." *Journal of Intercultural Communication Research* 38 (3): 193–209.

Eisenstadt, Shmuel Noah. 2000. "Multiple Modernities." *Daedalus* 129 (1): 1–29.

Escoffier, Jeffrey. 2009. *Bigger Than Life: The History of Gay Porn Cinema from Beefcake to Hardcore*. Philadelphia, PA: Running Press.

Fox, Ragan. 2007. *Gays in (Cyber-)Space: Online Performances of Gay Identity*. Saarbrücken: VDM Verlag Dr. Muller.

Funatsu, Tsuruyoa, and Kazuhiro Kagoya. 2003. "The Middle Class in Thailand: The Rise of the Urban Intellectual Elite and Their Social Consciousness." *Developing Economies* 41 (2): 243–63.

Garcia, J. Neil. 2009. *Philippine Gay Culture: Binabae to Bakla, Silahis to MSM*. Hong Kong: Hong Kong University Press.

Gill, Rosalind, Karen Henwood, and Carl McLean. 2005. *Body Projects and Regulation of Normative Masculinity*. London: LSE Research Articles Online. Retrieved March 24, 2014, from http://eprints.lse.ac.uk/archive/00000371/.

Hall, Donald E. 2003. *Queer Theories*. New York: Palgrave Macmillan.

Halperin, David M. 2002. *How to Do the History of Homosexuality*. Chicago: University of Chicago Press.

Harrison, Rachel V., and Peter A. Jackson, eds. 2010. *The Ambiguous Allure of the West: Traces of the Colonial in Thailand*. Hong Kong and Ithaca, NY: Hong Kong University Press and Cornell University Southeast Asia Program Publications.

Heat. 2002. Issue 1.

Hennen, Peter. 2008. *Fairies, Bears, and Leathermen: Men in Community Queering the Masculine*. Chicago: University of Chicago Press.

Herman, Didi. 2003. "Bad Girls Changed My Life: Homonormativity in a Women's Prison Drama." *Critical Studies in Media Communication* 20 (2): 141–59.

Herzfeld, Michael. 2010. "The Conceptual Allure of the West: Dilemmas and Ambiguities of Crypto-Colonialism." In *The Ambiguous Allure of the West: Traces of the Colonial in Thailand*, edited by Rachel V. Harrison and Peter A. Jackson, 173–86. Hong Kong and Ithaca, NY: Hong Kong University Press and Cornell University Southeast Asia Program Publications.

Hey! 2008. Issue 1.

Hin, Lee Wing. 2008. "Centering the Center: Finding the 'Hetero' in Heteronormativity." *Graduate Journal of Social Science* 5 (1): 5–32.

Hooven, F. Valentine, III. 2002. *Beefcake: The Muscle Magazines of America 1950-1970*. London: Taschen.

I Am Guy. 2007. Issue 5.

Ibson, John. 2002. *Picturing Men: A Century of Male Relationships in Everyday American Photography*. Washington, DC: Smithsonian Institution Press.

Ikemoto, Yukio, and Mine Uehara. 2000. "Income Inequality and Kuznets' Hypothesis in Thailand." *Asian Economic Journal* 14 (4): 421–43.

Jackson, Peter A. 1989. *Male Homosexuality in Thailand: An Interpretation of Contemporary Thai Sources*. New York: Global Academic Publishers.

——. 1995. *Dear Uncle Go: Male Homosexuality in Thailand*. Bangkok: Bua Luang Books.

——. 1997a. "*Kathoey* >< Gay >< Man: The Historical Emergence of Gay Male Identity in Thailand." In *Sites of Desire/Economies of Pleasure*, edited by Lenore Manderson and Margaret Jolly, 166–90. Chicago: University of Chicago Press.

——. 1997b. "Thai Research on Male Homosexuality and Transgenderism: The Cultural Limits of Foucauldian Analysis." *Journal of the History of Sexuality* 8 (1): 52–85.

——. 1998. "Male Homosexuality and Transgenderism in the Thai Buddhist Tradition." In *Queer Dharma: Voices of Gay Buddhists*, edited by Winston Leyland, 55–89. San Francisco: Gay Sunshine Press.

——. 1999. "An American Death in Bangkok: The Murder of Darrell Berrigan and the Hybrid Origins of Gay Identity in 1960s Thailand." *GLQ: A Journal of Lesbian and Gay Studies* 5 (3): 361–411.

——. 2000. "An Explosion of Thai Identities: Global Queering and Reimagining Queer Theory." *Culture, Health & Sexuality* 2 (4): 405–24.

——. 2001. "Pre-Gay, Post-Queer: Thai Perspectives on Proliferating Gender/Sex Diversity in Asia." In *Gay and Lesbian Asia: Culture, Identity, Community*, edited by Gerard Sullivan and Peter A. Jackson, 1–25. Binghamton, NY: Harrington Park Press.

——. 2003. "Performative Genders, Perverse Desires: A Bio-History of Thailand's Same-Sex and Transgender Cultures." *Intersections: Gender, History and Culture in the Asian Context*, no. 9. http://intersections.anu.edu.au/issue9/ jackson.html.

——. 2004a. "The Thai Regime of Images." *Sojourn: Social Issues in Southeast Asia* 19 (2): 1–39.

——. 2004b (BE 2547). "Phet: Wathakam Pheun-Meuang Khorng Thai, Thammai Torng Prap-prung Thareutsdi Foucault Nai Kan-seuksa Watthanatham Thai" [*Phet*: An indigenous Thai discourse; Why Foucault's theory of sexuality must be adapted in studying Thai culture]. *Warasan Phasa Lae Watthanatham* [Journal of language and culture] 23 (1): 57–66.

——. 2009. "Capitalism and Global Queering: National Markets, Parallels Among Sexual Cultures, and Multiple Queer Modernities." *GLQ: A Journal of Lesbian and Gay Studies* 15 (3): 357–95.

——. 2010a. "The Ambiguities of Semicolonial Power in Thailand." In *The Ambiguous Allure of the West: Traces of the Colonial in Thailand*, edited by Rachel V. Harrison and Peter A. Jackson, 37–56. Hong Kong and Ithaca, NY: Hong Kong University Press and Cornell University Southeast Asia Program Publications.

——. 2010b. "Postcolonial Theories and Thai Semicolonial Hybridities." In *The Ambiguous Allure of the West: Traces of the Colonial in Thailand*, edited by Rachel V. Harrison and Peter A. Jackson, 187–205. Hong Kong and Ithaca, NY: Hong Kong University Press and Cornell University Southeast Asia Program Publications.

——. 2011a. "Capitalism, LGBT Activism, and Queer Autonomy in Thailand." In *Queer Bangkok: 21st Century Markets, Media, and Rights*, edited by Peter A. Jackson, 195–204. Hong Kong: Hong Kong University Press.

——. ed. 2011b. *Queer Bangkok: 21st Century Markets, Media, and Rights*. Hong Kong: Hong Kong University Press.

——. 2013 (BE 2556). "Cultural Pluralism and Sex/Gender Diversity in Thailand: Introduction." In *Phet Lak Chet-si: Phahuwattanatham Thang-phet Nai Sangkhom Thai* [*Cultural Pluralism and Sex/Gender Diversity in Thailand*], edited by Narupon Duangwises and Peter Jackson, 14–27. Bangkok: Princess Sirindhorn Anthropology Centre.

——. 2016. *First Queer Voices from Thailand: Uncle Go's Advice Columns for Gays, Lesbians and Kathoeys*. Hong Kong: Hong Kong University Press.

——. 2020. "Beyond Hybridity and Syncretism: *Kala-thesa* Contextual Sensitivity and Power in Thai Religious and Gender Cultures." *Journal of Anthropology: Sirindhorn Anthropology Centre* 3 (1): 4–37.

Jackson, Peter A., and Gerard Sullivan, eds. 1999. *Lady Boys, Tom Boys, Rent Boys: Male and Female Homosexualities in Contemporary Thailand*. Chiang Mai: Silkworm Books.

——. 2001. *Gay and Lesbian Asia: Culture, Identity, Community*. Binghamton, NY: Harrington Park Press.

Jagger, Gill. 2008. *Judith Butler: Sexual Politics, Social Change and the Power of the Performative*. London: Routledge.

K-Mag. 2001. Issue 9.

K-Mag. 2002. Issue 19.

Käng, Dredge Byung'chu. 2015. "White Asians Wanted: Queer Racialization in Thailand." PhD diss., Emory University.

——. 2017. "Eastern Orientations: Thai Middle-Class Gay Desire for 'White Asians.'" *Culture, Theory and Critique* 58 (2): 182–208.

——. 2021. "The Duty to Transform: Properly Refining the Body and (Re)defining Oneself in Thailand." *Asian Studies Review* 45 (2): 272–89.

Kapac, Jack S. 1998. "Culture/Community/Race: Chinese Gay Men and the Politics of Identity." *Anthropologica* 40 (2): 169–81.

Karl, Irmi. 2007. "Gender, Sexuality, and the Techno-Politics of Everyday Life." In *Queer Online: Media, Technology, and Sexuality*, edited by Kate O'Riordan and David Phillips, 45–66. New York: Peter Lang.

Khetara Sriyaphai. 2007 (BE 2550). *Parithat Muay Thai [Muay Thai in review]*. Bangkok: Matichon Books.

Kimmel, Michael S. 1994. "Masculinity as Homophobia." In *Theorizing Masculinities*, edited by H. Brod and M. Kaufman, 126–27. Thousand Oaks, CA: Sage.

——. 2001. "Masculinity as Homophobia: Fear, Shame, and Silence in the Construction of Gender Identity." In *The Masculinities Reader*, edited by Stephen M. Whitehead and Frank J. Barrett, 266–87. Malden, MA: Blackwell.

Kittiwut J. Taywaditep. 2001. "Marginalization Among the Marginalized: Gay Men's Anti-Effeminacy Attitudes." *Journal of Homosexuality* 42 (1): 1–28.

Kleinhuber, Andrea. 2000/2001. "The Politics of Identity in Lesbian and Gay Anthropology." *NEXUS* 14:43–55.

Kodmhai. n.d. Thai criminal code in Thai. Accessed September 18, 2015. http://www.kodmhai.com/m2/m2-2/m2-276-287.html.

Kongsakon Kawinraweekun. 2002 (BE 2545). "Kan-sang Rang-kai Phonlameuang Thai Nai Samai Jorm-phon P. Phibunsongkhram Ph. S. 2481–2487" [Constructing the body of Thai citizens during the Phibun regime of 1938–1944]. MA diss., Faculty of Sociology and Anthropology, Thammasat University, Bangkok.

Kukdej Kantamara. 2010. *Mae Mai Muay Thai: The Art of Self-Defense*. Bangkok: Chulalongkorn University Press.

Lap Chaphor (Chao Si-muang) [Top Secret: Lavender People]. 2001. Issue 121.

Lim, Eng-Beng. 2005. "Glocalqueering in New Asia: The Politics of Performing Gay in Singapore." *Theatre Journal* 57 (3): 383–405.

Luther, J. Daniel, Jennifer Ung Loh, and Matthew Waites, eds. 2024. *Queer Asia: Decolonising and Reimagining Sexuality and Gender*. London: Bloomsbury Academic.

Male. 1995. Issue 15.

Male. 1996a. Issue 5.

Male. 1996b. Issue 23.

Male. 1996c. Issue 27.

Malebranche, Jack. 2006. *Androphilia: A Manifesto*. Baltimore, MD: Scapegoat.

Man. 2010. Issue 1.

Marketingoops! 2014. "Thai Kheun Thaen 'Gay Yoe' Mak Thi-sut Andap 10 Khorng Lok" [Thailand ranks 10th in the world for having the most gay people]. October 8, 2014. Accessed January 23, 2024. https://www.marketingoops.com/reports/thai-gay-population-global/.

Martin, Fran. 1998. "Fran Martin Responds to Dennis Altman." *Australian Humanities Review*, online edition. Accessed August 14, 2021. http://australianhumanitiesreview.org/2008/05/01/fran-martin-responds-to-dennis-altman/?utm_source=rss&utm_medium=rss&utm_campaign=fran-martin-responds-to-dennis-altman.

Max. 2009. Issue 81.

McGlotten, Shaka. 2007. "Virtual Intimacies: Love, Addiction, and Identity @ The Matrix." In *Queer Online: Media, Technology, and Sexuality*, edited by Kate O'Riordan and David J. Phillips, 123–38. New York: Peter Lang.

McGrath, Matthew D. 2006. "The New Male Consumer: Appearance Management Product Advertising and the Male Physical Ideal in Men's Interest Magazines from 1965–2005." PhD diss., Florida State University.

McLelland, Mark. 2000. *Male Homosexuality in Modern Japan: Cultural Myths and Social Realities*. Richmond, UK: Curzon.

——. 2005. *Queer Japan from the Pacific War to the Internet Age*. Oxford: Rowman and Littlefield.

McNally, David, dir. 2000. *Coyote Ugly*. Touchstone Pictures.

Medhi Krongkaew. 1993. "Poverty and Income Distribution." In *The Thai Economy in Transition*, edited by Peter G. Warr, 401–37. Cambridge: Cambridge University Press.

Messner, Michael A. 1997. *Politics of Masculinities: Men in Movements*. New York: Sage.

MGR Online. 2011. Accessed November 8, 2011. http://www.manager.co.th/QOL/ViewNews.aspx?NewsID=9480000171685.

Midway. 1986. Issue 1.

Midway. 1987a. Issue 13.

Midway. 1987b. Issue 15.

Midway. 1989. Issue 28.

Midway. 1990a. Issue 39.

Midway. 1990b. Issue 40.

Midway. 1991a. Issue 31.

Midway. 1991b. Issue 47.

Midway. 1991c. Issue 51.

Midway. 1995. Issue 75.

Midway. 1997. Issue 82.

Midway. 2000. Issue 97.

Midway. 2001. Issue 100.

Mthai. n.d. In Focus. Accessed November 8, 2011. http://men.mthai.com/infocus/33140.html.

Mthai. n.d. Men.mthai forum topic 137021. Accessed November 8, 13, 17, 2011 and January 4, 2012. http://men.mthai.com/forum/topic/137021.

Mithuna Junior. 1984a. Issue 1.

Mithuna Junior. 1984b. Issue 2.

Mithuna Junior. 1984c. Issue 3.

Mithuna Junior. 1984d. Issue 6.

Mithuna Junior. 1984e. Issue 7.

Mithuna Junior. 1984f. Issue 8.

Mithuna Junior. 1984g. Issue 45.

Mithuna Junior. 1985a. Issue 9.

Mithuna Junior. 1985b. Issue 13.

Mithuna Junior. 1985c. Issue 15.

Mithuna Junior. 1985d. Issue 18.

Mithuna Junior. 1985e. Issue 21.

Mithuna Junior. 1985f. Issue 27.

Mithuna Junior. 1986a. Issue 30.

Mithuna Junior. 1986b. Issue 31.

Mithuna Junior. 1986c. Issue 32.

Mithuna Junior. 1987a. Issue 40.

Mithuna Junior. 1987b. Issue 42.

Mithuna Junior. 1987c. Issue 46.

Mithuna Junior. 1987d. Issue 47.

Mithuna Junior. 1988a. Issue 49.

Mithuna Junior. 1988b. Issue 50.

Mithuna Junior. 1988c. Issue 51.

Mithuna Junior. 1988d. Issue 52.

Mithuna Junior. 1991a. Issue 60.

Mithuna Junior. 1991b. Issue 65.

Mithuna Junior. 1992. Issue 69.

Mithuna Junior. 1993. Issue 77.

Mithuna Junior. 1994. Issue 80.

Mithuna Junior. 1995a. Issue 87.

Mithuna Junior. 1995b. Issue 91.

Mithuna Junior. 1997. Issue 96.

Morakot. 1987. Issue 16.

Morakot. 1991. Issue 58.

Morakot. 1995. Issue 105.

Mutchler, Matt G. 2000. "Seeking Sexual Lives: Gay Youth and Masculinity Tensions." In *Gay Masculinities*, edited by Peter Nardi, 12–43. London: SAGE Publications.

Narong Petpraseret. 1992. "White Collar Workers in Thailand." PhD diss., La Trobe University, Australia.

——, ed. 2005 (BE 2548). *Khon Chan-klang Thai Nai Krasae Thun-niyom* [The Thai middle class under capitalism]. Bangkok: Political Economy Study Center, Faculty of Economics, Chulalongkorn University.

Narupon Duangwises. 2003 (BE 2546). "Pleuay Nai Baep: Nangseu Po Lae Kamarom Nai Chiwit Gay Thai" [Naked male models: Pornography and the sexual life of Thai gay men]. *Rattasartsarn* 25 (2): 164–203.

——. 2010a (BE 2553). "Khabuan-kan Khleuan-wai Khorng Gay Nai Thai: Phak Patipat-kan Lae Krabuanthat" [The gay movement in Thai society: Practices and paradigms]. PhD diss., Thammasat University, Bangkok.

——. 2010b (BE 2553). "Nittayasan *Mithuna*: Banthatthan Khorng Gay Thai Chon Chan-klang" [*Mithuna* magazine: The founding of Thai gay middle-class normativity]. *Rattasatsarn* 31 (3): 89–132.

——. 2024. "Transcultural Deterritorialization of Gay Dance Party and Songkran Festival in Thailand." *KKU International Journal of Humanities and Social Sciences* 14 (2): 1–39.

Narupon Duangwises, and Peter A. Jackson, eds. 2013 (BE 2556). *Phet Lak Chet-si: Phahuwattanatham Thang-phet Nai Sangkhom Thai* [Cultural pluralism and sex/gender diversity in Thailand]. Bangkok: Princess Sirindhorn Anthropology Centre.

——. 2017. "Review of Studies of Gender and Sexual Diversity in Thailand in Thai and International Academic Publications." Paper prepared for the Thailand Research Institute, Bangkok, and presented at the 13th International Thai Studies Conference, Chiang Mai, July 15–18, 2017.

——. 2021a. "Effeminacy and Masculinity in Thai Gay Culture: Language, Contextuality and the Enactment of Gender Plurality." *Walailak Journal of Social Science* 14 (5): 1–23.

——. 2021b. "A Homoerotic History of Bangkok's Gay Middle Class: Thai Gay Bars and Magazines in the 1980s and 1990s." *Journal of the Siam Society* 109 (2): 59–77.

——. 2023. "Evolving Thai Homoeroticism: Male Nudity and Multiple Masculinities in Gay Magazines Since the 1980s–2010s." *Asia Social Issues* 16 (2): 1–24.

National Statistics Office (Thailand). n.d. Accessed July 25, 2013. http://www.nso. go.th/.

Nattaphat Navigcheewin. 1978 (BE 2521). "Lai-sak Kha Thi Ban Chiang" [Leg tattoos in Ban Chiang]. *Meuang Boran* 4 (4): 93–98.

Nattapol Wisuttipat. 2022. "Spicy: Gendered Practices of Queer Men in Thai Classical String Music." PhD diss., University of California, Riverside.

Nayti Soontravaravit, Kettawa Boonprakarn, and Porntipa Banthomsin. 2011 (BE 2554). "Phap-lak Lae Tua-ton Khorng 'Gay' Nai Pheun-thi Cyber" [Images and identities of gays in cyberspace]. *Warasan Silapasat—Journal of Liberal Arts* 3 (2): 117–30.

Neon. 1985. Issue 11.

Neon. 1986. Issue 13.

Neon. 1990. Issue 49.

Neon. 1991. Issue 61.

Nikom Chantarawitoon. 2007 (BE 2550). "Raeng-ngan Kap Rat: Sam Thatsawat Haeng Kan-phatthana" [Labor and state: Three decades of development]. In *20 Pi Pathakatha Phiset Puey Ungphakorn* [20 years special lecture: Puey Ungphakorn], edited by Pokpong Chanwit, 22–97. Bangkok: Open Books.

Ockey, Jim. 1999. "Creating the Thai Middle Class." In *Culture and Privilege in Capitalist Asia*, edited by Michael Pinches, 230–50. New York: Routledge.

O'Riordan, Kate. 2007. "Queer Theories and Cybersubjects: Intersectional Figures." In *Queer Online: Media, Technology, and Sexuality*, edited by Kate O'Riordan and David J. Phillips, 13–30. New York: Peter Lang.

Pantip. n.d. Discussion board topic 30039518. Accessed November 22, 26, 2011. http:// pantip.com/topic/30039518.

Pantip. n.d. Discussion board topic 30323517. Accessed November 21, 24, 2011. http:// pantip.com/topic/30323517.

Pantip. n.d. Discussion board topic 32503265. Accessed October 8, 2014. http://pantip. com/topic/32503265.

Pantip. 2015. "Ma Hai Khanaen App Gay Na Khrap" [Let's rate gay apps]. February 20, 2015. Accessed January 23, 2024. https://pantip.com/topic/33264373.

Pavadee Saisuwan. 2016. "Male Femininity in Thai Among Men Who Identify with Non-Normative Male Roles." PhD diss., Queen Mary University of London.

Peerasek Borisudbuathip, Anupong Sukkasem, and Waiyawut Yoonisil. 2020 (BE 2563). "Kan-seuksa Phreutikam Kan-chai Ngan Application Ha Khu Khorng Phet Chai (Chai Thae, Gay Lae Bisexual)" [Study of behavior in dating applications use among Thai men (heterosexual men, gays and bisexuals)]. *Warasan Sathaban Wijai Lae Phatthana Mahawitthayalai Ratchabhat Ban Somdet Chaophraya (Journal of the BRUS-Research and Development Institute* 5 (1): 33–50.

Pendergast, Tom. 2000. *Creating the Modern Man: American Magazines and Consumer Culture, 1900–1950*. Columbia: University of Missouri Press.

Phillips, D. J., and C. Cunningham. 2007. "Queering Surveillance Research." In *Queer Online: Media, Technology, and Sexuality*, edited by Kate O'Riordan and David J. Phillips, 30–44. New York: Peter Lang.

Phorphan Uiyanont. 1999 (BE 2541). "Kha-jang Raeng-ngan Nai Prawattisat Thai" [Labor wages in Thai history]." In *Prawattisat Raeng-ngan Thai: Chabap Ku Saksi Kammakorn* [The history of Thai labor: Restoring the dignity of Thai labor], edited by Chalong Suntrawanich, Suwimon Rungjaroen, Sakdina Chatrakul Na Ayutthaya, and Sanam Jaemburi, 61–112. Bangkok: Museum of Thai Labour.

Phujatkan 360 rai-sapda [Manager weekly]. 2011. March 22.

Phuwin Bunyawetchiwin and Natthanon Sukthungthorng. 2021 (BE 2564). *Lok Khorng Y: Siri Y Prakotkan Y Hua-nom Wai-run Chai Lae Wayaphiwat* [The world of Y: Y TV series, the Y phenomenon, teenage boys' nipples and Y-isation]. Bangkok: Institute of East Asian Studies, Thammasat University.

Pimpawan Boonmongkol, Ronnapoom Samakkeekarom, Wachira Chanthong, Phanuphan Phumphruek, and Chayanan Manokasemsuk. 2008. *Sexuality and New Media: Context of Risk and Encouragement in Sexual Health*. Bangkok: Woman's Health Advocacy Foundation.

Pimpawun Boonmongkon and Peter A. Jackson, eds. 2012. *Thai Sex Talk: The Language of Sex and Sexuality in Thailand*. Chiang Mai: Mekong Press.

Poirier-Poulin, Samuel. 2021. "'Can You Toss Me That Shirt Behind You?': Beefcakes, Ambiguous Masculinities, and Pornographic Bodies in the Video Game 'Coming Out on Top.'" *Synoptique* 9 (2): 139–58.

Positioning. 2006. January issue.

Postjung. n.d. Board posting 650355. Accessed October 8, 2014. board.postjung.com/650355.html.

Pranee Tinnakorn and Chalongphob Sussangkarn. 1998. *Total Factor Productivity Growth in Thailand: 1980–1995*. Bangkok: Thailand Research Development Institute.

Prathern Mahakhan. 1991 (BE 2534). *Sinlapa Kan-sak-lai* [The art of tattoo]. Bangkok: Odeon Store.

Prempreeda Pramoj na Ayutthaya. 2003 (BE 2546). *Kan-chuang-ching Atthalak Kathoey Nai Ngan Khabare Cho* [Contesting identities of *kathoey* in cabaret shows]. MA, Faculty of Social Science, Chiang Mai University, Thailand.

"Queer Asia as Method." 2021. Roundtable convened by Hongwei Bao, J. Daniel Luther, Liang Ge, and Victor Fan at King's College, London, on September 4–5, 2021. Accessed August 10, 2024. https://queerasia.com/qamethod2021/.

Rat Raman. 2003 (BE 2546). *Sak Yan: Itthirit Reu Mon Dam* [Tattoos: Supernatural power or black magic?]. Bangkok: Animate Group.

Reynolds, Craig J. 1999. "Gendering of Nationalist and Postnationalist Selves in Twentieth Century Thailand." In *Genders and Sexualities in Modern Thailand*, edited by Peter A. Jackson and Nerida M. Cook, 261–74. Chiang Mai: Silkworm Books.

Ronnapoom Samakkeekarom and Pimpawun Boonmongkon. 2011. "Cyberspace, Power Structures, and Gay Sexual Health: The Sexuality of Thai Men Who Have Sex with Men (MSM) in the Camfrog On-Line Web-Cam Chat Rooms." In *Queer Bangkok: 21st Century Markets, Media, and Rights*, edited by Peter A. Jackson, 121–40. Hong Kong: Hong Kong University Press.

Ronnapoom Samakkeekarom, Pimpawun Boonmongkon, and Wachira Chantong. 2008a (BE 2551). "Camfrog Lae Phetwithi Khorng Wai-run Chai Rak Chai Pheun-thi Saiboe Khrong-sang Amnat Lae Amnat Nai Ton Thang-phet" [Camfrog and the sexualities of Thai gay youth: Cyberspace, power structures, and sexual agency]. In *Phetwithi Seuksa Nai Sangkhom Thai* [Sexuality studies in Thai society], edited by Pimpawan Boonmongkon and Thawatchai Pachuen, 230–40. Bangkok: Center for Health Policy Studies.

——. 2008b. "Camfrog and the Sexuality of Young Gay Men: Cyberspace, Power Structures and Sexual Authority." In *Report of the 1st Annual Meeting on Sexuality Studies in Thai Society*, edited by Thawatchai Pachuen, 230–39. Bangkok: Charoen Dee Kan Pim.

Salinee Niyomburana. 2015 (BE 2558). "Luat-lai Lae Reuan-rang" [Body ornamentation]. MA diss., Silpakorn University, Bangkok.

Sanook. n.d. Accessed October 7, 2014. http://money.sanook.com/68862/california-wow.

Sarayut Rotchanawanichkul. 2008 (BE 2551). *Tua-ton Lae Phetwithi Khorng Gay Nai Sangkhom Online: Korani Seuksa Program Camfrog Horng Gay Freestyle* [Gay identity and sexuality in online society: Case study of Camfrog, gay freestyle room]. Paper presented to the Southeast Asia Studies Program, Faculty of Arts, Thammasat University, Bangkok.

Schmiedgen, Peter. 2007. "Homo-Normativity, Hetero-Normativity and Socio-Spatial Difference." Paper presented at Conference of Queer Space: Centres and Peripheries, Faculty of Design, Architecture and Building, University of Technology, Sydney, February 20–21, 2007.

Siam Thurakit. 2011. September 21.

Sinnott, Megan. 2004. *Toms and Dees: Transgender Identity and Female Same-Sex Relationships in Thailand.* Hawai'i: University of Hawai'i Press.

——. 2011. "The Language of Rights, Deviance, and Pleasure: Organization Responses to Discourses of Same-Sex Sexuality and Transgenderism in Thailand." In *Queer Bangkok: 21st Century Markets, Media, and Rights,* edited by Peter A. Jackson, 205–28. Hong Kong: Hong Kong University Press.

Siriporn Yodkamolsart. 2005 (BE 2548). "Kan-niyam Chon Chan-klang Nai Sangkhom Thai" [Defining the middle class in Thai society]. In *Chon Chan-klang Thai Nai Krasae Thun-niyom* [The Thai middle class under capitalism], edited by Narong Petprasert, 145–78. Bangkok: Adison Press Products.

SOLID: Aspiring Fitness Magazine. 2012. Vol. 1.

Stibbe, Arran. 2004. "Health and the Social Construction of Masculinity in Men's Health Magazines." *Men and Masculinities* 7 (1): 31–51.

Suwipha Bussayabuntoon. 2013 (BE 2556). "Poet-Phoey California Wow" [Revealing California Wow]. Accessed June 26, 2013. Retrieved from http://www.than online.com/index.php?option=com_content&view=article&id=188688:-1-&catid=216:2011-03-07-07-53-38&Itemid=607#.VDIyiBbaKhk.

"Thailand Gay Guide City Directory." 2011. Accessed December 7, 2011. http://www.dreadedned.com/directory/index/.

Techsauce. 2016. "BLUED Application Sangkhom Gay Thi Yai Thi-sut Nai Lok Poet-tua 'Live' Feature Mai Khrang Raek Thi App Gay Samat Lai Dai" [BLUED, the world's largest gay social application, launches a new 'live' feature. First time a gay app can stream live]. August 11, 2016. Accessed January 23, 2025. https://techsauce.co/pr-news/blued-gay-community-application-grand-opening-live-feature.

Thaksin Pawatha. 2015 (BE 2558). "Phon-krathop Khorng Kan-khai Borikan Thang-phet Phan Program Camfrog Khorng Klum Chai-rak-chai Nai Changwat Chiang Mai" [The impact of homosexual men selling sexual services via the Camfrog program in Chiang Mai province]. MA diss., School of Digital Communications, Maejo University, Chiang Mai.

Totman, Richard. 2003. *The Third Sex: Kathoey—Thailand's Ladyboys.* Chiang Mai: Silkworm Books.

Truehits. 2011. Accessed November 8, 2011. http://truehits.net/index_ranking.php.

Tuay (pseud.), ed. 2003 (BE 2546). *Sinlapa Haeng Muay Thai—Glimpses of Muay-Thai: The Siamese Art of Buddhatantric Self-Defense.* Bangkok: P. Watin Publications. (In both Thai and English.)

Van Esterik, Penny. 1999. "Repositioning Gender, Sexuality, and Power in Thai Studies." In *Genders and Sexualities in Modern Thailand*, edited by Peter A. Jackson and Nerida M. Cook, 275–89. Chiang Mai: Silkworm Books.

——. 2000. *Materializing Thailand*. Oxford: Berg.

Violet. 1993. Issue 2.

Warren, William. 2001. *Celebrating 100 Years of the Royal Bangkok Sports Club*. Bangkok: Mark Standen.

Waugh, Thomas. 1996. *Hard to Imagine: Gay Male Eroticism in Photography and Film from Their Beginnings to Stonewall*. New York: Columbia University Press.

Weekend Men. 1992. Issue 25.

Worayut Phaiphayu. 2018 (BE 2561). "Kan-seuksa Kan-chai Prayot Lae Khwam-pheung-phor-jai Khorng Application Ha Khu Bon Thorasap Meu-theu Khorng Klum Chai Rak Chai" [Study of benefits and satisfaction of using dating applications on mobile phones by gay men (MSM)]. MA diss., National Institute of Development Administration, Bangkok.

Yue, Audrey, and Jun Zubillaga-Pow, eds. 2012. *Queer Singapore: Illiberal Citizenship and Mediated Cultures*. Hong Kong: Hong Kong University Press.

Index

Figures and tables are respectively indicated by the letters "*f*" and "*t*" placed after a page number.

kala-thesa. See gender: contextuality of
kathoey, 13, 19, 31, 35–36
  changing meaning of, 2
  differentiation from gay, 2, 29, 31, 49
  language use by, 33–34
K-Mag magazine, 113
Korea, 12, 170, 222

Lee, Bruce, 88
lesbians, 8, 33, 239n3 (introduction)
  language use by, 40–41
Lumphini Park, 47, 104–5, 240n2 (chap. 4)

mai sadaeng ork. See closeted gay men; straight
    acting
male escorts, 114
  See also male sex workers; masseurs
Male magazine, 102f, 108
male nude, representation of, 119–20
  See also pornography
male sex workers, 19, 29, 55–58, 60–62, 67, 95
  declining popularity of, 110
  female customers of, 151
  payments to, 151
  See also centerfold models; go-go boys; male
    escorts; masseurs; middle class; working
    class
man, meaning in Thailand, 14, 27, 49–50,
    190, 219
  See also masculinity
market. *See* capitalism
marriage equality, 8
masculinity
  commodification of, 81, 214–15
  gay alternation with effeminacy, 25
  as gender hierarchy, 203–9, 212, 215, 220–21
  language of, 40–42
  middle class, 3, 20
  as multiple and fluid, 3, 20, 88, 122–23,
    199–200, 224–26
  normative patterns of, 91
  and sexual role, 83, 190
  in sexual settings, 25
  Thai state policy, 141
  working class, 3, 20
  See also bi; bodybuilding; bottom, sexual role;
    Buddhism; Camfrog; centerfold models;
    dark/intense masculinity; fashion, and
    masculinity; gay; gay gendering; gay sex,
    masculinization of; hegemonic masculinity;
    internet; *man*, meaning in Thailand;
    metrosexual; Muay Thai; slim physique,
    as masculine ideal; straight acting; tattoos;
    top, sexual role; white/fair masculinity

masseurs, 114
  See also male escorts; male sex workers
media
  in gay history, 11
  sensationalism, 8
metrosexual, 108–11, 114, 117
  and bodybuilding, 133
  consumerist lifestyles, 136
  and fitness culture, 136–39
  and masculinity, 106
  and Thai economy, 135
  See also centerfold models; middle class;
    white/fair masculinity
middle class, 46–47, 106
  aspirational status, 146–47, 164,
    167, 214
  and Thai gay identity, 47, 82, 138, 214
  See also capitalism; class difference;
    consumerism; fitness culture;
    homonormativity, of Thai middle
    class; masculinity: commodification of;
    metrosexual; *Mithuna Junior* magazine
Midway magazine, 19, 44, 49, 67f, 68, 96, 98
  centerfold models in, 101–2
  closure of, 109
Mithuna Junior magazine, 19, 29, 44, 96
  centerfold models in, 71–72, 101, 103
  closure of, 109
  history of, 49–56, 81–86, 211
  and gay bars, 56–57, 64, 72
  and gay identity, 74–75
  and gay middle class, 65, 75–76
  and homonormativity, 80
  personal classifieds in, 76–78
  promotion of commercial sex, 121
Morakot magazine, 19, 44, 49, 66f, 68, 96
  centerfold models in, 101
  closure of, 109
MPlus organization, 4
Muay Thai
  and Buddhism, 129–31
  and masculinity, 86, 91, 128, 198
muscular physique, as masculine ideal, 102
  See also bodybuilding; fitness culture;
    metrosexual; middle class; slim physique,
    as masculine ideal

Natee Teerarojjanapongs, 52–53, 79, 85
Neon magazine, 19, 29, 44, 49, 76, 96
  centerfold models in, 103
  closure of, 109
Num-sao magazine, 93

OnlyFans. *See* social networks